Ellen –

Thank you for all your support! I hope you enjoy reading as much as I did writing. Please share your thoughts with me as you read!

With love,
Colby Hopkins
6.14.13

Another World *IS* Possible:
Freedom, Economic Truth, and Creating a Society of Humanness

Colby Hopkins
The Humanness Project Press
New York, New York

Another World *IS* Possible: Freedom, Economic Truth, and Creating a Society of Humanness

Colby Hopkins

The Humanness Project Press, New York
Thehumannessproject.org

Copyright © 2013 by Colby Hopkins

All rights reserved. Printed in the United States of America. No part of this book may be used or reproduced in any manner whatsoever without permission except for brief quotes used for critical articles or reviews.

For requests for permissions or any other information contact colbyhopkins.com or the Humanness Project at thehumannessproject.org.

Email: thehumannessproject@gmail.com

ISBN: 978-0-9891086-0-7

Printed in the United States of America
Edited by Simran Sachdev
Cover design and graphics by Colby Hopkins

The Library of Congress has catalogued this paperback edition as:
Hopkins, Colby
Another World IS Possible: Freedom, Economic Truth,
and Creating a Society of Humanness

2013905724

This book is dedicated to open-minded and openhearted people everywhere who strive to make our world a better place by prioritizing human beings and nature over money and material goods. Another world is truly possible and you will make it so.

Contents

Acknowledgements..ix
Preface..xi

Part 1: Liberty and Freedom in Human Society............1

Chapter 1: Freedom for All in a Society.............................3
Notions of Freedom and Government......................................3
Breaking the Bonds of Indoctrination: Understanding Freedom in a Societal Context..7
Coexisting and the Impossibility of Freedom..........................11
Redefining Freedom...15
Rights and Restrictions: The Freedom Trade-offs..................17
Balance Rights and Restrictions to Achieve Freedom for All.............20

Chapter 2: Lifting the Fog: Americans' Quest for Democracy in America...25
Call It Democracy and They Won't Ask for Democracy......................25
Democracy, Freedom, and Accurate Information: Getting Past the Truth Obstructers...31

Chapter 3: Democracy and Freedom: The Human Element...46
Humanness: What It Really Means to Be Human..................46
Real Democracy as Freedom in Society.................................50

Part 2: Challenging the Economic Status Quo: *Considerations of Reality and Humanness*..53

Chapter 4: The Foundation We Built the Economy On.........55
Human Nature: Fixed, Selfish, Rational, and Competitive....................60
Incentive: Your Motive is Money..63
Rational Man, Rational Person: The Path of Least Resistance...........64
Rational Choices: The Human Computer..............................65
Competition: Winners Win and Losers Lose.........................66
Innovation: The Key to Everything..67
Supply and Demand: The Language of the Herd...................67
Wealth Creation: How to Grow a Pie.....................................69
Economic Growth: The Productive Potential of Us...............70
Economic Measures: The Example of GDP..........................70
Standard of Living: The Boats Are Rising.............................72

Quality of Life: Livin' the Good Life...73
This Process Can Continue Forever!...74

Chapter 5: The Great Debate: Influential Thinkers and What We Don't Know About Human Nature..................................75
Fixed ... orrrrrrr Not...76
Self-interested and Competitive ... But Also Generous and Cooperative...80
Rational ... Okay, Come On, You Know We're Irrational..................86
So How Sure Are We About That Human Nature?.........................89

Chapter 6: Assumed Truths (and Ignored Realities)............90
Economics: It's Called a Science, So It Must Be Right......................92
Human Nature: Just Accept It, You're Sort of a Jerk.....................103
Incentives: Nothing Matters Except the Green................................107
Rational Man and Rational Choice: You're Not an Animal, But a Computer...112
Competition: You're Not Rich, So You Must Be Lazy.....................121
Innovation: You Think, Therefore You Profit................................129
Supply and Demand: If You Ignore Enough Factors, It Really Works!...135
Wealth Creation: They Don't Care About Your Drinking Water, They're Sharing Pie...145
Economic Growth: The Fatter the Better..152
Economic Measures: Good − (-Bad) = Good..................................155
Standard of Living: You Have 1, He Has 99, Therefore, You Each Have 50..162
Quality of Life: No, Seriously, Your Life Is Good...........................165
This Economic Process Can Continue Forever! (We Assume).........168

Chapter 7: Our Societal Structures Oppose Political and Economic Freedom, Democracy, and Humanness................169

Part 3: Creating a New Society of Humanness............177

Chapter 8: American Revolution 2.0..............................179
A Seed Was Planted...179
Occupying Wall Street..186
The Message of the 99%..188

Chapter 9: Principles of Humanness..................199
Guiding Principles for a New Society..................199

Chapter 10: Methodology of Humanness in Social Movements..................216
Actual Space: Utilize and Democratize the Commons..................216
Direct Actions: They Speak Louder Than Words..................219
Technology: The Great Equalizer..................220
Working Groups: People Get It Done Together..................220
Direct Democracy: Anything Else is Not Democracy..................221

Chapter 11: Bringing It On Home: How Engaging in Your Community Will Change the World..................238
Make a Difference Starting Now..................240
Leveled Horizontal Organizing..................241
Self-organizing for Social Change..................244
Extend from Home: Organizing with a Small Group of People Around You..................249
Form Your Group: Meeting Your Partners for Change..................251
Build a Local Base: The Redistribution of Power..................253
Community: The Building Blocks of a New World..................260
How Does This Actually Work?..................267
Actions: Communities Moving for Change..................269
Imagine Another World..................270

Appendix: Organizing Resources..................279
Endnotes..................283
Index..................293

Acknowledgements

I wish to thank all of my friends at Occupy Wall Street and in movements for social justice everywhere. These are extraordinary people working tirelessly and often jeopardizing their own safety to make the world a better place. In large part, this book has originated from many hours of discussion and days of action with them. There are just too many people to mention, but I would like to thank a few: Rivka Gewirtz Little, Bruce Little, Walter Hergt, Yotam Marom, Kelly McGowan, Nathan Fishman, Andy Smith, Michael Premo, Daniel Latorre, and Lisa Fithian.

I would also like to thank my friends and family who have been not only remarkable in listening to and informing my ideas, but also in providing the crucial feedback that allowed me to make this book what I wanted it to be. Thank you Vincent Petronelli, Eric Dimbleby, Chris Conte, Denise Petronelli, and Jamie Hopkins. I want to thank Jeff Wall for helping with the cover design and for his generosity during my last few months of writing. I'd like to thank Professor Michael Vocino who inspired me to pursue my beliefs, which led to this book.

I would like to thank my editors. They all fit into the group above, but they have also provided content inspiration since long before the first page was written. They volunteered their time and skillfully directed this project from conception to actualization with love and support. I am lucky to have people in my life who help guide me toward the person I want to be. Thank you to my sister, Kristen Hopkins, my mother, Gail Conte Wall, and my best friend since childhood, Peter Aguiar. Additional thanks are needed for my mother for her heartwarming hospitality during my last few months of writing.

I especially want to thank my partner Simran Sachdev. She has been my constant support and inspiration in every way imaginable. She walks next to me on the front lines of protests, guides me through the day-to-day struggles, and motivates me to always be better. Through productive, attentive, and thought-provoking conversation; emotional support and encouragement in both the writing and the activist lifestyle that led to it; and countless hours of book work and editing, this project would not be what it is if it were not for her. She is a true inspiration for a better world.

Preface

In September of 2011, I went to Liberty Square to join the Occupy Wall Street protests. People coming together in real open dialogue and engaging in democratic conversations with people from all different belief systems inspired me. It amazed me how people from such different backgrounds and political beliefs could unite and passionately fight our collective oppression. They realized that political and economic systems oppress all of us. They believed that they could work with people with different opinions and find common solutions. Gradually, I watched friends and family turn against the Occupy Movement (and therefore against my beliefs) as they fell victim to the corporate media's hijacking and distorting of the movement and its messages.

I wrote this book because, like most Americans, I am sick of two things: I am sick of the political polarization in the national debate and I am sick of the extreme power of the political, corporate, and financial elites. Our current social and political structures do not respect the variability in human beings or how humans impact each other. We do not live in a democracy, but I want to.

Unfortunately, our dominant media is owned and operated by colossal corporations. They are more interested in drumming up dramatic fights to boost ratings than they are in productive dialogue and democratic processes.

Once at an Occupy march, I was gathering with a group of friends when a man on the way to his Wall Street job walked by. He started cursing at the protesters and yelled, "Why don't you get jobs you goddamn socialists?!" I persuaded this man to stop and talk to me so I could explain a little bit about Occupy Wall Street that he may not know. I told him about the methods Occupy uses to be a platform for all voices, how the media spins the real dialogue, and some of my critiques about capitalism and the 1%. After only a few minutes, he conceded that he misunderstood Occupy and, while he may not come down to Liberty Square (as I had suggested), he hoped we could succeed in changing the national discourse.

The fact is that people do not disagree on fundamental issues. In this book, I include quotes from leading political figures, scholars, social critics, and artists to highlight various beliefs in the mainstream discourse and to show that we do not agree and disagree with others the way we think we do. Of course, we can find things to disagree about and we can fight over them, but if you break any issue down to the roots, there is little disagreement. Unfortunately, we are conditioned not to find common solutions, but to fight. When we have political conversations we look to prove the other wrong rather than seek the depth of that person.

Let me provide an example: if someone wants universal healthcare, they are likely to be ridiculed and called a socialist by opponents of universal healthcare. But even levelheaded conversations will be about how we cannot afford to pay for that and, on the other side, how unethical it is to let people be sick. The common ground is simple. How can we provide healthcare to everyone at an extremely low cost? Now, you might think that is impossible, but I don't. My belief is that when people come together from different points of view, in honest and open-minded dialogue, they are able to come up with creative solutions for all of our social ailments. Why is it that we believe that people are so creative and innovative that we can fly around space, create the Internet, and transmit messages instantaneously to the other side of the planet, but we cannot organize ourselves to improve our society in a way that meets our needs?

You'll notice how I stray from the normal discourse: I am not talking about compromise. The best that Washington politicians can do is talk about compromise. To use our healthcare example, they will try to cut other programs, raise some taxes, and water down services, so Republicans can please their base and Democrats can please theirs while both parties cater to the medical, pharmaceutical, and insurance industries. We cannot trust them to solve this problem, nor can we trust the corporations. We need to solve these problems ourselves. How can we dramatically cut medical costs and provide quality services to everyone? If people come together and democratically create their own solutions, it can be done.

Once we begin to approach problem solving by engaging

others in productive dialogue for common solutions, we will realize several things: First, freedom is for everyone. If we really believe in freedom, it only makes sense that everyone shares the same freedom. As much as we value individual freedom, we must recognize that it's important to limit our own freedom when it unreasonably infringes on others' freedom.

Now if these restrictions are inflicted on us from some far-off government institutions, we may oppose them and we should challenge them. But if these restrictions derive from collective agreements that we were a part of making (through real democracy), then it is an act of self-determination. This is the importance of a government by the people and for the people as opposed to our current government.

Next, we will realize that freedom is not only a political issue. Economic freedom is fundamental to a free and democratic society. We must engage with our fellow citizens to create a society that fosters economic freedom for everyone. To accomplish that, we must recognize that the world does have some ecological limitations and what one person does affects others' ability to live freely. We don't have to allow unlimited plundering of the earth and exploitation of the people to have a free society. Nor do we have to punish small business owners and other people who work hard, so we can provide services for those not working. We can value individual freedom and collective freedom.

Most people recognize the importance of a social contract—that is, people believe it is important to have laws that protect people from the possibility that others will harm them. As much as we don't like to say it, these laws restrict freedom to protect people and enhance overall freedom. Being that we accept the social contract, it doesn't make sense to advocate for unchecked perpetual economic individual freedom any more than it would make sense to advocate for removing all of our laws.

Finally, we will realize that the structure of our economy fosters a plundering of our common resources and exploits people. What one person does, affects other people. The global economic structure, based predominantly on individual freedom, outright ignores this fact. Therefore, the economic system oppresses freedom for all of us, and such oppression has led to massive wealth inequalities and people's sense of disenfranchisement. People suffer largely because of systematic flaws—not because of laziness or personal inadequacies.

The common discourse tells us that the economy fosters freedom and that people don't all succeed because they are free to fail. There's no coddling in this economy and only the strong survive. But those who believe this do not understand the way the economy actually functions.

In this economy, it is not that you are simply free to fail. Rather, most economic factors are far outside the control of the people. When we cannot impact our own situation, we do not have freedom and self-determination. How can we have no quarrels about touting the exceptionalism and importance of American freedom on one hand, and minimizing every sign of oppression against others with a "life isn't fair" or "it's better than any other country" on the other hand?

Now, I never imply that it is impossible for some people to work hard and succeed: it is possible. But that isn't the whole story. The fact is that the chips are stacked against the people, and even those who work hard their whole life and make good choices are not bound to success—they might not even get by. Meanwhile, our simple and common everyday actions, like shopping at the supermarket, funnel wealth to the wealthy and chip away at our livelihood and environmental stability.

I believe that the government does not represent the people. And I believe that a small group who exploits people and the planet for their own personal profits controls the economy. I also believe in freedom and justice. Finally, I believe in real democracy. I did not write this book because I have the answers to our collective problems. I wrote this book because I believe that if people have access to accurate information and can engage with each other in real dialogue, then people are capable of governing themselves. If you believe this too, then I wrote this book for you.

When we come together in our communities with open dialogue, we are capable of fostering both individual and collective freedom. We are capable of building common solutions that meet the needs of all of us. Of course, this method takes time and work, but we know we cannot trust political, business, and financial elites to govern our lives. If we want freedom, we must govern our own lives together.

The remedy to restraint on freedom is the expression of freedom. Individuals can maximize freedom in a society through open dialogue, mutual respect, and participatory democracy, which have historically been exhibited in many communities. Individuals may, and should, live freely, but not to the extent that they hinder other's freedom. This book lays out steps people can take to implement true democracy in their own communities at the local, national, and global levels.

To many people, creating a new society of humanness sounds impossible. It is difficult to engage someone that we so strongly disagree with, and it seems impossible to find common solutions. But people do not disagree with each other the way they think they do. While reading this book, you may disagree with some of my points or what you infer I am trying to say in my writing, but I strongly believe that you and I do not disagree on most issues, no matter what your position is. At the root of our beliefs we would find enough common ground to stand on and we could build common solutions.

All I ask is that while reading this book you understand that nothing written here is intended as an attack on any person or beliefs. I ask that you proceed without prejudging my intentions or what you think my agenda is and read through the content with an open mind. Try to interpret what points I am making—not assume what points I am making based on the standard public discourse. The actual purpose of this book is to move beyond the regular, polarized discussions and find the roots of our commonalities. I believe that the only way to solve our collective problems is to engage with each other and work together to build a new way of living. I believe this course of action requires everyone to collaborate rather than mobilize one side to defeat the other. I believe another world really is possible and I believe that we can create one if we work together. That's what this book is about.

Part 1: Liberty and Freedom in Human Society

The first part of this book is based on the idea that freedom is essential to the human experience. By using humanness as the foundation for analyzing freedom, it follows that all forms of societal organization must correlate with the complex notion of free humans living together in a society.

Chapter 1 explores the idea of freedom for all in a society as it relates to government and other social institutions, specifically corporations. It then considers true democracy as a method of social organization conducive to freedom, which should extend beyond government institutions.

Chapter 2 argues that we do not have a system of true democracy in the United States and that elements of our society that do have democratic tendencies are manipulated by leadership through various means of controlling information—information that is essential to real democracy.

Finally, Chapter 3 examines the notion of humanness and all its complexities to highlight that while we may not have true freedom and democracy, if we consider humanness when organizing our society, we can and will have both.

Chapter 1: Freedom for All in a Society

"Freedom and justice cannot be parceled out in pieces to suit political convenience. I don't believe you can stand for freedom for one group of people and deny it to others."
—Coretta Scott King

"We allow our ignorance to prevail upon us and make us think we can survive alone, alone in patches, alone in groups, alone in races, even alone in genders." —Maya Angelou

Notions of Freedom and Government

"Civilization has been a continuous struggle of the individual or of groups of individuals against the State and even against 'society,' that is, against the majority subdued and hypnotized by the State and State worship." —Emma Goldman

"A government is the most dangerous threat to man's rights: it holds a legal monopoly on the use of physical force against legally disarmed victims." —Ayn Rand

"If [the government] be the agent of the people, then the people alone can control it, restrain it, modify, or reform it … It is, Sir, the people's Constitution, the people's government, made for the people, made by the people, and answerable to the people."
—Daniel Webster

Liberty and freedom, these words are very familiar to the American ear. They are part of our everyday life, history, and culture. The great welcoming monument of our nation is the Statue of Liberty. We have a Liberty Bell. America is the "land of the free." Americans have "liberty and justice for all," in fact; we *demand* that we are given liberty or death. The list of symbols and phrases goes on and on. We know, as Americans we enjoy certain freedoms on a daily basis, simply because we were born in the United States of America. Politicians stir patriotic notions of Americanism and emotions of pride, honor, and love by shouting words of freedom from the hilltops … Capitol Hill that is. Pundits and scholars alike drum up feverish support for their own opinions by highlighting the rich history of the struggle of Americans for freedom and equality. Since we are undoubtedly immersed in freedom and liberty in everything that we do, these terms should be easy to define.

The American Heritage Dictionary's definition of freedom yields the following: (1) The condition of being free from restraint

(2) Political independence (3) Possession of civil rights, immunity of arbitrary exercise of authority and (4) The capacity to exercise free choice, free will.[1]

Freedom from restraint? Immunity from arbitrary authority? Free choice? These definitions probably encompass most Americans' ideas of freedom and what we feel freedom is. Therefore, it is difficult to disagree with these definitions. They make sense because these definitions are ambiguous. Who would disagree that freedom includes "political independence?" However, freedom is much more than political independence (which can mean different things to different people).

While we might not disagree with these definitions, we could all debate and argue the deeper meaning within them. If we were to extrapolate on these definitions, and apply them to specific issues, we would have many different interpretations of their meanings and how they should apply. Consider how two politicians always use the same rhetoric around freedom even if one is arguing for a bill and the other against it. Scholars, professionals, artists, and people from all walks of life tackle the concepts of freedom. There are endless amounts of books, poems, paintings, songs, emotional diatribes, and all types of expressions that attempt to explain and interpret freedom. Freedom is an idea: it is a concept.

More importantly, freedom is a feeling. It is not concrete, and it is not black and white. We know when we feel free and when we don't, but no one feels completely free all the time, unless they are ignoring the obvious—life has restrictions. Whether they are natural, physical, mental, societal, governmental, or individual, there are always forces restricting our freedom, no matter how little we feel the effects.

There is a misconception that government provides freedom; it does not. Freedom is inherent to all people. Many people fear government control and the risk of its infringement on freedom and thus create ways to mitigate it, as they should. Governments, by nature, restrict freedom. This is true even in a democracy. All government action is inherently coercive. At the least, government action requires taxes, which are not optional. If we consider government and the people as the two components of society, then an increase in the size and strength of government would certainly consist of an affront on personal freedom. However, society is not just made up of two exclusive and opposing sides of the people and government. Freedom is not only freedom from government. Society includes other institutions, like corporations and banks. While people make up every institution, including government, corporations and banks do not act like people: they are large institutions whose only purpose is to make profits. Furthermore, people within these institutions often have opposing interests. CEOs of large corporations do not have the same concerns as most Americans, like feeding their family and earning enough to make rent. But their actions impact us all, and often restrict our freedom. So people have to worry about more than just the government creating restrictions on freedom. Freedom is the absence of coercion whether it is by government, private institutions, or individual people. Government ensures that some inherent freedoms of people are protected from other elements in society, like other individuals and institutions.

Citizens accept a certain amount of government restriction on freedom because they want it to protect other freedoms. For example, most people are willing to stop their cars when the government's traffic lights tell them to because they know that it benefits all of society and helps protect people.

We call codified freedoms that are protected by the government, rights. However, government control over us can go too far. When it does, citizens will resist the infringement on their freedom. For example, the continuous growth of the size and reach of the federal government provoked an anti-big government movement in the form of the Tea Party movement that took the 2010 mid-term elections by storm. While the press only focused on outrageous tactics of a small number of people in the movement, and even though the Republican Party co-opted and minimized the impact of the movement, it showed that there are a lot of Americans fed up with the inefficient, over-spending of American tax dollars. Many feel that governments are inefficient, and inadequate to provide social services. Many also feel that our government spends too much money, creates too many restrictions, and kills too many innocent people in the name of providing security.

With people holding such concerns, they must always check the government (or any system of power) to ensure that their restrictions on freedom are justified. Our nation was founded on this basis. The founding fathers and mothers worked to create an alternative form of government to break away from the tyranny of the British government, but also to prevent another tyrannical government from developing in the new land. We still need to be vigilant and constantly active about getting and keeping the government in check to prevent such tyranny. However, we must also be cautious of infringement on freedom from other sources, especially ones that we as people, have little or no control over.

Consider two things. First, total freedom for everyone is not only impossible: it is undesirable. If everyone had total freedom, I am not certain that a Hobbesian state of nature would emerge where life of man would be "solitary, poor, nasty, brutish, and short" because everyone's distrust for one another would cause constant preemptive attacks on individuals. However, if everyone were completely free, without restriction, then maybe something closer to a Lockean scenario would ensue where people without a strong conscience could exploit and hurt others for their own gain and without consequence.

For Hobbes and Locke, people enter into a social contract to mitigate or prevent this type of behavior. They argue that this is why people consent to having a government. (I would argue that there might be other methods to accomplish protection and justice without a government body, but that's beside the point.)

Second, achieving desirable freedom, whatever that may include, necessitates a balance of forces. Therefore, a check on *ALL* sources of illegitimate power is necessary, not just on government power. But before we know what freedom we have (or don't have), we still have to know what freedom is, right? Through the rest of this chapter we will explore freedom with the purpose of redefining it to include a system of balance, thinking about how to process information to pursue this balance, and considering how to account for the human element—what freedom is to human beings.

Breaking the Bonds of Indoctrination: Understanding Freedom in a Societal Context

"None are more hopelessly enslaved than those who falsely believe they are free."
—Johann Wolfgang von Goethe

Structured societies condition people to believe certain things automatically. In the United States, most citizens believe communism, for example, is a very specific thing: it is bad. They believe democracy is communism's opposite and, therefore, good. People are told the American government projects "American ideals." Government leaders put American soldiers in harm's way to protect freedoms. The American government, which we are told is a democracy, therefore, should somehow coincide with terms like freedom and liberty, which are ingrained in our national history. We are likewise taught to believe that capitalism is our economic system and it is the only system that coincides with freedom. This is how we are indoctrinated.

Freedom is such an ambiguous term and idea that it does not align with any form of government or economic structure more than another. To clarify, true democracy promotes freedom in a societal context. However, when we speak of freedom, as in rights, or as in individual freedom, it could exist in any system to some degree (and depending on how one defines freedom). People could live freely and feel untouched by their king in a monarchy, that is, if the king chose to implement policies that allowed it.

Joseph II, the Holy Roman Emperor from 1765 to 1790, instituted policies that spread education, reduced the power of the church, protected freedom of worship, removed class and ethnic requirements for government positions, and he ended serfdom. Joseph II issued over 6,000 edicts and over 11,000 new laws aimed at increasing the happiness and freedom of his people, but his empire was not a democracy.

Many monarchs have instituted polices that increased people's freedom or brought prosperity to them. The problem is that there are no guarantees that such freedom will last. Even the greatest, benevolent monarchs will eventually pass on and be succeeded. With a benevolent monarch, people may have the freedom to work, eat, and live happily and freely, but may have no say in their political structures whatsoever. They may even be persecuted for speaking out against the ruler. In a democracy, people can starve to death on the street but can verbally lash out at the President on their deathbed. So, who is more free?

Looking at communist or socialist regimes (which Americans are conditioned to despise) with some objectivity reveals that these systems are not inherently opposed to freedom. Instead, historically, it was leaders within these regimes that instituted policies that hindered freedom. For example, during the Cultural Revolution in China, Mao Zedong expected the arts in China to reflect the ideals of a socialist society. As a result, artists that were considered bourgeoisie or anti-socialist were prevented from working and persecuted under Mao. This is the opposite of what Americans consider freedom; however, authoritarian policies like these are the result of authoritarian leadership, rather than inherent to a social theory (especially those that are economic systems like socialism and communism).

To put this into perspective a bit, consider that in the U.S., Black Americans are less than fifteen percent of the population. After the abolition of slavery, state and local governments began to institute Jim Crow laws, designed to make Black Americans second-class citizens. This happened democratically, according to the U.S. system. Throughout the 20th century, the U.S. Supreme Court began overturning Jim Crow laws (against the majority of voters). However, if U.S. law functioned based solely on majority rule, the country could have permanently implemented Jim Crow laws even if there had been equal voting for people of color. According to some definitions of democracy, that would have been democratic, but not freedom. This gets to the core of the freedom discussion.

Americans think of freedom, in the context of a democracy, as the right of every person to express themselves socially and religiously as they choose, pursue economic security and expansion, and participate equally and purposefully in the government process of decision-making. To boil it down, freedom is self-determination. Freedom (and justice) for all requires that these conditions occur without directly hindering the same conditions for others. This is where it gets tricky.

For example, most people want to enjoy the benefits of their labor. Certainly the harder a person works the more comfortably they can live, but not relative to the amount of labor they put in. Most middle and lower class folks understand that people can excel at their jobs, work extra hours, even work a second job, and still not get ahead because wages are low, expenses continuously rise, jobs are outsourced, and owners and executives keep profits from businesses. Does that make sense?

People cannot advance relative to their labor. Of course some people will get ahead in life when they work hard, but the majority of jobs pay so low, wage increases are so small, and prices of total goods and services rise so fast that over a lifetime most people who work long, hard hours, year in, year out, will never get ahead. Therefore, self-determination is not easily accessible in the economic sense, and government is not the only institution that gets in the way.

Beyond the restraints of employment and wages, and economic forces outside an individual's control, self-determination is also limited by others who use or damage things that belong to everyone. Those plundering the limited resources of the earth that affect every global citizen, to increase personal profits and shareholder profits, restrict self-determination of others to some extent. One person's pursuit of self-determination should not include destroying things for other people.

For example, the British Petroleum oil spill in 2010 saw 4.9 million barrels of oil flood out of the ocean floor into the waters of the Gulf Coast. Additionally, 1.9 million gallons of Corexit dispersants were used to sink the oil. No one will ever know the full damage of the oil spill, but some effects are obvious. Fishermen from the Gulf regularly find mutated fish in their catches including eyeless shrimp, clawless crabs, and fish covered in lesions. Local fishers have lost up to 75 percent of their income.

Freedom to pursue profit and freedom to plunder the earth to pursue profit are two different things. Destroying the earth, wasting resources, and other practices that hinder the freedom of others cannot be justified by the value of one individual's freedom to pursue profits. However, it has become ingrained in American culture, and thus, industrialized countries' cultures, that capitalism is the economic system of democracy and that both capitalism and democracy align with freedom—people have the freedom to plunder the earth for personal profit. Furthermore, over the last century, this style of corporate capitalism has become the way a capitalist system is "meant to be" and that system is called freedom, even if at the expense of others. In reality, this is all a lie.

The basis for the idea behind capitalism, both in method and purpose, is individual freedom—the noblest of capitalists' causes. Many advocates of capitalism hold individual freedom as the highest virtue. Milton Friedman, a leading proponent of capitalism wrote, "we take freedom of the individual, or perhaps the family, as our ultimate goal in judging social arrangements. Freedom as a value in this sense has to do with the interrelations among people." However, upon further analysis of the notion of freedom, we realize that unchecked individual freedom naturally hinders freedom of other sorts, including individual freedom of others.

A free market system means that individuals function in markets free from the restraints of their governments. People and corporations are able to function as they choose—buy, produce, sell, etc.—without government interference. It does not mean that businesses competing in those markets are free from each other. Actually, it's the opposite. In a free market system, businesses are at the mercy of one another and the hope is that the free market system functions to allow the best—most productive and efficient—businesses to thrive, while the others collapse. Furthermore, a free market system does not mean that individual people are free from the restraint of others. The free market system functions on competition so people are subject to the restraints of the dominating forces. Whether you believe that to be good or bad is a different story, but it is the reality.

People generally prefer and accept the government's control over our society (albeit, to varying degrees) rather than being unpredictably controlled by whoever finds a method of power over us (whether it be corporations at home or foreign powers abroad). Americans accept this because citizens are supposed to have some say in the government. However, the point remains that any government exists to control the people that it governs. Once this is understood, it easily follows that absolute freedom is impossible. Ironically, freedom in a society requires restrictions. There must be restrictions if people are to coexist. And with that knowledge, we can work to live in a free society that acknowledges all people and allows self-determination.

Coexisting and the Impossibility of Freedom

"Liberty may be endangered by the abuses of liberty as well as by the abuses of power." —James Madison

"Political freedom means the absence of coercion of a man by his fellow men. The fundamental threat to freedom is power to coerce, be it in the hands of a monarch, a dictator, an oligarchy, or a momentary majority. The preservation of freedom requires the elimination of such concentration of power to the fullest possible extent and the dispersal and distribution of whatever power cannot be eliminated—a system of checks and balances." —Milton Friedman

"Capitalism today commands the towering heights, and has displaced politics and politicians as the new high priests, and reigning oligarchs of our system. So capitalism and its principle protagonists and players, corporate CEOs, have been accorded unusual power and access ... These are the new high priests." —Ira Jackson

Freedom means you can do as you please. You can act, think, and believe how you want and you are able to express thoughts and beliefs, as you want. Freedom on an individual basis is rather easy to conceptualize. We can think of it as the limitlessness of the individual. Especially as Americans, most of us feel free in some sense of the word. Most Americans probably feel as though they can pretty much do as they wish and live as they choose without other people getting in their way. At least those with good paying jobs may feel unrestricted. Do some people feel as if no forces hinder them from living their lives as they choose? Or maybe they don't feel free but blame their jobs for their restrictions? What are the impediments to their freedom? Taxes? Of course, freedom is also more than just being able to act however we want.

What about those of us who are working and cannot seem to make ends meet? I would bet that some feel as though they are unable to live as they wish. Maybe they think it's outside forces preventing them or maybe just circumstances. Many Americans struggle more than others. People are marginalized and oppressed; those living in poverty have a more difficult time elevating their quality of life than those who are not. Perhaps even low-income people feel that they are able to live as they choose, but probably not to the same degree as the American middle class and elite. Furthermore, there is an inherent disconnect between the labor one pursues and their own self-determination. This contributes to an underlying feeling of discontent among workers even if most people can ignore it or put up with it. Karl Marx wrote of the impacts of laboring for someone else's profit:

> *Labor is external to the worker, i.e., it does not belong to his intrinsic nature; that in his work, therefore, he does not affirm himself but denies himself, does not feel content but unhappy, does not develop freely his physical and mental energy but mortifies his body and ruins his mind. The worker therefore only feels himself outside his work, and in his work feels outside himself. He feels at home when he is not working, and when he is working he does not feel at home. His labor is therefore not voluntary, but coerced; it is forced labor ... It is therefore not the satisfaction of a need; it is merely a means to satisfy needs external to it.*[5]

Conversely, freedom for all as a general condition is almost impossible to conceptualize, and to think we have freedom for all is ridiculous. For two or more people, limitless freedom is impossible because what each person does, will impact the others. In the U.S., freedom means access for everyone to life, liberty, and the pursuit of happiness. Conflict arises when acting on beliefs and pursuing happiness infringes on someone else's ability to do the same. Because society is made up of more than one person, we have to accept that one's capability to act freely must be limited to the extent that those actions do not hinder someone else's freedom. Society should work to allow everyone to equally act freely.

It seems that many prosperous people, who consider themselves free, try to disconnect themselves from people who are not. There is, however, a connection between them. People of extreme wealth maintain and increase power by controlling and exploiting the people without it. Sometimes this exploitation is intentional and conscious; sometimes it is the result of functioning in the system that necessitates it. The American people are included in this condition. Some wealthy Americans invest and own businesses that exploit the environment and the people. There are many poor and exploited citizens who are oppressed in work. We are coerced into contributing to the destruction of the environment to earn a living. This is not to say we do not have freedoms in America, as we do have many. But we do not have freedom equivalent to what we feel the word freedom means.

Government plays an interesting role in the concept of freedom. On one hand, it seems that government provides freedom by instituting laws that grant freedom. On the other hand, government cannot provide what is inherent to humans. Humans are inherently free; therefore, government can only protect what already exists in people. Now, on the third hand, another way to look at the relationship is that government hinders freedom. The truth is, the government both protects and hinders freedom. While government hinders freedom by placing restrictions on people, it also protects freedom by restricting other people from hindering it. If the government controls our freedom, then we are not totally free. But the core purpose of government is to maintain order among the people it governs. It is a created institution with the sole purpose of providing and enforcing rules that regulate the masses of people.

The very existence of government assumes that if it were not there then some people would unjustly dominate over others. Ironically, to protect people from controlling each other in society, the government itself has to have a certain amount of control over the people. This is the idea of the social contract propelled by the works of Thomas Hobbes and John Locke who had significant influence on the foundations of American government and society.

People consent to a certain amount of governing power over them, to ensure that the government protects against other hindrances to freedom by other individuals. It's not necessarily a bad deal, especially if America was a true democracy where the people had control over the government (or even better, if they were the government). That would mean the people govern themselves.

Opinions vary on how much freedom the government should restrict in order to protect overall freedom. Some politicians even argue that government cannot regulate institutions like banks and corporations because that would be an infringement on their freedom.

13

In America, we enjoy many freedoms. Some of the notable ones are freedom of speech, freedom of religion, and freedom of the press. Even with these, it is somewhat of a fallacy to believe we are a free society. The government, private corporations, and banking institutions determine a great deal of our existence. If everyone had total freedom, with no governmental control, then the more powerful people in society would be free to exploit others and the environment without repercussions (even more than they currently do).

The government obstructs the people's freedom, but it should also protect it. Sure, people should be free to conduct their businesses as they choose, but that allows power to accumulate in unaccountable hands that obstruct other people's freedom. The result is that the government ends up protecting the freedom of a few individuals, whose actions hinder the freedom of the rest. And now the situation is out of control because the worst elements of both sectors, government and private, seem to be working together all the time! So what do we do?

This conundrum has brought our society to a critical point where we, as people, need to make some choices. Those choices need to be conscious and specific. Somewhere along the line, through the guise of rhetoric, freedom became defined as the ability to gather as much unnecessary wealth as possible by exploiting the planet and its people while the government cuts you a break on your taxes. We need to take back control of the terminology. We need to understand what freedom really means to us, and not allow our politicians to abuse and exploit the meaning and create policies of oppression in the name of freedom.

I still believe in the real thing. I still believe that freedom is the ability to find happiness and self-determination, which does not come from a gross abundance of wealth, but from family, people, community, and one's ability to participate meaningfully in the decisions that impact one's life and social structures. I just have to ask, why not? Why can't we have it? The answer is simple: we can.

While unlimited freedom for everyone may be impossible, knowing that means we can consciously find a balance and collectively protect our freedoms. This is what it means to coexist. We only need to further our understanding of freedom and include the notion of balance in our new definition of it.

Redefining Freedom

"Don't regard yourself as a guardian of freedom unless you respect and preserve the rights of people you disagree with." —Gerard K. O'Neill

"This country will not be a good place for any of us to live in unless we make it a good place for all of us to live in." —Theodore Roosevelt

Think for a moment about the word "freedom." What an ambiguous term. Freedom is one of those words like "love." When you say the word love, you may feel like you know *exactly* what you mean. But love, like freedom, can translate to very different feelings to different people and can be easily misconstrued in the language. You may not even realize it until you dig deep into the details of specific examples. When you hear people talking about freedom, or that we live in a free society, we are all using the same words, but we are thinking and feeling different things. Furthermore, because of the impossibility of unlimited freedom we must figure out what balance of freedom and restrictions is right.

Hopefully, we will conclude that when a freedom is right for one, then it is right for all. We must consider our own freedom as something inherently tied to the freedoms of others. This can be tremendously difficult because freedom is an emotional topic. We often identify the nation with freedom and we want only to protect that ideal. But part of what makes the U.S. an amazing country is that we are able to challenge the government and societal institutions. When we challenge the notion of freedom in our society, if we do not get defensive and actually hear other ideas, and dig deep within our own belief systems, we will find more similarities than differences about what freedom means to us.

Definitions of freedom include the absence of things like fear and want. It also means the absence of physical force or any other form of coercion. However, in a social context, definitions of freedom may vary based on individuals' interactions with others. Freedom is not one universal concept.

Because we live in a society where a person's actions affect others, total freedom is impossible for everyone to have, and there must be limitations. Therefore, we must redefine our understanding of freedom to include a system of balance between allowances (rights) and restrictions (regulations). Restrictions protect individuals from other citizens or institutions that could hinder freedoms. Once this mindset is established, people can start to analyze the trade-offs that must be made to maximize everyone's freedom in an equitable way. Most likely this is not actually a redefinition, rather a combination of getting to the root of what people believe freedom really is and expanding that concept so it applies to everyone. This is the critical first step toward progress.

Over time, Americans have learned and are still learning, that if we allow our government to put restrictions on others, then, because it is only fair, we must accept those same restrictions on ourselves. Similarly, if we are allowed a certain freedom, then other people should have that same freedom, whether we agree or disagree with what they do with it. This is the prerequisite for a discussion on freedom in society. What is true for one person should be true for all people. If we cannot accept this one simple truth, then we are hypocrites and don't really believe in freedom for all.

For example, if we support freedom of speech, we must support it even when we do not like what another person says. We may wish to condemn the words but we cannot condemn the act of using them. Dictators support free speech as long as the speaker agrees with their view, but that is not free speech. Supporting freedom of speech means everyone is free to say what they choose and the government, institutions, or other people cannot prevent it. The challenge is to find the balance of allowance and restrictions as it best serves all people. Freedom of speech may therefore be limited in the event that the speech infringes on someone else's freedom. But how do we collectively find this balance?

Government or some other body of the people must regulate freedoms as well as restrictions to ensure the success of such freedoms. There must be a way to allow people to freely pursue self-determination while ensuring that people are not also restricting other individuals' ability to do the same. Since we, the American people are supposed to be the government (of course through our elected representatives) we must use our political power to control our balance of freedoms and restrictions. That is the purpose of government, and that is what our duty is as the people that are the government.

The difficulty is, since the bulk of Americans do not actively participate in government, representatives are free to act as they choose and do not acknowledge different views regarding what freedom actually is. This is perpetuated by the fact that government officials hide information from us and skew the information they provide so we are largely uninformed. Furthermore, the dominating corporate media misinforms, manipulates, and polarizes the people, which misdirects focus to concern for political parties and hinders effective participation. If we, the masses, inform ourselves and become actively involved in the process of self-governance, we can easily find and implement the tradeoffs between rights and restrictions.

Rights and Restrictions: The Freedom Trade-offs

"My freedom to move my fist must be limited by the proximity of your chin."
—*Former Supreme Court Justice William O. Douglas*

Each freedom we have restricts other freedoms at the same time. So when we consider freedom, we have to be able to accept, or deal with, the limitations put onto us by others having that same freedom. On one side, democratic "liberals" press for a certain amount of services like housing, medical care, food, and other basic needs for all. By doing this, government coerces other people in society who have more property to pay for those services through taxes, thereby infringing on their freedom. We have watched this debate go back and forth throughout the history of our nation.

Currently, the debate is that the wealthy should pay taxes because it is fair that everyone pay their fair share. Furthermore, the wealthy earn profit by exploiting people and the earth so they need to contribute more taxes to make up for the damage they do. However, the wealthy make society better by creating more jobs for everyone. If you let them work, unhindered by taxes, society will improve. Any monetary contributions to society should be a voluntary choice for charity, not coercion by taxing. But the jobs they create are few, low paying, and going to people in other countries.

So freedom of the most vulnerable, we are told, comes at the expense of freedom of those with more wealth. Some people argue that healthcare is a human right and, therefore, access to basic medical needs is an essential component of freedom. On the flip side, others might argue that because healthcare costs money, and those that cannot afford it would have to rely on others to pay for it, that the payers' freedom is jeopardized. Furthermore, they argue that by providing free services we are removing the incentive for people to advance themselves.

When it comes to social safety nets, perhaps the trade-off would be diminished if we implemented them with a long-term strategy to minimize them. Currently we use social safety nets to maintain capitalism and mitigate its natural effects on society. However, if society actually allowed people to flourish, these would only be necessary for people with severe medical needs. Regardless, in our current system, we must choose between paying taxes or giving up social programs and choosing one means giving up the other.

The right to bear arms offers a stark example of freedom trade-offs. The Constitution of the United States sets the foundation for our government, but before agreeing to ratify it, some of the nation's founders decided it was necessary to codify some rights (freedoms) so no one, in theory, could restrict these particular freedoms. They wrote up the Bill of Rights.

The right to bear arms means we all have the right to unlimited access to have any guns, right? Maybe that is exactly what it means, maybe not. None of us can be sure, which is why people can turn it into a controversial issue. The rights to protect one's property and one's family are extremely important. However, the freedom to do so restricts other people's freedoms. I know that we would all protect our families at any cost, but let's just acknowledge that this freedom impacts other people's freedom. Whatever your stance on this issue, exercising this freedom necessitates a balance as to not restrict other freedoms.

With this great freedom of bearing arms, the bearer

exercises the right to feel protected because they have a gun, which makes them feel safe. This is considered a freedom from fear because having a gun is a way to protect us from harm. However, when one person has a gun, other people around that person are restricted on their freedom from fear, because now they are likely to be fearful of the person with the gun. Even if others get guns too, it doesn't remove fear of the original gun carrier, it only helps to level the fear.

I'm not trying to defend or condemn this right. My only point is that with rights come natural restrictions. Even if you are willing to accept them, the point is that they exist. Some restrictions are more obvious than others because, like with guns, they threaten our physical safety directly. People may debate whether guns are necessary or they may believe that the second amendment is the end of the discussion, but we all know guns are weapons that can be used to hurt others.

The freedom of speech, codified in the first amendment, offers another example. There are some obvious examples when freedom of speech can put our safety at risk; therefore we accept some restrictions on it. For example, yelling, "fire!" in a theater is against the law if there is not a fire because people could hurt others trying to escape.

If we allow everyone to have freedom of speech, then we have to allow people to say things that we might think are unacceptable and can make our society worse. This applies especially to people on television and radio because they are in positions to reach a large amount of people and possibly affect their opinions. Depending on one's opinion, it is possible that these people are corrupting our society. Thus, the freedom to speak freely hinders everyone else's freedom from the resulting consequences of speech that we do not like or think may harm society.

For example, we may get upset that certain programs are allowed on television in the name of free speech because we do not want our children seeing sexual or violent scenes. Many people would love to shut up Jon Stewart or Rush Limbaugh, but to do so we have to restrict freedom of speech and press. It is a hard line to draw no matter what right you consider.

This, however, does not mean that having certain freedoms is not worth the trade-offs; rather, trade-offs are inherent to freedom in a society. These are just some examples that highlight the conundrum of the notion of freedom. Remember, what is true for one must be true for all, so we need to find what trade-offs maximize freedom for everyone, how we can overcome restrictions, and find a balance.

Balance Rights and Restrictions to Achieve Freedom for All

"For to be free is not merely to cast off one's chains, but to live in a way that respects and enhances the freedom of others." —*Nelson Mandela*

While some may be content with government restrictions, many of us are adamantly opposed to them depending on the reason for them. Questioning, challenging, and opposing government restrictions are things every American should constantly engage in. However, such engagement should not depend on which party is in power. We must question the legitimacy of all forms of authority. We all benefit from our government, but to balance rights and restrictions it is crucial that all people have a meaningful voice in what the government does.

There is considerable distrust of government in America, but by not allowing government to restrict others, our freedom may be in more jeopardy than if we allowed the actual restrictions. BIGGGGGGG GOVERNMENT! Wow. Read that out loud a couple of times, it even sounds bad. It sounds horrible, but how horrible is it? Some of us think big government is awful and that government should stay out of the way and let society flow as much as possible. Is big government in and of itself bad, or is it simply that our current big government is bad?

Let us forget for a moment what we are always told: that big government cannot work. Just because something is not working, does not mean it cannot work. What if it could; then would big government be so bad? And what is it about big government that we should oppose? Social programs? The military? All of it?

We often hear that we don't want the government deciding

how to spend our money. "Damn right I don't want the government spending my money. I want to spend my own money!" Then again, if you lost your job and your healthcare and a family member got sick, and the government provided your healthcare, you might feel differently about it. Government healthcare may not be the solution, but the need for treatment is very real. So the issue is not how big the government is, but whether it makes society better. We know that our current government systematically works against our best interests.

There is a misconception that protesters in the Occupy Wall Street Movement, and maybe protesters or even liberals in general, are lazy and want "handouts." An online blog called *We Are the 99 Percent* allows people to post their messages, telling the stories of their struggles. One message that received a lot of attention was from a man who had cancer and could not get treatment:

> *I am an American. I pay taxes. I worked. I was the guy who worked in his field for 20 years until the economy collapsed. Then I was the guy who brought you your pizza. You know, a job? Not unemployment? Then I got cancer. Minimum wage and part-time insurance meant I needed Arizona's welfare, AHCCS (Access), or I needed to gather my affairs. Minimum wage meant I made too much money, according to Access, and I was denied Access. Cancer solved the problem and removed my ability to work. Access approved. Despite what you've been told, the hospital <u>will</u> turn you away if you're broke. Despite what you've been told, churches and private institutions will <u>not</u> pay your medical expenses. I was diagnosed April 1st, 2011 and had major surgery on May 12th. I am still recovering from radiation and chemo treatments ended in August. I am alive because I'm unemployed. Does any of this make sense? I am the 99%.*

His question is one we should all consider: does any of this make sense? Our government is not of the people or by the people. If it were, we would not have so much disdain for the government or politicians. If the government were truly of and by the people, we would be having a very different conversation with and amongst ourselves. We would be looking in the mirror and toward our communities to find change, not bickering about how much we hate the Republicans or Democrats.

What if a network of community based governments spanned across the country and provided similar services in healthcare, education, and social security as the federal government provides? What if our government could be by the people and for the people; then why would anyone oppose it whether it was big or small? If we had the power to make decisions together, then maybe we wouldn't have a problem helping people like the man who posted the story above.

Most people know that the government is NOT by or for the people, but the beauty of the American government—the one thing that does make this country the greatest country in the world—and why people should all love living in America, is that ultimately the people do have a say. But political games in Washington and in the corporate media polarize every message and practically force people to choose sides so there is never a reconciling of differences. You either win, and get what you want, or you lose and your voice is ignored. Just under half of the population's desires are ignored at any given time. We cannot find balance this way.

Additionally, we are force-fed so much misinformation that it is almost impossible to figure out if what we believe or value is really in line with what we think is right. People are not being represented in the government and if the people are not being represented, I know whose fault it is. We love to blame the Congress, and the President, and the corporations, and the liberals, and the conservatives, and whoever else we can point the finger at. And they are ALL guilty.

But the truth is that if we are not represented, we have to demand it. It is our responsibility to fight through all the propaganda and nonsense on TV. It is our responsibility to be heard. Maybe big government is only bad when the people are left out of it. It is a great misconception in our society that what we say doesn't matter. But we have to do more than just vote in the national elections. We actually have to do something!

Many of us have been convinced that we do not have a say, we cannot change things, our vote does not count, and we do not have a voice. If that's how you feel, you may have been fooled. Do not give up. Albeit, it has been getting increasingly more difficult to make our voices heard. We have little choice but to spend most of our time just getting through the day-to-day struggle, trying to make ends meet, and care for our children. But we *can* mobilize and we *can* participate and we *can* find the balance we need to make this country what we want it to be.

I'm not saying everyone needs to march on Washington (although that does help) but it is crucial that we come together to figure out what we believe in, our similarities and differences, and how this country should function—what's important, what's not important, what freedoms we want citizens to have, and what restrictions we can accept.

All the back and forth bantering can, and must, stop. Instead of picking sides against each other, we must create some new solutions to achieve balance. Balancing does not mean we have to find compromises and meet in the middle; it means we can combine ideas and construct new solutions that meet the needs and beliefs of all of us. Furthermore, we all need to consider what we are willing to contribute to make this happen.

Forget what the 1% wants you to believe: society cannot function if everyone is only pursuing their own best interests all the time—that's chaotic. We have to be willing to help each other and find mutually beneficial agreements that may not involve money, but have significant value. Once we figure all that out, we need to do something about it. We need to create a balance between rights and restrictions by freely and collectively contributing to society. This way, we will be our own government and we will need the current government institutions less and less.

I bet most of us don't differ in opinion on a lot of issues, but just disagree on the versions of issues that are plastered all over the mainstream "news." Some of us or all of us, are not doing our job, our duty as citizens, to let our opinions be known. Don't be fooled, voting is not enough. How many times will we choose between the lesser of two evils? There must be a better way. You only have essentially two choices when you vote and neither side represents you completely so you need to make your opinions known.

But this is why you and I are here right now. That's what this book is about: how you can have a say. No matter what your beliefs are, they are valid and important. How can you take control over your own destiny? Let's find out.

We do not have to figure out what the forefathers thought or wanted on all the specific issues. They were a group of people, with differing opinions so we can be certain they didn't all want the same things entirely. What we know they agreed on is that the government they created would be accountable to the people and the people would be able to change and adapt it. That is the genius of the U.S. Constitution. What we need to do is decide what kind of country we want to live in, and make that happen. Do we want a society that promotes as much freedom, liberty, and self-determination as possible? Do we want as much participation from citizens as possible?

For government to work in accordance with freedom, and therefore balance rights and restrictions, it matters who has a say in that government and what the process of participation is. If democracy were truly a system of governance where everyone had an equal say and differences were reconciled, maybe the government would be the best way to promote freedom. Part 3 of this book describes how we can govern ourselves and create true democracy in America. True democracy could be the tool to transition government from a body that oppresses freedom and supports others that hinder freedom to one that is the exercise of freedom in a society.

However, democracy is another term that has been hijacked and exploited to the point that when it is used, most people will feel good and agree that it is good, but they may actually have different definitions of "democracy." As with freedom, we have to consider what democracy really means to us, what system of government we actually have, and what system we want.

Chapter 2: Lifting the Fog: Americans' Quest for Democracy in America

"We become slaves the moment we hand the keys to the definition of reality entirely over to someone else, whether it is a business, an economic theory, a political party, the White House, Newsworld or CNN." —B.W. Powe

"Those who do not move, do not notice their chains." —Rosa Luxemburg

Call It Democracy and They Won't Ask for Democracy

"People will believe a big lie sooner than a little one, and if you repeat it frequently enough, people will sooner or later believe it." —Walter Langer

"Democracy must be something more than two wolves and a sheep voting on what to have for dinner." —James Bovard

The premise of this section is that the American government, which Americans tout as a democracy, is not a democracy because it doesn't include any self-governance or self-determination. We are no longer forcibly beaten or coerced into compliance, but corporate and political leaders use the language of freedom and democracy to manipulate the masses into complacency, rendering our democracy illusionary. However, the positive impact of the exploitation of words like freedom and democracy is that most Americans believe whole-heartedly in these ideals. Therefore, true democracy is an achievable goal and will foster self-determination and freedom for all.

There is no universal definition of democracy; however, it is some version of a system of governance where all citizens have equal and meaningful say in the government's laws and policies. Democracy is considered an evolution of society that lifts people out of the totalitarian systems of oppression by advancing self-determination—people govern themselves.

While a true democracy would offer self-determination and a process to find the balance between rights and restrictions, America was not built to be a democracy. The founding fathers did not describe the government they created as a democracy. In fact, the word democracy is not in any of the founding documents.

James Madison said of democracies that they "have ever been spectacles of turbulence and contention; have ever been found incompatible with personal security or the rights of property; and have in general been as short in their lives as they have been violent in their deaths."[6] Similarly, John Adams wrote, "Democracy never lasts long. It soon wastes, exhausts, and murders itself. There never was a democracy that did not commit suicide."[7]

Instead of a democracy, the forefathers built a republic, which is a system of government where citizens elect officials, who have a say in making laws and policies. This representative government requires the people to consent to being ruled by leaders; they don't rule themselves. We should have access to good information so we can make informed decisions and pressure our representatives to do what we want. Instead, we are suffering from impacts of advertising, public relations, and media campaigns that keep the populace largely misinformed. Meanwhile, the structure of this political system is that most Americans vote every few years for one of the two choices they have and then sit back and let the winner rule over them with little or no resistance. Therefore, the people do not govern, are simply misled, and appeased to the extent necessary, to allow the elite to continue to govern and reap the spoils of regular citizens' complacency. There is a fundamental difference between a system where the public votes to choose between two people who then govern over them and self-determination where people govern themselves.

America is an oligarchical republic led by the extremely wealthy with a few laws that mitigate some of the inherent inequalities of the system. For example, checks and balances are essential elements of our republic. In theory, the branches of government check and balance one another and prevent the consolidation of power, but ordinary citizens must use their power to check and balance branches as well. However, checks and balances in a republic still do not equal democracy or self-determination.

Some believe democracy simply means a government chosen by the people, even if it is representative government. Citizens choose their representatives by voting, but there is no political self-determination in a republic; it is leaders making decisions for you. Although voting is one of America's most democratic characteristics, it isn't an equalizing of voices or a process of self-determination; it is a silencing of voices that are not in the majority and requires citizens to submit to authority.

Western countries, like the U.S., often focus on elections in developing countries to prove the existence of democracy. However, even tyrannical leaders, like President Mahmoud Ahmadinejad of Iran, allow elections to legitimize their rule. This doesn't mean they are a democracy. In the U.S., all the president needs is to win by a slim majority and they claim to have political capital to spend, meaning they do just about whatever they want. Not only do they ignore the desires of those who did not vote for them, but they often ignore the desires of those who did.

Representatives are supposed to vote on legislation based on their constituents' interests. In practice, we know this does not work because representatives are basically free to decide how they should represent their constituents who have a variety of different needs. Even in the best scenarios, most representatives support actions that appease a small majority of folks (usually those with money), rather than find solutions that work for everyone. In other words, citizens consent to being ruled, with no self-determination beyond choosing between two similar rulers every few years. This is an extremely narrow view of democracy and does not amount to any definition of self-determination.

Perhaps self-determination could be achieved with representation if officials were actually accountable to their constituency, which is only possible with a small constituency. There can be no self-determination through representatives on a national level that are only accountable every few years. Instead, political and corporate leaders manipulate the public into consent so they can maintain their power and wealth even while their leadership forces the masses into political, economic, and social turmoil.

As a republic where leaders rule over the citizens and citizens consent to such rule, the U.S. has political and economic institutions that shift the exercise of power from forceful oppression to manipulation. Politicians and institutional leaders use emotionally big and vague words like freedom and democracy in manipulative ways to gain support of the people and their consent. Every politician claims to support freedom, but whatever choices they make, they will vote against someone's freedom. It is not a question of whether they support freedom, but rather, what they value in the balance it requires.

In President Obama's address to the United Nations General Assembly in 2012, he eloquently reminded the world of the promises of American freedom:

> *True democracy demands that citizens cannot be thrown in jail because of what they believe, and that businesses can be open without paying a bribe. It depends on the freedom of citizens to speak their minds and assemble without fear, and on the rule of law and due process that guarantees the rights of all people. In other words, true democracy, real freedom is hard work.*[8]

In stark contrast to his propagandist remarks regarding freedom, President Obama has steadfastly pursued policies of oppression. Not only did he continue the Bush Administration's policies of indefinite detention without charge or trial, but also he expanded the power of indefinite detention to include American citizens when he signed the National Defense Authorization Act in 2011 and again in 2012. In an unprecedented use of presidential power he began assassinating U.S. citizens abroad, including the 16-year-old Abdulrahaman al-Awlaki, without charge or trial.

The Obama Administration has also impeded press freedom by attempting to scare and intimidate the free press, for example, by attacking legally protected whistleblowers. President Obama has prosecuted twice as many cases under the Espionage Act, a law that prohibits free speech that interferes with military operations, promotes insubordination, or shows support for U.S. enemies, as all other Presidents combined.

One such case involves John Kiriakou, a CIA veteran who served from 1990-2004. He played a role in the capture of Al-Qaeda member Abu Zubaydah in 2002 but later revealed that

Zubaydah was tortured using the technique of waterboarding. Kiriakou faced charges including revealing the identities of covert officers, leaking classified information, and lying to a CIA review board. Because of his efforts to hold the U.S. to a higher standard of human rights and alert the public of their government's policy of torture, Kiriakou faced charges that carried a penalty of up to 20 years in prison. In October 2012, he pleaded guilty to one account of disclosing information by identifying a covert agent and was sentenced to two and a half years in prison.

President Obama is not the only guilty party. Almost all leaders, pundits, and citizens talk about democracy as if it means extremely idealistic things, and talk about the American government as if it is a democracy. They talk about our voting system and call it democracy. They talk about democracy and call it freedom. By this logic, the American political process should be the essence of a free society. But democracy is not just voting. It is also not synonymous with freedom. By throwing these terms around and constantly bundling them together, the words lose the importance of their individual meanings and confuse honest dialogue. The American political process is not a democracy.

Without understanding the context of the word when used and the speakers' meaning behind it (as well as the process to achieve it), people are left to have an emotional response based on their own perceptions of the word and perhaps of the person using it. We are manipulated to associate words like democracy with freedom, and believe that democracy is the American form of governance and that it is good because it is associated with freedom. Navigating the discourse becomes very difficult in all this confusion.

As a result of all the twisting of grandiose language, most people have an idealistic view of what democracy means even though they don't live in an actual democracy. Americans closely associate democracy with American ideals of freedom and equality. It is almost as if American democracy and freedom go hand-in-hand. When you hear the word democracy what do you think of? Some definitions that cross your mind might be along the lines of "freedom," "equality," or "America."

Americans use the word democracy as a term encompassing all civil and political rights such as freedom of speech, freedom of the press, due process, and the notion of all citizens being equal before the law. These ideas are not the same as democracy. However, a truly democratic system would foster freedom, equality, and self-determination for all people.

Self-governance is a requisite of self-determination, which is an individual's birthright and expressed in the American foundation as the inalienable right of an individual to "life, liberty and pursuit of happiness." The word democracy is comprised of the Greek root words "demos," meaning people and "kratos," meaning power. True democracy is the capacity of people to participate freely and self-govern in their society to their fullest potential. In a true democracy people have equal and meaningful say in decisions that affect their lives, hence, self-determination.

Self-determination is achievable through true democracy. It comes from individuals' control over their own lives within a community. Therefore, a person self-governs on an individual level and participates meaningfully in a community that governs over itself. When citizens personally participate in the decision-making processes of the government, it is called direct democracy. This is an active, highly participatory approach, far beyond simply voting.

When direct democracy occurs in a non-hierarchal, leaderless process, where everyone's voices are heard and respected equally, it is referred to as horizontal (direct) democracy. Direct democracy occurs largely in groups and assemblies because it requires people to interact and collaborate. However, with technological advances in communications there are increasingly more elements of democratic participation that can occur via the Internet. Direct, horizontal, participation of all citizens is how democracy can foster self-determination.

So many people think there is not enough time to participate in society in this way. I encourage everyone to think of two things: First, how much time we spend on other pastimes like watching television. And second, how much time we could free up by working together in our communities and helping each other accomplish goals. What we lack is not time, but community.

People can consent to be governed but they must be able to govern as well. Without accurate information, citizens are neither able to vote or act in their own best interest, nor can they find commonly constructed tradeoffs and solutions. For a democracy to function, people need a free press because they must have access to accurate information as to adequately inform them so they can make the best decisions to pursue self-determination.

However, corporate media destroyed the freedom of the press by crushing independent, objective media and becoming a tool to divide the masses and manipulate them into a state of apathy. When people speak out against the government, it is usually in a polarized, media-framed debate that everyone chooses a side in, rather than speaking out for constructive actions that benefit everyone. To find democracy, citizens first have to get past the corporate media and government-controlled messages.

Democracy, Freedom, and Accurate Information: Getting Past the Truth Obstructers

"In our struggle for freedom, truth is the only weapon we possess." —*14th Dalai Lama*

The difficulty in determining the best courses of action in pursuing freedom and democracy for everyone, is navigating through the controlled messages (more honestly called rhetoric) of the political and economic institutions including corporate media. To determine what kind of society we want to live in, we need access to accurate information. We need accurate information in its proper wider context, both current and historical. We need the whole picture, not carefully selected, cherry-picked pieces of it. In short, we need to know the truth.

It is up to us as individuals to find what realities correlate with our actual beliefs and make sure our actions are pursuing those beliefs. Often we are not pursuing our beliefs, even when we think we are, because the messages we act on are so inaccurate. Considering additional truths in conjunction with our own beliefs will help us embrace an open-minded approach, expand our understanding of self and others, and help us see commonalities instead of differences.

For example, let's say you believe in the American dream. You believe that a person can come to America and work hard and be able to prosper. Without changing that belief, you can also believe that people can come to America and work hard and barely get by. Of course once those two beliefs are combined you have a clearer version of truth—not everyone who works hard can succeed. The next step can be an open-minded discussion about why some people find prosperity and others do not, what factors are in our control as a society, and what we can do to influence those factors.

Whether we choose to watch the news on TV, read magazines, blogs or books, and whether we choose progressive, conservative, or middle of the road sources we are asked to choose a side. I am asking you for something different. The discussion that I am asking you to embark on will not be like others that you have had in the past. I am not going to attempt to impose what I believe as truth on you by trying to prove your beliefs and truths wrong. As you will see, I don't even think that could be done—because I don't think what you believe is wrong or false.

This discussion, rather, will ask you to further embrace your own ideas as truth, to really understand their value, and then understand other ideas as additional truths. The beauty in this exercise is that you won't have to give up a thing! There is no changing your personal beliefs or ideas; it is simply to understand them and others, and to understand your beliefs in the context of others. Nothing more.

The truth can be a pretty funny thing. People think they know what is true and when they talk they confidently spew facts to assure everyone that they know what they are talking about. Yet, the truth is quite elusive. Sure, it's never too difficult to find out something that happened, some event, or perhaps a fact regarding a particular situation. Unfortunately, no truth exists in a vacuum. Truth, of one simple thing, can consist of many different elements—so many different factors that it is almost impossible to consider them all.

In this complex context, finding out why something occurred or why something is the way it is, can be much more problematic. Furthermore, there are many of us who have truths that do not require factual evidence. We believe certain things as truth based on faith, and what we have faith in is our truth. So what to do? Should we just believe what we are told? How can we figure out what the truth *really* is?

In this section we are going to identify common methods by which information is presented or understood in a narrow and manipulative way. These methods of presentation limit the truth to a specific thing, and are not inclusive of all the many things that actually are truth. People, especially media pundits, scholars, business leaders, and politicians, use these tools to push their opinions onto the public and hide additional truths. We will refer to these methods as truth obstructers because that's what they do—obstruct truth.

Truth obstructers are methods, practices, habits, and tactics that prevent us from experiencing more truth (or the whole truth if that is possible). The truth obstructers are assuming totality, unjustifiably omitting the other, ignoring hypocrisy, disingenuously selecting evidence, creating duality, dividing into sides, using ambiguous language, and framing issues.

Identifying these obstructers will make it easier to interpret all information from any source. You see, truth is almost never one exact thing. It is a bundle of different things. We have all created our version of truth: our truth is what we believe. We did this by accepting some things as right on certain issues, while finding wrongs in the other sides of those issues. These choices constructed our beliefs. There are always more than two sides to an issue. And, either side can appear right depending on how the argument is presented and who is having it.

Corporate and political leaders always have hidden agendas. These are usually malicious and self-serving. Leaders make decisions to line their own pockets and to stay in power. A 60 Minutes report in November of 2011 revealed the magnitude of congressional members using their positions of privilege and access to information to engage in insider trading.

While the nation was debating universal healthcare in 2009, House Minority Leader, John Boehner was leading the fight against Obama's public option. Boehner bought health insurance stocks just days before the public option was demolished at which point they immediately increased. Similarly, former Speaker of the House, Nancy Pelosi, purchased five thousand shares of Visa stock at a low price of $44 per share as a bill that would hurt credit card companies made its way through congress. The legislation was killed before it ever reached the house floor and stock prices rose to $66 per share.[9]

However, it is important to remember while we discuss this, most people believe their own values, opinions, and actions to be noble. These may range from values like "I'm just doing my job" to "I want to make a better life for my family," or beliefs like "this is just how the world works." Many people believe that if everyone who runs a corporation does everything in their power to make as much profit as possible, society benefits from the total of all individual actions. Some corporate leaders believe that they are in better positions to create positive change because of the power corporations have.

For example, Interface, the largest designer and producer of carpet tiles in the world, seeks to stand out in the corporate world by being "the first company that, by its deeds, shows the entire industrial world what sustainability is in all its dimensions: People, process, product, place and profits—by 2020—and in doing so we will become restorative through the power of influence."[10]

Realize that although you may not agree with their opinions, most people's intentions are good so you can at least respect them and attempt to understand. More often than not, when people do terrible things, it is largely because they live and function in a terrible social structure. This is true for both sides.

When truth obstructers are present, and they always are, it is important to realize that most of the time it is not due to malicious intent. There is good reason to believe almost anything. And once you believe in something, it can be easy to dismiss things that may contradict that belief. Opinions are often presented as fact, and partial information is presented as if it is the whole picture. This is what I call **assuming totality** and it is the first of our truth obstructers.

Assuming totality is having a belief and assuming that this

belief is the total truth. When this happens, we tend to hinder our ability to expand on that truth or accept additional truths. Here I am not referring to religious beliefs. Perhaps your religious beliefs serve as a definitive and total truth to you. I wish to leave religion out of this portion of the discussion, except as it pertains to social and governmental action.[i] When I discuss assuming totality as a truth obstructer, I am referring to any truth besides religious beliefs. Because religion is faith in things beyond the natural world, total belief in religion in and of itself is not a truth obstructer in a social and political sense. Religious beliefs will serve as truth obstructions to other religions (believing in one religion, as the total truth will prevent belief in other religions) but not to social and political matters. However, when religious beliefs are applied to social and political issues, then they are treated like any other assumption of totality and will obstruct other truths.

We already discussed a perfect example of assuming totality. In the U.S. and other western countries it takes the form of a simple statement: "communism is bad" or "communism doesn't work." These statements are largely accepted as true and most people who believe them accept them as total truth. These perceptions of totality assume so many things that simply are not true. It assumes communism is one specific thing, it has been implemented, it failed, we understand what it means to fail, and the reason it failed is only because it doesn't work.

In reality communism is an idea that could be implemented in many ways on different scales. It does not need to be forced on a nation by a dictator. We typically define economic failure by a lack of growth, but as you will see in Part 2, the way growth is calculated should not determine success. Finally, any nation ever considered communist by the U.S. was targeted by economic and military operations aimed at smothering them. In any example, outside forces, other than the would-be-communist economic system, had a large hand in failures. There is simply good things

---

[i] In other words, if you believe that the government should enforce your religion, then you do not believe in freedom in a society because others are not allowed to believe something different. That is why the founders of the nation discussed separating church and state. Religious laws are not compatible with freedom as they force the beliefs of some on to everyone. That said, religious beliefs might be a total truth for you.

and bad things in most social theories but assuming totality, like "communism is bad," strangles productive dialogue.

In social or political (or really any earthly) beliefs it is important to remember that just because one thing is true does not mean its opposite is false. But information is presented to show something as true and that because it is true that other things must be false. This is another truth obstructer called **unjustifiably omitting the other**. More than one thing can be true, or right. Therefore, dismissing something simply because you believe something else, is not justifiable. The goal here is to avoid assuming a totality of one truth so we can recognize why other people believe things different from you and acknowledge the value of their truths.

Of course, everyone believes in more than one thing, but what this exploration should do is allow you to realize that you can believe more than one thing about a single issue that may appear as opposites in the mainstream discourse. You can believe in free healthcare and small government, pro-life and pro-choice. How is this possible? Because pro-life and pro-choice are not opposites; they are only presented as such. The opposite of pro-choice is anti-choice, but pro-life believers are not fundamentally against the right to choose; they just want to protect what they believe is an innocent life. The opposite of pro-life is pro-death, but people who support a woman's right to choose do not want to kill others; they just support a woman's right to control her own body including a fetus, which they don't believe is a person.

Because of the religious nature of this debate, pro-life and pro-choice supporters are generally considered irreconcilable. However, groups like The Common Ground Network for Life and Choice have brought these would-be opponents together in workshops and consensus building dialogues with some significant successes. Their website tells the following story:

> *In St. Louis, Andy Puzder, the pro-life lawyer who helped to author Missouri's legislative restrictions on abortion, and Ms. B.J. Isaacson-Jones, the director of Reproductive Health Services, the largest abortion provider in the state, which sued to stop the legislation, sought a new approach after the Supreme Court ruling upheld the law. Andy had suggested in a newspaper article that it was time to put aside hostilities and*

find ways to cooperate to help the women and children whom both sides claimed to protect.

After a series of cordial discussions, they were joined by others prominent on each side of the debate, and for more than four years have focused common attention and resources on issues of mutual concern: assistance to crack-addicted pregnant women, preventing unwanted pregnancies, providing women support during pregnancy, teaching abstinence to teenagers, reducing infant mortality, and financing school breakfast programs.[11]

I am suggesting that we simply open up to other possibilities and factors to understand many perspectives in the world because other factors do exist and are relevant to the makeup of reality. Doing so will help us avoid attacking an individual person and focus on the issues that matter. If we accomplish this goal we can all accept additional truths into our belief systems without having to change our current beliefs. Once we are able to see the issues objectively and understand them from all angles, we can start to work together to solve them. Then we can work to better society as a whole and make huge gains on all types of issues so that everybody wins! Stick with me on this and you will see how it can be done.

Next, in the name of fairness and justice, everyone must concede to the rules of sincerity. That is, people interested in honest dialogue cannot be hypocrites. Unfortunately, information is almost always presented using the next truth obstructer: **ignoring hypocrisy**. If there is something that you or I really believe in, then we have to acknowledge that rules, regulations, or freedoms that govern the belief apply to us and to other people. We cannot expect to have a right without other Americans having that same right, even if we don't like what they do with it.

When someone pushes the limits of American freedom in certain ways, we as citizens should get mad and yell and scream about it, but we should not argue against the freedom of others or concede to the government restricting that citizen's freedom. If we want something to apply to us but not to someone else, then we are simply ignoring our own convictions and obstructing our own truth. Some American patriots repeat the words of Evelyn

Beatrice Hall: "I detest what you say, but I will defend to the death your right to say it."

There are still national debates on whether we should be able to make children stand and say the Pledge of Allegiance when it forces them to admit the nation is "under God" and they may not believe in God. Additionally, for many children, the very act of standing and reciting a pledge to the flag violates their faith. Whatever stance we take, we must acknowledge that the same rules must apply for everyone. You may passionately believe that the Pledge of Allegiance is important to you and to the country, but do you believe that you should be forced to express your love for the country in ways that you do not believe are right or violate your religion? If you believe in freedom of speech and freedom of expression then you must support a person's right to abstain from this type of forced obedience—even if the Pledge of Allegiance is dear to your heart.

Another typical defect in societal dialogue that obstructs truths is that evidence from one social element or another is used to support a point, belief, or side; meanwhile other pieces of evidence from that same genre are ignored as to not disprove the point. This is a trick that everyone uses. This truth obstructer is called **disingenuously selecting evidence.**

Everyone picks and chooses evidence as proof when it is convenient to their argument but easily dismisses (or will not even mention) contradictory evidence, or evidence that might just offer additional truth. This is the challenge we face because almost all our sources of information have biases and agendas to satisfy. Their goal is to paint a specific picture for consumers, rather than to actually inform them of the truth.

It is the responsibility of avid truth seekers to look past the headlines and find the whole story. Of course, one source is not enough. It is essential to think critically, so if there is not enough time to investigate through multiple stories, simply understanding that anything you read is written from a particular angle is important. We have to read between the lines.

Statistics can also be misleading as statistical evidence is often manipulated. We need to consider how the statistic was calculated, what was left out, whether or not it is valid, and if it proves the point. Maybe if some other things were considered and calculated, the statistic would prove something different. A statistic is never the whole story. Furthermore, while such statements or pieces of evidence might make a particular point true, they most likely do not disprove opposing or different points of view. As stated earlier, just because one thing is true, it does not mean the opposite is false.

For example, pundits use history as evidence to back up one side of a particular debate. Unless the discussion is about the historical event itself, this form of evidence makes little sense. Historical language and intentions are ambiguous and debatable. Using such things as evidence is simply a tactic to stack the deck in one's favor.

The right to bear arms seems pretty cut and dry, and pundits use the phrase all the time. However, the second amendment of the Bill of Rights actually reads, "A well-regulated Militia, being necessary to the security of a free State, the right of the people to keep and bear arms, shall not be infringed." Now that may mean exactly what we said before: you have the right to bear arms. However, it doesn't look as cut and dry when it's phrased this way.

A militia is an army of ordinary citizens, not part of the national army. During the time the Constitution was written there was no U.S. Army, and militias were formed to provide public safety, so ordinary citizens needed weapons of their own in case they were called on to defend the nation or their state against foreign aggression. A "well-regulated militia" is no longer necessary for the security of the state. Today we have the biggest and most powerful military in the world. So, you and me? Chances are we are not going to be called on by the governor to take our rifle off the shelf and go shoot some Canadian intruders. Uncle Sam has that one covered.

Also, a "well-regulated militia" sounds like it might not mean every individual citizen gets to run around gun slinging. Well-regulated sounds like there might be some kind of regulation on this rule. Your right to keep and bear arms shall not be violated, but there could be some guidelines.

Finally, the weapon of choice during the American Revolution was the muzzle loading flintlock musket, not the Glock 17 semi-automatic pistol or assault rifles that ordinary people own today. So the historical argument of arms does not exactly translate. Weapons now have a much greater capacity to destroy life, and their impact on society is different. Historical evidence can be used to argue strict unchangeable views or one that calls for some regulation.

Although we use historical content as an argument, it is not always valid. Times change and people change. The beauty and genius of the Constitution is that it was set up so it could be changed. The Constitution itself lays out the powers of Congress, the executive branch, the judicial branch, and the states. The Bill of Rights is a list of ten amendments to the Constitution that grants certain rights and protections to "the people." The definition of "the people" has expanded over the years, and for the better. Just as these amendments were added to the Constitution in 1791, many more have been added as well.

It's Article Five of the Constitution that grants our Congress the power to add and change such amendments. The amendments are passed by a two-thirds vote in Congress and with the ratification of three-fourths of the states. This is not an easy thing to do, but this is good because it is important to have major public support to amend the Constitution. However, the notion of change is ingrained in our foundation. So, any pundit who points to the Constitution in support of their argument should also acknowledge the founders set it up to be changeable over time. This should inform any historical argument.

The fact is that there is much more than one truth to an issue and there is evidence of this multi-truth existence everywhere. We have to assume that when someone is supporting their belief, on any side of any issue, they are leaving out certain facts that would support something different. Often it is not only evidence to the contrary that is ignored; information that might be in between sides, or third perspectives are ignored as well. The gray scale is left out.

This leads me to the next truth obstructer: **creating duality**. So many people appear to think in dualities: black and white, right and wrong. Maybe we have been conditioned to think this way because it is how information is constantly presented to us or how society is structured. Some people don't feel like thinking or questioning things. Constantly changing their minds or reevaluating their positions or beliefs takes too much energy. Maybe it's pride. Changing one's opinion is almost like admitting you were wrong. Not having definitive answers is like admitting we do not know the answer. It's easier to just have a conviction and stick with it.

With definite answers comes a feeling of security that human beings like. People like knowing the definitive answer even if it is wrong, or more precisely, incomplete. It's easy to live with incomplete because it can be ignored. Life, of course, is not so simple. Nothing is definite. It seems easier to oversimplify the understanding of issues while overcomplicating how they are dealt with. But nothing is a simple as two opposing views.

Duality provides an easy path for people to **divide into sides**, which can be a truth obstructer by itself. It's obvious how the lines are drawn: liberal vs. conservative, Republican vs. Democrat, capitalist vs. environmentalist, pro-life vs. pro-choice. Dividing into sides obstructs truth because people tend to oppose things because someone from the other side supports it, or let representatives get away with doing that. The major flaw here is that these groups are not opposites and almost no one fits into one particular mold, yet the biggest national debates occur across these lines.

Members of Congress and the corporate media often try to present Congress as having two opposite sides. The Republican and Democratic parties are not drastically different on most issues but the media presents them like polar opposites. Where there are distinctions, members within each party have many different beliefs and support or oppose things to different degrees. They are, in fact, human beings. There is also a wide world of different ideas and beliefs that extend far beyond the narrow confines of the Republican and Democratic parties. Unfortunately, voting is a system that compartmentalizes beliefs into a black or white, yes or no, mentality.

When society divides into sides it has detrimental effects. First, it forces people to align with a position against their own interests. Americans face this challenge every election because they believe they must choose the Republican or the Democrat candidate. Most people do not closely align with either of these sides, but they choose one or the other because they know a third party candidate won't win in the U.S. Another negative effect of dividing into sides is it narrows the debate. Every challenge we face as a society has a plethora of possible solutions or approaches we can take. By letting the debate split into sides we remove other possibilities out of the public discourse.

Many Americans get their information from limited sources—corporate television news and maybe a newspaper or two. People generally choose a news source that is along the lines of their beliefs whether it is FOX, CNN, MSNBC, or NPR. There is simply not a good way of getting accurate information from any one of these sources, but there is a fallacy among people that says if you want to be informed you have to look at the conservative media and the liberal media, and the truth is somewhere in the middle of the two sides. In addition to the reality that these sources don't cover many stories, don't investigate their stories, and make up facts, the truth is not an average of two sides especially narrowly differing ones. The truth is more accessible with a combination of many stories and an open-minded perspective that requires thinking beyond what any story tells you.

The people that mainstream media refer to as liberals have the greatest intentions. When liberals say we need to do more to protect the environment, which we all know we need to do, why are average Americans dividing into sides on it? The mainstream media has made the argument about whether all of global warming is created by human actions. They have also made it about whether the belief is liberal or conservative. We all know we can and should do better to protect the environment. This isn't even a question. We know we don't want huge amounts of trash filling up landfills, toxins in our air, or chemicals in our drinking water.

Why is a clean environment considered a liberal issue? We all could make proactive changes to help control pollution, with little change to our daily life. If anything, only profits of big corporations would be affected because they would have to spend some money cleaning up their act, but why is that so bad? They shouldn't be profiting from polluting the environment to begin with. Other businesses will still profit from the changes, either in the cleanups or in alternative energy sources.

Helping the environment in a huge way hardly affects our daily lives at all, except that we will have better health. Why are we even debating this issue? Does anyone care if their milk comes in a bag instead of a carton? Does anyone mind turning the water off when they brush their teeth or mind getting power from a windmill instead of coal burning? Some people have turned against the environment, which we all enjoy and rely on, simply to take a stance against a fictitious side.

These issues are polarized as "liberal values," but everyone benefits from a clean environment. People can find ways to reconcile caring about the environment with conservative principles of smaller government and allowing entrepreneurs to prosper but the debate is too polarized for productive dialogue. The media compartmentalizes people who want to protect the environment and people who want to promote economic growth and pit them against each other as if they are mutually exclusive and opposing interests. This divisiveness perpetuates to the point where people hate one another simply because they are labeled the other side, liberal or conservative: isn't that crazy?

For the most part these so-called sides believe in the same things, especially when you talk to regular Americans. It might be hard to believe since everyone gets into heated debates with friends or family, and that other person seems like the polar opposite. Take healthcare, for example. The mainstream progressives believe in universal healthcare, which means that every American should have access to healthcare.

The craziness of this debate is that conservatives, especially the average American conservatives, believe the same thing. Nobody wants other people to be left without healthcare. In fact, you would have to be heartless to look at a poverty-stricken 8-year-old human and think, "he doesn't deserve healthcare." We all want other people to be cared for. The people who might be against the progressive version of universal healthcare are against it for other reasons. For example, they might believe the government should not provide health coverage, but they would like to create another way for everyone to have access to coverage. Many folks believe America could accomplish this through the free market, supplemented by charity.

One major reason that people end up disagreeing with each other is that most leaders in society purposely use the truth obstructer of **ambiguous language** that is inflammatory and divisive when speaking on an issue. Besides hiding an issue or using misleading evidence, speakers often attempt to gain the support of an audience by evoking emotion using ambiguous terminology that almost anyone would agree with.

We have already seen how this concept applied to the use of the words freedom and democracy. Everyone believes in freedom, but there can be dramatically different interpretations of what freedom is, who should have it, and how to get it. Politicians and business leaders all use ambiguous language to push their agenda. This is why so many of them say the same things but often yield very different results, and more likely than not, what they mean is very different than how most Americans interpret what they say.

Besides ambiguous language, leaders use very carefully crafted specific messaging to obstruct truth, using what is called **framing issues**. Framing is a process of using selective messaging to influence perceptions of words and issues. Some techniques are using the same words over and over again and using positive language that blurs the issue but creates the perception that it is a good thing. We often see this technique in the titles of laws like the "No Child Left Behind Act" and the "Clean Air Act." The titles of these bills would convince people they are inherently good, without providing any real content about the laws (when in reality these names are completely misleading). As politicians and media control our perception of our government by connecting it to democracy and connecting democracy to freedom, they constantly frame debates.

In a Republican Governors Association meeting in Florida in late 2011, Republican strategist Frank Luntz instructed attendees on how to frame discussion coming out of Occupy Wall Street. For example, Luntz told the governors not to say, "government spending" but instead to call it "waste."[12] In this conversation, most of us, who do not have time to look into all of the government's financing, will hear the word waste and assume that whatever we are talking about is bad. Waste is bad. However, others may look at that and think, "no it's not waste!" But, therein lies the problem: we agree or disagree based on the frame, not the content of the issue.

To find the real story we would have to ask, what are we spending the money on, how much money are we talking about, where will the money come from, and what are the benefits of spending the money on this? Of course, discovering the answers to these questions will require breaking through multiple frames. Linguistics expert George Lakoff suggested that occupiers frame their own debate. For example, promote the message "strong wages make a strong America."[13] Finding out what the truth is, and how different truths relate to our own beliefs requires critical thinking.

Once we can reorganize and see through the truth obstructers, it is easy to see the actual reality we live in, which consists of countless truths. Furthermore, by acknowledging the numerous truths, it is easy to see the many similarities among people and appreciate the differences. If we can do this, we can collectively begin to transform our society toward one in which true freedom and true democracy are customary, thereby recognizing humans for what they are. By working together, we can accomplish and maintain a free and democratic society by using a process that respects humanness. This is when we can start collectively deciding how we can accomplish the society we all want—one that offers freedom, fosters democratic self-determination, and allows our humanness.

Chapter 3: Democracy and Freedom: The Human Element

Humanness: What It Really Means to Be Human

"The most authentic thing about us is our capacity to create, to overcome, to endure, to transform, to love and to be greater than our suffering." —Ben Okri

Consider for a moment what we hold most dear. For most of us, we value our freedom because we want to express ourselves without reservation. We want to be ourselves, do what makes us happy, and feel the invigoration of life experiences. More importantly, we want what is best for our families. We want to raise them, teach them, and care for them. We want to have the capability of ensuring that those we love will experience the best possible life. This is what makes such freedom essential.

To be human means to be free and real democracy is a way to achieve freedom in a society. Freedom, as a system of balance that allows us to be and feel as free as possible, and democracy, as a system of self-governance that allows every individual to fully participate in the decisions that impact their lives and leads to self-determination, are practices that correlate with humanness.

Distinguishing humanness from human nature, a commonly understood phrase, is rather tricky. The difficulty in discussing human nature may be a result of human nature itself, or a result of our societal conditioning that instructs us to understand everything scientifically. It seems we want everything we observe to fit into neatly packed categories with clearly defined boundaries. We typically debate and define human nature as one set of criteria. And when we define human nature as one thing, we dismiss the opposite, for example, "human nature is rational, therefore, it is not irrational." Of course, this is not true. Human nature is both rational and irrational. There is a lengthy discussion regarding human nature in Part 2 of this book. For the purpose of this section, I only want to clarify the difference between human nature and humanness.

Human nature refers to characteristics common to all humankind that result from the natural origin of human beings: something inherent from our genetic make-up. In contrast, humanness refers to what it means to be a human, the qualities and characteristics that just are, regardless of why or where they came from. It includes the nature versus nurture debate (meaning the argument about whether humans act a certain way based on their inherent nature or by social conditioning), society, culture, history, and biology: all of it.

Being a human today may be very different than two hundred years ago, yet similar in some ways too. Being a human in America will be very different from being a human in Kazakhstan but there will be many similarities as well. Humanness includes the desire to be alone and the desire to be around others, which may depend on how a person feels on any given day. Humanness includes all our social conditioning and all our imperfections. It is everything human. If we consider all the things that make us human, the variations throughout humanity, and the need to express them within each individual, freedom is an essential component of humanness.

We are physical beings. We are part of a physical world of air, water, and earth that we interact with to nourish and maintain our own bodies. Our bodies are limited in the short term so we are active and work but need rest. Our bodies are also limited in the long term where we are vulnerable to disease and death. We often hear the phrase "I'm only human" when someone makes a mistake or meets a limitation.

We are dependent beings. No matter how independent we want to be, we all rely on other people for our well-being. We are surrounded by family and friends throughout our lives, we require doctors to care for us, teachers to educate us, farmers to grow food to nourish us, and on and on. Beyond being dependent on other people, we are dependent on the earth for health, nourishment, and resources for our survival.

We always hear that humans are rational beings. We are curious. We think. We solve problems. Humans are also irrational. We are full of a variety of emotions that impact the way we think and act. Emotional experiences such as love, admiration, or joy, make us feel good; and others such as hate, envy, or sorrow, make us feel terrible; but all are part of humanness. Emotions drive motivation and motivation causes human action. Some people act more on emotions than others, but emotions affect all of us. We often make mistakes based on not thinking things through before we act. Even when we are not acting on our emotions, emotions are a significant part of what we are. Sometimes we make mistakes by thinking through things too much—sometimes we should "follow our hearts." To deny either the rational or the irrational elements of humanness is to deny something vital to what it means to be human.

We are moral. We all have different morals but most of us have a general idea about right and wrong and have compassion toward others. Beyond morality, we are spiritual. Certainly, we are not all religious but humanness includes a connectedness beyond the self, which is ones' spirituality. For many, spirituality manifests in religious beliefs. For others, it is simply a consciousness of something greater than themselves, perhaps a being, perhaps something like energy. Some interpret spirituality as a connection to nature, humanity, or the depths of the inner-self, among many other interpretations of spirituality.

We also work. Sigmund Freud said, "Love and work are the cornerstones of our humanness." We are servants. We all serve others, whether it is caring for our family, showing an act of kindness by helping a stranger, volunteering, or something else. Service is the giving of self. In a world dominated by profit motives and mass consumption, serving others is an exchange that has human value outside of monetary measurements. Serving others helps shift our mindset away from selfishness toward selflessness and helps foster communities.

We are social creatures. As humans, we are continuously interacting with others. Of course there are those that prefer isolation, and all of us need it at times, but over the course of a lifetime, we immerse ourselves in the lives of others. Interactions occur at many different levels and with advancements in technology, the amount of interactions and the levels of interaction are continually expanding. Telephones, cell phones, Internet, emails, social media, and video calls allow us to create and maintain interactions over great distances. Television provides us with information and may increase our understanding of people and places far from us, but of course the relation is not the same as interacting with people. Part of being human is having intimate interactions. While technology allows us to interact and connect at great distances, it does not replace the need for face-to-face interactions and intimate relationships.

There is a human element to meeting up with close friends and family in person and having face-to-face discussions and interactions. Seeing the whole of a person, in real time, while you interact with them has immeasurable human value. There is a distinct difference between communicating with many people over the Internet or being in a crowd of people and speaking to the crowd, or walking through the crowd and interacting with people and small groups within the larger crowd. There are multiple dynamics of human relationships going on all at the same time. Any of us who have been to a concert, rally, club, or sports event know what this feels like.

Humans are communal beings. Beyond simple interactions with others, we use various methods of communication to express ourselves, exchange ideas, and build and navigate complex social structures. As communities form, people become free to interact with others to exchange, share, and co-exist, creating a sense of commonality and connectedness. Human societies develop cultures made up of stories, histories, myths, legends, rituals, ceremonies, celebrations, rules, norms, ethical codes, values, beliefs, and habits. We identify with these communities and cultures. We say things like "I am Mexican," "I am Jewish," "I am Black." Those identities have value to us.

We are also creative, both in our work and for self-expression. We make things and we express ourselves in abstracts. We write poems, books, and business plans. We paint replicas and abstracts. We draw pictures and blueprints. We build sculptures and skyscrapers. We sing, dance, and play instruments, which we created. In our work, service, art, community, and family, we want to feel valued. We want to know, on some level, that we matter.

Every human is different. Aspects of humanness vary to different degrees from person to person. Any system of social organization that fosters freedom must account for the vast differences in and among people. Humanness necessitates flexible and inclusive political and economic practices if humans are to be truly free in a society with other people. By participating in a truly democratic process that actually allows us to contribute freely to our fullest potential to the societal decisions that affect us, we are participating in the continual creation of the society in which we exist. As a result, the society reflects and reciprocates our humanness to the extent we participate and have an impact.

Real Democracy as Freedom in Society

"Democracy is not merely a form of Government. It is primarily a mode of associated living, of conjoint communicated experience. It is essentially an attitude of respect and reverence towards our fellow men." —Bhimrao Ramji Ambedkar

"The common interests very largely elude public opinion entirely, and can be managed only by a specialized class whose interests reach beyond the locality." —Walter Lippmann

"If we put our trust in the common sense of common [people] and 'with malice toward none and charity for all' go forward on the great adventure of making political, economic and social democracy a practical reality, we shall not fail." —Henry A. Wallace

"Those who own the country ought to govern it." —John Jay

Society, including government, is not a static thing. It is fluid: constantly changing. But to constantly change it must continuously be created. This happens even when we don't participate. Currently, Congress, the President, and banking and business leaders are creating the bulk of our society in their favor. If we actively and continually collectively participate in the creation of our own society, we will bring humanness to freedom. This process, that we call direct democracy, connects our political governance, that is our method of coexisting, to our humanness and thus is freedom for all. It is the balance of freedom in a society. This is the connection. This is finding what it really means to be human.

Real democracy requires patience. It takes time. But let us not confuse efficiency with effectiveness. As Harry S. Truman pointed out, "When you have an efficient government, you have a dictatorship." Instead, we can embrace our humanness and embed it in our political and societal structures. The bigger the group, the longer it will take to get everyone accurate information, allow them to form opinions and exchange ideas, and share what they have to say. Therefore, most political interactions should be local and engaging.

Instead of occupying your time in front of the television and complaining about the government and the community to your friends without having an impact, imagine a different lifestyle. Imagine the joy of bringing your family down to a local assembly, engaging with them in discussions of issues that impact all of your lives, and having your voices be heard! What more could parents want than teaching their children the beauty of self-determination, compassion, and respect for others? Simply put, we can all experience what it really means to be human and free.

Freedom is essential to human beings. True democracy nurtures freedom among humans in a society. Unfortunately, we do not have true democracy in America. To achieve freedom in a society, we must interact democratically in a way that considers and respects the realities of humanness. However, our government and social institutions hinder freedom because they do not correspond with actual humanness. Although we are told society is organized in a way that accounts for human nature, it actually only accounts for the narrowest view. Part 2 of this book analyzes the foundation of economic thought and policy to highlight how it does not respect humanness. By highlighting these inadequacies, it will become apparent why the economic system forces great divisions among people and destroys the planet we live on. More importantly, it will be clear how we need to change the economic system to account for the realities of humanness.

Part 2: Challenging the Economic Status Quo: *Considerations of Reality and Humanness*

Part 2 challenges the foundation behind our current economic structure. Keeping in mind the ideas of freedom in a society based on humanness developed in Part 1, Part 2 argues that the current economic structure opposes humanness and, therefore, freedom. This is a direct contradiction to the mainstream discourse, which establishes capitalism as the only economic system to promote freedom.

Chapter 4 revisits the foundational discourse behind capitalism. By laying out the linear thought process of the capitalist structures and explaining each step individually, Chapter 4 illustrates the building blocks that justify the status quo. This is essential because the entire description, from human nature to improving the quality of life for everyone, is rarely presented in full. Instead, pundits and politicians assert narrow phrases that emphasize one aspect of one piece of the foundation, thereby making it accepted and common knowledge without the merits ever being challenged. This thought process begins with the notion of human nature.

Chapter 5 challenges the commonly accepted idea that human nature is selfish, competitive, and rational by examining philosophers whose ideas were used to create that perception. The chapter shows how these prominent philosophers who are credited with the idea that human nature is selfish, competitive, and rational were not as definitive and certain as we are led to believe. It also explores ideas of some other highly respected philosophers who transformed social thinking but had views on human nature that contradict the mainstream discourse.

Chapter 6 confronts every step of the capitalism justification thought process by explicitly asserting all the falsehoods one must assume as whole and accurate truths to make this foundational thought function. By accepting these misrepresentations as truth, we ignore many realities and consequently forgo our humanness.

Chapter 7 connects the dysfunctional economic thought to notions of freedom in a society and explains how the capitalist economy hinders freedom in a society because it does not align with humanness.

Chapter 4: The Foundation We Built the Economy On

"The fundamental issue that must be decided in this, country ... whether to have real freedom for the mass of people, not only political but economic, or whether we are to be governed by a group of economic overlords." —Harold Ickes

"The forbidden truth is that we are living by a set of lies, which are necessary for short-term profit, at the expense of human physical and psychological life and global environmental integrity. We are living in a system where power ensures that the requirements of profit take priority over the requirements of living things—including the need to know that this is the case." —David Edwards

Part 1 shows that we must analyze our social and political structures to determine that freedom requires a balance and to understand how to achieve it. Similarly, we must analyze our economic structures to discover what economic freedom in a society looks like. Unchecked individual economic freedom hinders other individuals' economic freedom to pursue a quality livelihood and realize self-determination. Therefore, it is crucial that we have some understanding of economics on multiple levels.

Obviously, we all should seek education in personal finance: we should have a budget and understand how to save money. However, America is an economic giant on the global scene, so if we are serious about impacting the economy in a productive way, we should understand how the economy functions throughout our nation and abroad, not just individually. This section explains the foundation and guiding principles of our economic system, as we know it—the way scholars and political leaders have always justified it to us.

We all know what "the economy" is. Not a formal definition, but when we refer to the economy we are generally referring to the network of the exchange of goods and services, using money as the medium of exchange, including labor, manufacturing, distribution, trade, and consumption, either within the limits of the country or throughout the global economy. An economic system is composed of institutions and laws, but it also includes people and relationships. We hear about it all the time: the shifts, if it's good or bad, the market, and so on. However, when we think of what we call "the economy," we should think about what economics is in the simplest of terms: economics is the study of how people deal with scarcity.

The world is a finite ecosystem. Economics is the study of how the limited resources are best distributed among people. Because there are limits and people's wants supposedly always exceed means, people are forced to make choices regarding what to do with resources. Some aspects of the environment are simply protected by laws preventing their exploitation. Most of these controls over resource allocation come in the form of private property rights and prices. Resources go to the highest bidder.

We consider some resources "renewable" (meaning unlimited). However, even the most renewable resources are only partially renewable and supplies diminish over time if they are overused. There may be exceptions to these categories; for example, sunlight appears to be neither renewable nor nonrenewable as the supply is unaffected by our usage.

An economic system attempts to answer this problem of scarcity by determining what to produce, how to produce it, and who has access to it once it is produced. Although not everyone desires it, an economic system may be associated with different goals as well. For example, besides growth, an economy may focus on liberty or equality. However, today, the world's largest economic institutions function based on a capitalist-type model, meaning that production and distribution are privately owned.

Capitalism has developed and expanded since the 16th century in Europe, spreading in the Western world after feudalism, and lead to the industrial revolution. It is based on individualism, which developed during the Enlightenment period in 18th century Europe. Essential to capitalism is the notion of private property rights where owners have control over the use and production means of their property and they own what is produced from it. Private owners make decisions regarding production and investment.

Capitalist systems vary including those from no government regulation, called anarcho-capitalist, to regulated market systems that aim for a more equitable distribution of wealth. In a laissez-faire system the government's role is minimal regulation where it only maintains peace and order to allow the economy to function. Regardless of type, most people agree that capitalism encourages economic growth.

In a capitalist economy, the goal is to maximize profits. You may have heard the story of the cyclical process of increasing profits. Private owners of the means of production act in their own best interest. Resources or factors of production—land, labor, and capital—are all owned by households. Firms buy or rent these factors to produce goods and services, which are sold back to households (keep in mind that firms are owned by other households). In markets for factors of production, money is exchanged to purchase land, labor, and capital.

Making profit is the owner's incentive to produce goods that consumers want. Prices function as signals that represent the relationship between supply and demand of goods and services and let the owners know what and how much to produce to optimize profits. They are competing with other firms who will do the same, driving prices down as firms seek ways to sell products at lower prices than their competitors. This process creates economic growth as producers will continually find more efficient ways to produce goods and services at lower costs to continue increasing profits.

Means of production are operated by laborers who sell their labor to the owners for a wage. Competition among laborers determines the price of labor through supply and demand. Laborers have an incentive to work to make money. They choose what work they do based on pursuing their own best interest.

Goods and services, that are produced from privately owned means through labor, are sold on the market. In markets for goods and services, money is exchanged for goods and services produced by firms. The same is true for the service of lending money. In financial markets, savers lend money to borrowers at a monetary price (interest) determined by supply and demand.

Supply and demand determine prices on the market that act as a signal to communicate to producers what goods and services consumers want and how much they are willing and able to pay for them. Consumers act in self-interest to find the best goods and services to make them happiest at the lowest cost. They purchase those goods and services with money, which is paid back to the owners of means of production as profits. In actuality there isn't usually a direct link from consumers to producers of goods. However, by using money as a common means of exchange, money flows back through retail suppliers and distributors back to the owners of production.

The owners reinvest some of the profit to invest in more means of production. They keep the remainder of profit, and the cycle continues all while accumulating wealth for owners and creating more jobs for labor. Competition between firms forces them to continuously innovate new ways to improve efficiency of production, make new and improved products, and lower prices. With continuously lower prices and more available jobs, the standard of living rises.

Of course this is just the cycle of one firm in the production sector. Many other firms and several other sectors will interact and overlap with this cycle at different points as it progresses. For simplicity, I will deconstruct this one cycle, highlighting the inconsistencies of the theory. What you should keep in mind is that these same assumptions and inconsistencies apply to the other firms and sectors, which continually interact, exponentially compounding the problems, exploiting the weaknesses, and blurring the reality. Economists study this cycle and break every piece down into near-perfect equations so they can track and predict how people function to make policy and decision-making much easier.

Economics is in a league of its own in the realm of social science. Unlike any other social science, economists approach problems and treat observation as if they are conducting experiments in a physical science. However, in reality, economics is a human science. It is like sociology or history. Historians may attempt to predict future events based on historical facts, but they largely avoid mathematical models to determine future behavior. What is worse than trying to predict human behavior based on quantitative analysis, is trying to control it based on quantitative measures.

The economic system is such an overwhelming piece of our societal and cultural makeup. It is how we interact with most people and it impacts the way we act. Many people argue that our current system isn't capitalism. However, mainstream economic thought and discourse are based on capitalist theory and tendencies.

Mainstream economics, that is classical and neo-classical, both function on a string of logical steps that create a foundation for all modern economic thought and policy. Then the details are debated in the mainstream discourse: more tax, less tax, who to tax, regulate, deregulate, etc., etc. We debate things like how much government intervention the market needs. Meanwhile, the foundations of such debates—theories, policies, practices, and measures—begin with some assumptions that are never questioned within the mainstream discourse.

Scholars say they have figured out over the last few centuries that humanity can structure a system of economics that is self-perpetuating and self-regulating. It will function naturally, as it obeys laws of nature. It begins with human nature. This foundation of thoughts and theories follow a logical process. The shorter version of the argument is as follows:

Human nature is rational and competitive and motivated by self-interest, therefore, given **incentives** of property protected by rights of ownership, these human **rational actors**, having **accurate information** will make the **best choices** as to what to produce, buy, sell, and/or do for work to make the most profit. **Competition** means increasing profits will be further invested into **innovating** ways to produce more goods for the lowest possible cost because innovation means producing goods cheaper and a greater supply of goods means a lower price, dictated by **supply and demand curves**. And, the cycle continues, **creating more wealth**. Producing more goods creates more jobs because more workers are needed to produce more goods, more goods cause even lower prices, and more people working means more people purchasing more goods that need to be made. This **economic growth** is measured by **gross domestic product** (**GDP**). Increased growth leads to more people having access to more lower-priced goods and allows more people to improve their **standard of living** and **quality of life**. And, the cycle continues!

However, if we explore this train of thought, the inaccuracies become so prevalent and we see that the entire foundation is an illusionary system strung together by partial truths and covered up through propaganda and rhetoric. This leads one to think, if the foundation of thought is so overwhelmingly misguided at every stage, how insufficient, inaccurate, and destructive are the policies and practices that were built on that foundation over the last century?

The remainder of this chapter provides the common explanation for each step of the mainstream economic foundational thought process. The doctrine and rationale are so embedded in our national discourse that the sequence is rarely discussed as a whole. Instead, small catch phrases like, "the essence of capitalism is freedom," "in capitalism the harder you work, the better off you are," and "the best succeed the most" are casually repeated, reinforce individual elements of the status quo, and are simply accepted as truth. However, when these components are considered together, their reliance on each other becomes obvious, as do the fragile roots of the generally accepted catch phrases.

Human Nature: Fixed, Selfish, Rational, and Competitive

"To feel much for others and little for ourselves, that to restrain our selfish and to indulge our benevolent affections, constitutes the perfection of human nature." —Adam Smith

Economic policies are largely constructed and justified by notions of human nature. We are told that this version of free market-esque capitalismishness that we operate in is the only way to manage an economy because it correlates with human nature. Anything else, we are told, goes against our fundamental humanness. The conception of human nature we are talking about is one that is fixed, self-interested, rational, and competitive. This analysis of human nature is based on a lineage of thought by western philosophers and largely supported in scholarly analysis.

When we think about human nature, we are trying to determine how human beings think and act based on their natural state. That is, if we can figure out what humans will do naturally, meaning what they are programmed to do, we can add some real life variables and hypothesize a likely outcome of how they will function in the market. The market is a collection of billions of individual face-to-face transactions, a seemingly infinite system to attempt to analyze. By determining human nature and predicting the actions of individuals based on that nature, economists believe they can determine large-scale trends—the behavior of the masses: "the herd."

Theories of human nature that support the mainstream economic discourse derive predominantly from western traditions. Determining human nature involves questioning what human nature is and how it is. For example, is human nature fixed or flexible? In the western tradition the ancient Greek philosopher Socrates, who is credited as the founder of western philosophy, considered human nature to be a fixed state.

According to his student, Aristotle, Socrates believed there could be no knowledge of things in flux and, therefore, knowledge of human nature meant that it is fixed. Socrates devoted his time to finding definitions of humans' moral virtues.[14] He believed that humans are what they are because of human nature. While many philosophers debate whether human nature is fixed, the idea that human nature is specific and identifiable is dominant. Furthermore, whether fixed or flexible, many scholars agree that it is human nature to pursue one's self-interest.

Aristotle conceptualized self-interest in the realm of human nature. He wrote, "surely the love of self is a feeling implanted by nature."[15] The man considered to be the father of modern economics, Adam Smith, extrapolated on self-interest motivated by the pursuit of property. In 1759, Smith published *The Theory of Moral Sentiments*. In 1776, he published *An Inquiry into the Nature and Causes of the Wealth of Nations*, one of the leading manuscripts in classical economic theory.

The *Wealth of Nations* has influenced all western economic theory and policy over the past two and a half centuries, and its ideas are embedded in the foundation of modern thought. Highlighted by his famous quote: "It is not from the benevolence of the butcher, the brewer, or the baker that we expect our dinner, but from their regard to their own interest,"[16] Smith argued that people act according to self-interest and this feeds the economic cycle.

In Leviathan, Thomas Hobbes, one of the most influential western philosophers, wrote, "no man giveth, but with intention of Good to himself; because Gift is Voluntary; and of all Voluntary Acts, the Object is to every man his own Good."[17] In nature, Hobbes theorized, humans are self-interested beings that seek out cooperation to protect themselves from the natural state that self-interest dictates: "nasty, brutish, and short."[18] In this sense, humans could escape their natural state and function outside of it because they could agree to. Of course, the root of society is still self-preservation and self-interest.

John Locke, whose philosophies precluded the founding documents of the United States, believed humans were rational but nature also allowed them to be selfish. He argued people will naturally pursue their self-interest and that everyone had a right to defend his "life, health, liberty, or possessions."[19] Therefore, people engaged in a social contract to ensure this protection and to resolve conflicts.

The social contact is a theoretical agreement that legitimizes the existence of government. The theory states that people concede to giving up a certain amount of power and abide by laws because they will be protected from others, either because others follow the rules or because a governing body is empowered to enforce them.

These philosophers have had a profound impact on our society today. Socrates' notion of a fixed human nature is entrenched in the societal discourse and in the justifications for the status quo economic structures. Hobbes' and Locke's notion of human nature being self-interested, based on pursuing happiness and property, is used to justify our constant pursuit of material and monetary wealth. In total, human nature is fixed, self-interested, rational, and competitive. Using this conception of human nature, many people believe that the economic system of capitalism is aligned with human nature.

Incentive: Your Motive is Money

"People are people, and they respond to incentives. They can nearly always be manipulated—for good or ill—if only you find the right levers." —Steven D. Levitt and Stephen J. Dubner

"Wake up, you idiots! Whatever made you think that money was so valuable?" —Kurt Vonnegut

If human nature is inherently selfish, then humans will pursue self-interest if they are given an incentive to do so. An incentive is something that motivates us to act and is a central assumption of economic study and policy. An incentive, as they say, is why you get up to go to work in the morning. This of course means monetary incentive, and it implies if such incentive did not exist, people would not do any work.

Economics assumes that people require incentives to choose a particular action. It drives rational choice, competition, and innovation. In capitalism, the incentive is property ownership. Because you know if you work hard, you can expect to make money, purchase things you want, and have legal ownership of them, you will do it. No one would go to work if they knew their pay would be taken away.

Incentives help guide people toward the right decision—that is, the rational choice. Incentives also guide firms. With profit as an incentive, firms will produce goods that people want to buy, which, in turn, is the incentive for consumers to buy their goods (because people are motivated to fulfill their wants). Furthermore, firms create incentives for workers to complete work with the promise of wages (and the risk of being fired).

Rational Man, Rational Person: The Path of Least Resistance

"Man is a rational animal—so at least I've been told. Through out a long life, I have looked diligently for evidence in favour of this statement, but so far I have not had the good fortune to come across it." —Bertrand Russell

While human beings may be very complex creatures, economists believe habits and choices are often predictable. As free agents, with free will, people will make choices to fulfill their desire to be happy. People are generally selfish (according to economists, but not necessarily in a bad way). Therefore, mainstream economic theory and policy is predicated on the idea that human beings are rational actors who pursue self-interest and have the ability to make decisions and actions toward this aim. There is a lot of support for this idea in scholarly literature dating back to the ancient Greeks.

Plato and Aristotle argued that human nature is both rational and irrational. The irrational side will succumb to desires; therefore, the rational side must regulate it. Rationality is what separates man from other species. John Locke believed humans were rational but nature also allowed them to be selfish. One could infer that this means people will naturally pursue their self-interest and will find rational ways to pursue it.

Another influential thinker, John Stuart Mill, determined that because man is a rational being, he would pursue self-interested goals for the least cost. Mill wrote that man is a "being who invariably does that by which he may obtain the greatest amount of necessaries, conveniences, and luxuries, with the smallest quantity of labour and physical self-denial with which they can be obtained in the existing state of knowledge."[20] The "economic man," as this theoretical being is called, conceptually evolved into a person who acts rationally, based on accurate information, because of the self-interest-driven desire for wealth.

Rational Choices: The Human Computer

"To live is to choose. But to choose well, you must know who you are and what you stand for, where you want to go and why you want to get there." —Kofi Annan

"Nothing defines humans better than their willingness to do irrational things in the pursuit of phenomenally unlikely payoffs. This is the principle behind lotteries, dating, and religion." —Scott Adams

Based on the theory of a rational man, economists developed rational choice theories that are at the roots of economic study, theory, policy, and measurement. Rationality is assumed for individuals and firms throughout economic models to explain and predict human behavior. People pursue their self-interests by making rational tradeoffs and choices to maximize profits. In other words, individuals pursue specific ends (like money) in the greatest amount possible with the least possible cost.

People make choices by evaluating how happy each option would make them, determining the constraints and opportunity costs of each option, and choosing the option where benefits outweigh costs by the greatest margin (a cost-benefit analysis). People compare the benefits and costs of a possible choice to the benefits and costs of similar possible choices and decide based on the greatest benefit at the least cost.

People also choose the work or business of their skill and interest, and trade that labor for the equivalent monetary value as determined by the market. In rational choice theory, these costs in pursuing wants are external to the individual. Internal costs like morals are not calculable; therefore, they are left out of the equation and ignored as if they do not exist. Economic models further assume that individual patterns of behavior that dictate choice can be extrapolated on to determine economic trends of society as a whole.

Competition: Winners Win and Losers Lose

"Competition is the keen cutting edge of business, always shaving away at costs."
—Henry Ford

Most people do not really believe the government has no place in the economy. Even the most hardcore free market advocates believe it is the government's responsibility to create stability through national defense and monopoly prevention. The idea is that markets function best when conditions are predictable and investors do not have to worry about instability, in the imaginary setting of perfect competition: that is a market where no specific participant has the power to set the price of a product produced by multiple participants.

Without the restrictions of imperfect markets and with an incentive as the motivator, firms and households will compete against other firms and households for a greater share of the market. Competition to secure business transactions under the most favorable conditions means all parties strive to be as efficient and innovative as possible. By competing against one another, firms continuously develop technologies and services to produce new and better products that consumers want to buy for the lowest possible cost. An increase in the availability of products drives price down even further.

Consumers will always choose to purchase the best goods and services they need and want at the lowest possible cost. This gives consumers the power to tell firms what goods and services to produce and how much they are willing to pay for them, based on what and how much they buy. Firms compete against each other, as do laborers and consumers. Even workers within firms compete against each other, making the firm as efficient as possible. By pursuing self-interest, a person's and a firm's choices will drive competition and benefit everyone.

Innovation: The Key to Everything

"Just as energy is the basis of life itself, and ideas the source of innovation, so is innovation the vital spark of all human change, improvement and progress." —Ted Levitt

Because rational people and firms compete against other rational people and firms pursuing their self-interest, they must constantly innovate to outdo their competitors. Competition maintains pressure for the creation of new technologies, more efficient processes, better products, and ideas that we call innovation.

Innovation implies progress. It is the life force of the modern economy as it is the enemy of stagnation. It is the intangible energy that nourishes unlimited growth, ever lifting the standard of living for all. Innovation is born from the creative mind and the laborers sweat. It brings us everyday conveniences from the light bulb to the cell phone to HD television and the Internet. Innovation has allowed us ever increasing efficient modes of transportation from railways across the nation to airlines across the globe. It has more than doubled our life expectancy through medical advances. It gives us the power to destroy entire cities within seconds by the push of a button.

In line with mainstream economic thinking, innovation comes from people, or privately owned firms, because they have the incentive to be innovative. Innovation fuels supply and demand curves by creating new products people want to buy (demand). It also means firms are finding ways to make more products at lower costs, increasing supplies, and lowering prices for consumers.

Supply and Demand: The Language of the Herd

"Need is not demand. Effective economic demand requires not merely need but corresponding purchasing power." —Henry Hazlitt

"It is important to reclaim for humanity the ground that has been taken from it by various arbitrarily narrow formulations of the demands of rationality." —Amartya Sen

Supply and demand is the single most fundamental model in economics. Markets consist of billions of people and firms, making trillions of transactions every day. How all these separate individual entities can communicate with one another in any coherent manner should seem impossible. Forget ever trying to create policy or make business decisions based on predicting this global cluster of people. How could we ever hope to navigate such a mess?

Economists tell us the answer is price. Prices serve as signals from consumers to producers almost instantaneously. It is the way producers communicate what they will make and consumers communicate what they will buy. Thus is born the supply and demand model in mainstream economics.

Supply of goods are determined by marginal cost, meaning firms will produce additional goods if the cost of producing more goods is less than the price consumers will pay for it. Whereas, demand for goods is the amount of goods consumers are willing and able to purchase at various prices. The willingness and ability to pay for goods are determined by factors such as income, available credit, desires, cost of the goods, and the availability and the cost of similar goods.

In true capitalism, the consumer is king (so we are told). Consumers tell firms what goods and services they want, how much they are willing to pay, and what amount of goods and services they will buy. In turn, firms produce what goods and services people want and the quantity they want because firms want to make a profit. All of this happens through the signals of prices and their relationship with supply and demand.

We are also told that supply and demand dictates the value of a person's work. In the free market there is equilibrium between the value added to society and the compensation earned for labor, as labor is similar to goods and services in markets.

Supply and demand tells us that, in a competitive market (of course), the price of a good will fluctuate while consumers purchase that good in whatever quantities they are willing to. The less products consumers are willing to purchase at a given price, the more producers must lower prices to sell them. They will lower the price until it is no longer profitable, at which point they will no longer produce the good. Conversely, if consumers are purchasing an abundance of the good, producers will raise the price. The fluctuation continues until the price of that good reaches an equilibrium at the price consumers are willing to pay for the good at the quantity producers are willing to make the good. This process should also occur while workers negotiate wages and choose the best jobs for the highest wages they can get. (Like any good relationship, communication is key.)

Wealth Creation: How to Grow a Pie

"Most economic fallacies derive from ... the tendency to assume that there is a fixed pie, that one party can gain only at the expense of another." —Milton Friedman

Capitalism demands the best of every individual but it rewards them according to their efforts and skills. Through the process of pursuing self-interest by making rational choices, competing, and innovating, people and firms earn profits and accumulate wealth. There isn't one accepted definition of wealth but we have a general idea of what it encompasses. Adam Smith described wealth as "the annual produce of the land and labor of the society."[21] It is the sum of owned resources and goods including things like money, property, and real estate. It is calculated by subtracting the value of one's liabilities (i.e. debt), from the total of their assets.

The economic process described so far creates wealth accumulation. By producing goods and services, workers add value to objects that were previously raw material. This increase in value is referred to as value added and covers the cost of labor plus a surplus for owner's profit. At this point in the cycle some of the accumulated wealth that resulted from the process is reinvested back into innovation to increase productivity (because self-interested human nature prompts rational choice to better compete through innovation). The reinvesting of profit into capital is wealth accumulation because it is owned property, but some profits are also saved as financial assets, which may be invested into other firms. All of this wealth accumulation and reinvesting causes increased economic growth as measured by GDP.

Economic Growth: The Productive Potential of Us

"If there is any one subject on which everyone [on the news] seems to agree, any one point of doctrine to which every political sect subscribes, it's that 'economic growth' is the highest goal, our ultimate goal as a country. And not only as a country—as states, as communities, as corporations, as individuals." —Bill McKibben

Economic growth is the increasing accumulation of wealth and the capacity of the economy to produce goods and services to satisfy growing needs and wants of society. The capacity to satisfy growing desires increases by innovating new products or ways to better produce existing ones. Increased productivity lowers the amount of inputs needed for a given output (product or service). Therefore, goods are produced at a lower cost, prices for products and services drop, and consumers can purchase more goods for their money, thereby raising the standard of living.

Economic Measures: The Example of GDP

"Gross domestic product (GDP) is the market value of all goods and services bought in a given period. In short, it measures how much money is spent. When more money is spent GDP goes up, when less is spent, GDP goes down. When GDP goes up, the economy is said to be growing, when GDP goes down, the economy is said to be shrinking. This implies, of course, that 'the economy' is nothing but a number." —John Kozy

The growth of the economy must be measured for many reasons, including finding out which firms or nations have strong economies to invest in. It is important for firms to show that they are growing (increasing profits) to attract investors. Very few people would put all that newly accumulated wealth from economic growth, into a business that couldn't prove it was going to make more wealth so businesses report growth in quarterly and annual reports to prove their worth.

Countries also need to show a growing economy to attract foreign investment. Stable and consistent growth in a nation's GDP shows investors that the nation is capable of maintaining a stable, secure, productive environment for businesses to thrive. National economic growth shows how all the measured economic factors in the country are doing as a whole. Economic growth is measured as a percentage change in GDP from one year to the next.

The most widely used method for measuring GDP is the expenditure approach, which functions on the notion that all products made will be bought by someone, therefore the value of the total product will equal total expenditures. The equation to calculate GDP using the expenditure method is $Y = C + I + G + (X-M)$.

The variables represent the following:

GDP (Y) is the sum of Consumption (C), Investment (I), Government Spending (G), and Net Exports (X-M)

Consumption (C) is the sum of private households' purchases of goods (durable and non-durable) and services. Investment (I) is the sum of firms' investments into new equipment. Investment also includes the private purchase of new housing. It does not include the purchase of financial goods such as stocks. Investment into stocks are only calculated when the firm invests the money from the stock purchase into the purchase of new equipment. Government spending (G) is the sum of government purchases for goods and services such as military spending and postal service. Government spending does not include transfer of payments (i.e. social security). Exports (X) measure the total exports from the nation. Imports (M) are subtracted because imported goods are all calculated elsewhere (in the C, I, or G categories).

GDP is a measure of economic growth and is supposed to show how well the national economy is doing. Actions taken to increase GDP indirectly raise the standard of living increasing the productivity of labor and alleviating poverty, so we are told.

Standard of Living: The Boats Are Rising

"A rising tide lifts all boats." —John F. Kennedy

"Of all the preposterous assumptions of humanity over humanity, nothing exceeds most of the criticisms made on the habits of the poor by the well-housed, well-warmed, and well-fed." —Herman Melville

While there is no exact definition for the standard of living, the term is essentially a measure of how easily a population is able to satisfy its wants and needs at a given time. It refers to the level of wealth, comfort, and needs met in a society. It includes income, employment, poverty rate, housing, healthcare, education, life expectancy, freedom, and economic growth.

There is also no single accepted measure for the standard of living. Many economists measure GDP per capita, which is the GDP divided by the population (what every person's portion of GDP would be *IF* it were divided equally), as an indicator of the standard of living. Another widely accepted measure of the standard of living is real income per person, or average real gross GDP per capita, which is measured by adjusting the GDP per capita for inflation. Basically this means finding the average income and comparing it to the rise in prices of goods and services (or the devaluing of the currency) because that will tell you how much goods and services people can purchase with a given amount of money at a given time.

Another way to measure the standard of living is the poverty rate. Poverty is determined by assessing the total cost of necessary goods and services as consumed by an average adult. The poverty rate is the change in the percentage of people who can afford this average cost. Other measures include education statistics, life expectancy, and access to a common good (like when pundits flaunt how poor people have microwaves and Play Stations to prove that being poor isn't so bad). Whatever the measure, we are told that growth means the standard of living has been rising over the last century because of capitalism.

Quality of Life: Livin' the Good Life

"Many persons have the wrong idea of what constitutes true happiness ... [it] is not attained through self-gratification, but through fidelity to a worthy purpose."
—Helen Keller

"One's life has value so long as one attributes value to the life of others, by means of love, friendship, indignation and compassion." —Simone de Beauvoir

Quality of life, while not exactly the same thing as standard of living, is a measure used to evaluate the well-being of a population. Standard of living is based primarily on income and materials, whereas quality of life factors are non-material indicators such as health, education, leisure time, and civil society. Clearly, quality of life is even less tangible than standard of living and therefore impossible to determine.

Researchers focus on surveys to test non-tangibles like emotional and mental health. Additionally, statistical measures paint a picture of quality of life through various indicators. In the quality of life index the following indicators are measured: health, by measuring life expectancy at birth (in years); family life, by measuring the divorce rate per 1,000 people of the population (converted into index of 1 through 5); community life, by measuring rate of attendance in social and community groups; material well-being, by measuring GDP per person at purchasing power parity (PPP) in dollars; political stability and security; climate and geography; job security, by measuring the unemployment rate; political freedom, through political indices, like the freedom index; and gender equality, by comparing average male and female incomes.[22] Again, we are told capitalism is responsible for human advancement, innovation, and the drastic increases in quality of life since the Industrial Revolution.

This Process Can Continue Forever!

"The promoters of the global economy ... see nothing odd or difficult about unlimited economic growth or unlimited consumption in a limited world." —Wendell Berry

If you recall from earlier, all of this is based on how we systematically divide up limited resources. While this may seem precarious, there are two answers to address the resource limitation problem. First, wealth accumulation is not created solely from extracting and using limited resources. In the production of goods and services, human creativity and innovation are injected into the production process, thereby creating additional value and wealth, exponentially. Because the synergy of the human mind is unlimited, it can create unlimited wealth. Economists tell us that we don't need to worry about dividing the pie because we just keep making the pie bigger. Secondly, in the event we run out of resources, humans will innovate their way out of the loss. When we run out of something, or get close to running out, people will realize it is a problem and figure out ways to handle the issue and keep progressing forward.

So this is where the debate begins. Everything you just read is generally accepted as truth in mainstream economics and is embedded in colloquial dialogue. These arguments are used as rationale and justification for economic interactions in society as a whole: "people are selfish" or "that's just human nature." Whether you believe all, some, or none of it to be true, this is the foundation for the world you live in. With that established, society debates opposing views: Do you want to live in a free market or a controlled economy? Do you want freedom or government control? Regulation or deregulation? Taxes or no taxes? How much? How many? Etc. All the while, almost no one challenges the foundation these debates stand on.

Chapter 5: The Great Debate: Influential Thinkers and What We Don't Know About Human Nature

"We are all human; therefore, nothing human can be alien to us." —Maya Angelou

While we are led to believe that the above foundational concepts are truth, or at the least, they are the leading ideas, they have all been subjects of debate since their inception. It is interesting that scholars, historians, politicians, and pretty much everyone, choose specific things that past scholars and philosophers said as if their words are some kind of unbendable rule, while ignoring other things the same person said, either contradictory to the same point or in opposition to a different foundational topic. Pundits and policy makers bounce from person to person through history and cherry-pick specific things each said that support the story they want to tell. However, anything that any one philosopher said should simply serve as a basis for discussion, rather than be accepted as fact.

Earlier I wrote that the conception of human nature that aligns with our economic structures is fixed, self-interested, rational, and competitive. I wrote that these analyses are largely supported by scholarly lineage, which is true. However, there is a large body of scholarly work, which opposes these notions as well. Furthermore, as you will see, many of the most influential thinkers, that are the basis of these claims, themselves had divergent beliefs on human nature.

Because mainstream economists harp on these philosophers as propaganda for our misguided course of action, I will discuss some of these individuals to highlight the inconsistencies. Before we have that discussion, there are some important things to consider. Like any writer, I will throw in quotes to support my argument as it is important to read the philosopher's own words, but I acknowledge these quotes are not the whole picture of each author. You should acknowledge that too.

Quotes are a small portion of any work and have a particular context to them. To really understand the complexity of a work, you have to read the whole work, which would still be insufficient because words and phrases can be ambiguous, get lost in translation, and change meaning over time. To understand one philosopher, you would have to read all of their writing, which would still be insufficient for the same reason mentioned above. Also, because people change and grow throughout their lives and from one work to another, so it's really impossible to fully understand a philosopher's beliefs. Even scholars of philosophy debate what these philosophers actually meant.

So, the options are that we can allow pundits to throw quotes at us and use historical figures as infallible gods of economics and social policy, or we can recognize that these figures were all people with different and varying opinions like anyone else. And, even if a particular figure was a genius and certain of their theories, that does not mean their theories were actually correct. Even if what they said was true, it does not make it the whole truth. What I intend for the following section is to simply highlight a few of the well-known thinkers that laid the foundation of our current economic and political structures and show that even back in their time, it was not as black and white of a picture as our elites paint for us.

Fixed ... orrrrrrr Not

One element of human nature that has always been debated is whether it is fixed. Is human nature one set thing? If so, are the divergences of people based on social constructs? Or, is it that human nature is actually not fixed? The notion of human nature as fixed dominates the discourse; in fact, it is virtually accepted as truth. We constantly hear what human nature is and it is used to explain why people perform certain actions. It is also used to rationalize and justify policies. While the notion of human nature as fixed dominates the discourse as if it is unchallenged, many philosophers have debated it over time.

Socrates' philosophy moved away from the typical study of his time, heaven to the study of human truths. For Socrates, human nature was fixed or had final cause. This means that human nature dictated what humans became in a way that makes human nature almost separate from humans themselves. Ideas, not the material world we experience through our senses, possessed the truth. This view of human nature carries a metaphysical element to it as human nature is considered something beyond the physical human experience.

Socrates theorized that human nature was fixed and that humans became whatever they became and acted however they did because of it. Aristotle and Plato had more complex visions of human nature. They considered human nature to be split into two parts. One side was the rational side, which consisted of logical and more spirited parts. The other side of human nature was ruled by desires and passions. For them, the pursuit of desires had to be controlled by the more rational side so man could achieve greater things.[23][24] In this scenario, human nature is fixed but there appears to be room for flexibility. At the very least, a split human nature has a little more complexity to it than Socrates' version.

The rise of modernism brought a rejection of the Socratic notions of human nature as being fixed and having final causes. Contrary to a metaphysical conception of human nature, the study of human nature became the study of determining actual human tendencies. While this transition did not dispel the idea of fixed human nature, modernists such as Thomas Hobbes and John Locke argued against it.

Hobbes understood humans as elements of the physical world, simply matter in motion. He wrote, "For seeing life is but a motion of Limbs ... For what is the *Heart*, but a *Spring*; and the *Nerves*, but so many *Strings*; and the [*Joints*], but so many *Wheels*, giving motion to whole Body."[25] However, this suggests more of a malleable notion of human nature. Hobbes implies that similarities exist in all men, but individual situations, not just fixed nature, affect the nature of the individual: "I say the [similarity] of *Passions*, which are the same in all men, *desire, fear, hope, [etc.]*; not the [similarity] of the *objects*, of the Passions, which are the things *desired, feared, hoped, [etc.]*: for these the [individual situations], and particular education do so vary."[26]

77

To understand another person, Hobbes argues, you must be able to put yourself through the experiences they have been through:

> *But there is another saying ... by which [man] might learn truly to read one another ... Read thyself ... to teach us that [similarity of] thoughts and Passions of one man, to the thoughts and Passions of another, whosoever [looks] into himself and [considers] what ... he [does] think, opine, reason, hope, [fear, etc.], and upon what grounds; he shall thereby read and know what are the thoughts and Passions of all other men, upon the like occasions.*[27]

John Locke also denounced the idea that human nature was fixed. He saw the human mind as a blank slate formed by experiences. Locke's theory that the human mind was a blank slate influenced many philosophers that followed him. In the *Essay Concerning Human Understanding*, Locke discusses his theory of moral knowledge that rejects the possibility of innate ideas: "All ideas come from sensation or reflection. Let us then suppose the mind to be, as we say, white paper, void of all characters, without any ideas ... the busy and boundless fancy of man has painted on it with an almost endless variety ... all the materials of reason and knowledge ... in one word, [this comes] from EXPERIENCE."[28]

He believed that humans were born without innate ideas, and the human mind developed ideas only through experiences and reflections: "I think I may say that of all the men we meet with, nine parts of ten are what they are, good or evil, useful or not, by their education."[29] So much of our social foundation is built on Locke's philosophy, like our notions of inherent rights to protect our property, which Locke defined as "life, liberty, and estate."[30] However, we staunchly maintain perceptions of innate selfishness as human nature, while Locke maintained the human mind was a blank slate.

David Hume of Scotland, one of the most influential philosophers from the 18th century, also argued against the existence of innate ideas. He maintained that humans derived knowledge from their personal experiences. According to him, ideas are derived from impressions of actual experience and perceptions of self are derived from actual experiences and ideas that are based on actual experiences. Therefore, humans do not have an inherent conception of self.

Another modernist philosopher, Francis Bacon, was critical of Aristotle's focus on metaphysical reasoning in addressing ideas of human nature. Bacon believed that understanding the human experience meant freeing one's mind from the distortions created by idols, which are conditions that create false truths among men.

For example, his "Idols of the Tribe" described illusions that derived from the nature of humanity in general. One such idol is that people tend to believe whatever they believe to be true and find evidence to support it and dismiss evidence to the contrary. He concluded that if people freed themselves from the idols, they would realize that there was no universal human nature, rather different characters and situations produced different outcomes.

Bacon disagreed with Locke and Hume that the human mind is a blank slate. He believed the human mind was a distorted reflection of reality. In other words, what we perceive as truth is not an objective perception, but rather, a truth distorted by our past perceptions of our experiences. He wrote, "All perceptions both of the senses and the mind bear reference to man and not to the universe and the human mind resembles those uneven mirrors which impart their own properties to different objects, from which rays are emitted and distort and disfigure them."[31]

Bacon thought we had to completely free our minds from these obstructions before we could begin to gain knowledge. To accomplish this, he developed the Baconian Method, based on observation and scientific reasoning, which was a precursor to the development of the scientific method.

Immanuel Kant, a prominent German philosopher from the Enlightenment Period, argued that the blank slate model of the mind was insufficient to explain our beliefs about objects that we have. Contrary to the argument that all experiences bring thoughts to the mind, Kant argued that some components of our beliefs must be brought by the mind to experience. While he recognized that many aspects of knowledge come from sensory experience, he believed that to be an insufficient explanation for all human knowledge.

Karl Marx, a Prussian philosopher and one of the most

significant social critics of all time, criticized philosophers' notion of human nature as inherent to the species. He rejected the idea that human nature is consistent and universal; rather, he emphasized the impacts of social relations.

Social and historical structures combined with elements of human biology, shape how humans behave and interact. Therefore, Marx believed that humans are capable of shaping their own nature to some extent. While human nature will continuously transform, not every aspect will be transformed; only the total will transform because of simultaneously varying parts of human nature: social relations, biology, etc. Marx analyzed the context of the human condition so he believed that human beings were the product of class, social relations, and their positions in the realm of material production. He wrote, "The essence of man is no abstraction inherent in each single individual. In its reality it is the ensemble of the social relations."[32]

To Rene Descartes, called "the father of modern philosophy," the mind and body belonged to two parallel but fundamentally different realms. Physical laws governed the body and the mind was of free will, meaning the mind had the freedom of choice to do or not do something. This allowed him to analyze humans as machine-like beings, products of their environments and experiences, while leaving room for explaining free will.

Self-interested and Competitive ... But Also Generous and Cooperative

Another element of human nature that we accept as truth, yet has always been debated among scholars, is the belief that human nature is selfish and competitive.

Aristotle argued that loving one's self was human nature, but that did not necessarily mean that selfishness was. He argued, "the love of self is a feeling implanted by nature ... although selfishness is rightly censured; this, however, is ... the love of self in excess."[33] Aristotle argued in favor of private property, not because humans selfishly pursued it, but because "The greatest pleasure [is] in doing a kindness or service to [others], which can only be rendered when a man has private property."[34] In this analysis, property ownership is the means to an end. Man will desire acquiring property to fulfill the greater pleasure of serving others.

Aristotle focused on additional elements of human nature. He believed human nature made man conjugal, communal, and curious. Therefore, man's natural course was to build a family along patriarchal lines, upon adulthood. Additionally, man has an inherent tendency toward building communities beyond the family structure. Building villages, towns, and cities, guided by laws and common agreements are a natural progression. Finally, man has an inherent curiosity and creativity, which will require him to experience life beyond engaging in politics. Clearly Aristotle believed human nature was more than just selfish and competitive.

Hobbes believed people were naturally selfish. He thought that it was necessary to restrict human nature in order to achieve a good society through the force of the state. He argues that without government, humans cannot have peace and security. This is because humans will compete violently against one another for basic necessities and preemptively fight others because of mistrust and fear. This is the premise for Hobbes' concept of the state of nature.

His state of nature is often cited as evidence that human nature is selfish and competitive. However, his model does not assume that selfishness and competitiveness are human nature. Hobbes argues that IN a state of nature people will act this way because they know some people are selfish and competitive. He uses this as a rationale for why government is needed: "the wickedness of bad men also compels the good [men] to have recourse, for their own protection, to the virtues of war, which are violence and fraud."[35]

Government is NOT a state of nature, so with a government, Hobbes argues, most people will not act selfish and competitive. This logic does not suppose a government changes human nature; rather it respects differences in humans and protects them from how some might act in nature. It appears that "self-interest" to Hobbes is less about pursuing selfishness and competitiveness, and more about self-preservation.

Similar to Hobbes, Locke believed human nature allowed humans to be selfish, writing, "self- love will make men partial to themselves and their friends."³⁶ However, Locke differed from Hobbes in that he thought human nature consisted of reason and tolerance. Locke also acknowledged that self-interest was part of natural law in that people must protect their property. He claimed, "For the strongest protection of each man's private property is the law of nature, without the observance of which it is impossible for anybody to be master of his own property and to pursue his own advantage."³⁷

However, Locke disagreed with theories that all men always act in their own interest. For example, Locke believed it was a duty to preserve one's self as natural law, but while man seeks self-preservation, if he is to be reasonable, he must likewise preserve others. He also claimed it was a person's duty to preserve others, and not act in ways that destroyed others, as long as it did not conflict with their own self-preservation: "Every one, as he is bound to preserve himself … so by the like reason, when his own preservation comes not in competition, ought he, as much as he can, to preserve the rest of mankind."³⁸

Finally for Locke, human nature suggested the pursuit of social and communal existence: "GOD having made man such a creature, that in his own judgment, it was not good for him to be alone, put him under strong obligations of necessity, convenience, and inclination to drive him into society, as well as fitted him with understanding and language to continue and enjoy it."³⁹ This is interesting in the context of western economic discourse because leadership uses Locke's "life, liberty, and the pursuit of property" as American values' historical justification for unlimited pursuit of material wealth at all costs. This goes far beyond Locke's notion of preserving one's self and in many cases, against his beliefs, by destroying other people's ability to preserve themselves.

Other thinkers like Immanuel Kant believed people were naturally selfish, therefore, it was essential to restrain one's human nature through rational thought in order to attain a good society. On the other hand, Jean Jacques Rousseau, a Genevan philosopher whose work influenced the thinking of the French Revolution, theorized that society is what causes humans to be selfish. He considered how in earlier periods of human history people did not always have language or rational political interactions; therefore, human nature was outside the realm of these interactions. Living in civilized societies that are based on reason is, therefore, unnatural. He believed that men were inherently born with the potential to be good; however, civilized social structure caused envy and made men bad.

Rousseau disagreed with Hobbes' assertion that because man did not know of goodness in a state of nature, that man was inherently evil. He claimed, "God makes all things good; man meddles with them and they become evil."[40] He wrote, "let us not conclude with Hobbes that because man has no idea of goodness he is naturally evil; that he is vicious because he does not know virtue."[41] Contrary to Hobbes, Rousseau believed morality was innate and had been corrupted by social constructs.

This is not to say that Rousseau believed man would act morally in a state of nature. However, he wrote, "were [Hobbes] to have reasoned on the basis of principles he establishes, [he] should have said that since the state of nature is the state in which the concern for our self-preservation is the least prejudicial to that of others, that state was consequently the most appropriate for peace and the best suited for the human race."[42]

Rousseau argues that Hobbes "injects into the savage man's concern for self-preservation the need to satisfy a multitude of passions which are the product of society and which have made laws necessary."[43] In other words, Rousseau argues that the things Hobbes claims make man selfish in a state of nature only exist outside the state of nature. Man may act like an animal if in a state of nature but remains outside the conditions of a political society, which Rousseau views as having a negative impact on morality.

Rousseau argues that man has an instinctively positive self-love, based on natural self-preservation and reason: "self-love only becomes good or bad by the use made of it and the relation established by its means."[44] Society transforms this love into pride, which leads to envy, fear, greed and spite.[45] Humans possess the need for self-preservation and a natural inclination toward compassion, as do animals. However, man uses free will to try to progress, but progress corrupts man further. He wrote,

"Man was born free, and he is everywhere in chains. Those who think themselves the masters of others are indeed greater slaves than they."[46]

Rousseau claimed that man developed society as a way to cooperate and escape the state of nature. Developments of agriculture, the institutions of law, private property, and division of labor created a society where man is in competition with others and there is conflict and inequality. To pursue self-preservation and remain free, man's social contract must be to the sovereignty of the people, not a government or republic.[47] He argued that the modern state was made by the rich and powerful, who tricked the people into surrendering their liberties to them.

Marx also believed that societal structures corrupted human beings. He did not believe that human nature ought to be suppressed for there to be a good society, but rather, a good society should allow people to fully express their human nature. Marx argues that capitalists are not motivated by inherent selfishness; rather that capitalism alienates them from their nature, which makes them selfish. He wrote:

> *The propertied class and the class of the proletariat present the same human self-estrangement. But the former class feels at ease and strengthened in this self-estrangement, it recognizes estrangement as its own power and has in it the semblance of a human existence. The class of the proletariat feels annihilated in estrangement; it sees in it its own powerlessness and the reality of an inhuman existence.*[48]

David Hume criticized the notion that human nature was simply driven by self-interest. While Hume admitted that selfishness might drive many political and economic decisions, social aspects of humans were even more malleable and could change if circumstances changed. Against the self-interest based human nature of Hobbesian thought, Hume argued that thousands of "instances are marks of a general benevolence in human nature, where no real interests binds us to the object."[49]

Furthermore, he believed people respected the benevolence of others even when it did not benefit them. People enjoyed making others happy but this did not mean it was out of self-interest (both benevolence and enjoyment may have motivated people to act but Hume argued that benevolent sentiments were separate from self-enjoyment).

People approved of benevolence because it benefited others and society as a whole, and prompted other virtues such as justice. This is crucial because, unlike benevolence, justice, according to Hume, was not part of nature. He believed people did not only approve of acts that promoted their own interests, in fact, personal interests were often different from the public interests. However, when social interests differed from personal interests, people did not always disapprove of the social interests.[50]

Adam Smith authored the most influential book to western capitalism, *The Wealth of Nations*. It focused on using free markets as a tool for increasing wealth and benefitting society. Prior to *The Wealth of Nations*, in 1759, Smith published *The Theory of Moral Sentiments*, which focused on man's sympathy for others. This work presents an irony because mainstream economists and the western leadership use Smith's *Wealth of Nations*, to push the message of individual pursuit of self-interest as the noblest goal.

Essentially, pundits argue that the government and society do not need to take care of others because the free market will automatically benefit everyone. However, these books taken together illustrate that Adam Smith himself knew the picture was more complex than self-interested pursuit (*Wealth of Nations* in and of itself shows this as well as Smith's frequent arguments for the need for government assistance and regulation of big business). Smith focused on different aspects of human nature and society in each book. Of course, these elements are not the whole picture, nor are they mutually exclusive.

Leaders exploit Smith's *Wealth of Nations* to push the message that if everyone pursues their own best interests then everyone would be better off. But Smith also warned against businesses, joint-stock companies, and against a true laissez-faire economy. He knew that business and industry leaders' interests do not align with the public. Referring to directors of joint-stock companies, Smith cautioned that:

> *Being the managers rather of other people's money than of their own, it cannot well be expected that they should watch over it with the same anxious vigilance with which the partners in a private copartnery frequently watch over their own. Like the stewards of a rich man, they are apt to consider attention to small matters as not for their master's honour, and very easily give themselves a dispensation from having it. Negligence and profusion, therefore, must always prevail, more or less, in the management of the affairs of such a company.*[51]

Rational ... Okay, Come On, You Know We're Irrational

Socrates was a rationalist, meaning he believed that ultimate truth could not be sought by sensory experience and observation; rather, it can only be reached through deductive reasoning. Plato and Aristotle argued that part of human nature was rational while part was governed by desire. To be a superior human meant the rational side controlled the passionate side.

Hobbes believed that people acquired reason; they were not born with it: "Children therefore are not endued with Reason at all, till they have attained the use of Speech: but are called Reasonable Creatures, for the possibility apparent of having the use of Reason in time to come."[52] He also argued that even as adults, people do not use reason:

> *And the most part of men, though they have the use of reasoning a little way ... it serves them to [little] use in common life, in which they govern themselves ... according to their differences of experience, quickness of memory, and inclinations to several ends; but especially according to good or evil fortune, and the errors of one another. For as for Science, or certain rules of their actions, they are so [far] from it, that they know not what it is.*[53]

Hobbes clearly does not think that people are fundamentally rational. He sees that they succumb to passion and desire. In fact, his entire notion of the state of nature is based on irrationality. In Hobbes' analysis, a man is not at risk because he is guilty of violence; he is at risk because another man may irrationally think he will be violent and preemptively attack him. The state of nature is based on the fear that everyone acts irrationally.

Hobbes argued that man may have desired to live sociably like other creatures, like bees, but this was because "men [were] continually in competition for Honour and dignity ... and consequently amongst men there [arose] on that ground, Envy, and Hatred, and finally [war]." To bees, common good and private good are the same, while man's joy came from "comparing himself to other men."[54]

Hobbes believed that self-interest and desire distorted reason; therefore, man needed science as a guide. Man had the same basic passions, but different experiences affected everyone differently. People used their own feelings, based on experiences, to judge others: "Men vehemently in love with their own new opinions ... and obstinately bent to maintain them, gave those their opinions also that reverenced name of Conscience, as if they would have it seem unlawful, to change or speak against them; and so pretend to know they are true, when they know at most but what they think so."[55]

Hobbes argues that the state of nature is a state of war. However, human nature also provides means to escape war. Rational people will understand that a state of war hinders the pursuit of one's self-interest, and so can agree that, "Peace is Good, and therefore also the way, or means of Peace which ... are Justice, Gratitude, Modesty, Equity, Mercy, & the rest of the Laws of Nature are good."[56] We will seek peace with others who want peace by giving up our "right to all things," by mutually submitting to the authority of a sovereign.

Locke's notion of human nature and rationality is also complex. He disagrees with Hobbes and instead believes "reason [is] the common rule and measure God hath given to mankind."[57] However, man has the capacity to be unreasonable and "live by another rule than that of reason and common equity, which is that measure God has set to the actions of men, for their mutual security."[58] Locke argues that self-love may actually turn man to irrational behavior: "ill nature, passion and revenge will carry them too far in punishing others; and hence nothing but confusion and disorder will follow."[59]

According to Rousseau, reason is not inherent to human beings; rather civil society may condition man through the use of reason:

> *The passage from the state of nature to the civil state produces a very remarkable change in man, for it substitutes justice for instinct in his behavior and gives his actions a moral quality they previously lacked. Only then, when the voice of duty replaces physical impulse and right replaces appetite, does man [who so far had considered only himself] find himself forced to act upon other principles, and to consult his reason before listening to his inclinations.*[60]

David Hume argued that desire, not reason, drives human behavior, writing, "reason alone can never be a motive to any action of the will; and secondly, that it can never oppose passion in the direction of the will."[61] Against the moral rationalists, such as Locke, who argue that moral judgments are based on reason, Hume maintained that reason could not provide motive to action. People need sentiment to give a preference to the useful tendencies of actions.

Hume also argues that natural human instinct, not reason, allows humans to make inductive inferences: "Nature, by an absolute and uncontrollable necessity has determined us to judge as well as to breathe and feel."[62] Hume concluded intrinsic moral and ethical sentiments caused human motivation and action; they provide reason for action. Morals motivate passion, and cause or deter actions, and morality does not derive from reason: "Reason is, and ought only to be the slave of the passions, and can never pretend to any other office than to serve and obey them."[63]

He was skeptical of humans' ability to reason largely based on the common use of inductive inference. Hume realized that people believed that patterns of the observed behavior of things continued even when the observation stopped. He argued that this is based on either demonstrative reasoning or probable reasoning, and both are insufficient. Hume strove to create a total naturalistic "science of man" that examined the psychological basis of human nature. Hume writes, "The science of man is the only solid foundation for the other sciences, so the only solid foundation we can give to this science itself must be laid on experience and observation."[64]

Finally, Rene Descartes' perception was that the essence of human nature lies in thought: "I am thinking, therefore I exist" and "the things we conceive very clearly and very distinctly are all true."[65] Absolute truths could only be determined by reason, as truths gained through experiences were susceptible to illusionary interpretations.

So How Sure Are We About That Human Nature?

"You don't really understand human nature unless you know why a child on a merry-go-round will wave at his parents every time around—and why his parents will always wave back." —William D. Tammeus

I am not arguing that these debates render the former concepts false; rather, my point is to illustrate how more than one truth exists. There are justifiable debates that impact every step of the foundation that guide our entire economic thinking and structure. The problem is that the ideas that correlate with the current system are handpicked and then presented as if they are unquestioned. So many aspects of the most well-known philosophers' theories are ignored. What is worse is how many voices are left out of the discussion. Where are the female philosophers in our historical, mainstream discourse? Where are the philosophers from other parts of the world? When you think of what is built on this foundation, you begin to realize the magnitude of a system built on only part of the story and the devastation caused by leaving the rest of the story out.

Chapter 6: Assumed Truths (and Ignored Realities)

"It is the case in every period of history where injustice based on falsehoods, based on taking away the right and freedoms of people to live and survive with dignity, that, eventually, when you call a bluff, the tables turn." —Vandana Shiva

Challenging the conventional economic theory and the arguments used to perpetuate the current structure will yield a clear picture that our current social organization of economics is based completely on inaccurate information.

To make capitalism appear to work (and here, by "capitalism" I mean the current version of capitalism in the United States that has been evolving since the Industrial Revolution), over the past century, political, business, and academic leadership have had to create an intellectual and philosophical bubble. They have accomplished this by strategically using omissions, clauses, and generalizations at the foundational level, throughout the justification process to conceal inherent limitations of economic thought. I call these "assumed truths." For assumed truths to be believable we also have to ignore realities.

An assumed truth is inaccurate or partial information generally accepted as true. An ignored reality is simply a truth that is ignored or trivialized. Both are required for capitalist theories to make sense. When I say "assumed truth," one might think I mean we came up with these ideas on our own. We just assume them. On the contrary, these ideas have been propagated and force-fed down the throats of the people so that, over time, they were just generally accepted, maybe even considered common sense. We assume these things to be true, but in no way was that accidental.

Once the general public accepted these falsehoods as truths, the rationalizations for a capitalist society could begin. When questions and concerns arose, they were brushed off over and over again until the dominant discourse left them out almost entirely. Thus was established the academic bubble, which assumes capitalism is the only possible economic system. The economic debate that occurs in this bubble is based on continual growth and individual relentless pursuit of wealth. Any arguments in the public discourse happen without challenges to those preconditions. The debate of how to manage the capitalist economy proceeds in the protected bubble of falsehoods without regard for the greater reality.

People all over the world have been indoctrinated in many different ways. For better or worse, we all believe certain things we are told. Many ideas, we, the general populace, just accept as true. There is a great danger when there is a total acceptance of assumed truths as facts, and we build our other beliefs or arguments on the basis of those "facts." We need to ask important questions: What if? What matters? Why? And how do we know? The challenge is that most of us believe the string of ideas that I outlined in the first Section of Part 2. These ideas led us to the logical conclusion that capitalism is the best method for economic organization. However, as we already saw, these ideas are far from the whole truth.

The following sections discuss the assumed truths and ignored realities required to make capitalism work at every step of its foundation. Once we challenge these assumed truths and see that they are, at best, partial truths (at worst, outright lies) we begin to see the inconsistencies, contradictions, and flaws in the foundation of the economic system, and hence, the flaws in our social structures. From there, it naturally follows that there must be a better way to organize society so that it isn't marked by flaws that perpetuate huge divisions among people, and is not detrimental to the earth and our livelihood. To begin, this section highlights some of the assumed truths and ignored realities about economics and economic systems in general. Then, it discusses the assumed truths and ignored realities in the steps of our economic foundational rationale.

Economics: It's Called a Science, So It Must Be Right

"Where there is politics or economics, there is no morality." —Karl Wilhelm Friedrich Schlegel

"Economics is extremely useful as a form of employment for economists." —John Kenneth Galbraith

Assumption: There are only two choices for an economy: centrally planned or free

When it comes to economic systems (the rules, regulations, institutions, and norms that dictate how the economy works), we are told there are two options: there is the free market or the centrally planned. Of course, there are other options that we do not hear about in the debate. For example, the mixed economy, which is simply any combination of the free market and planned economy, is not mentioned.

While most people know that our economy is mixed, the discourse leads us to believe that it is predominately a free market economy. Furthermore, the battle continues to privatize all public enterprises into a free market system because we are told the free market is the best. Regardless of the disagreements, we are told that in the battle of ideas, the idea of free market capitalism won out.

"The battle of ideas"—consider how infantile this statement is. It is an insult to our intelligence. Ideas are not static, concrete, finite objects that wage war against one another to leave only one victor standing on the open field when the smoke finally settles. Ideas change. They apply differently in different situations. Ideas evolve.

We are told these two ideas of free market and centrally planned were tested against each other when the communist bloc of the Soviet Union, Eastern European countries, China, Vietnam, North Korea, and Cuba existed simultaneously with the capitalist bloc of the U.S., Britain, and their allies. On November 9th, 1989, the Berlin Wall came down, marking the fall of the Soviet Union and the final collapse of communist opposition. To the Western world, this momentous event proved beyond a doubt that communism does not work. Communism and socialism are dead, so they say. The free market is the sole survivor.

For this analysis to hold true, we must ignore what communism and socialism are, and assume that the governments of the Eastern Bloc were truly communist and socialist. At the least, we would have to assume that these governments implemented the only types of communism and socialism possible. These ideas are discussed in a way that simplifies and confuses the issue. Although there is a direct link between politics and economics, government systems and economic systems are separate, interconnected structures. Different combinations of governments and economies will yield different outcomes. Many combinations have never been tried. There is no reason to believe a democratic government is necessarily conducive to a free market and capitalism. There is also no reason to believe a dictatorship is conducive to communism or socialism.

Socialism is not a type of government, but rather, it is an economic system where the means of production are socially owned and the economy is managed cooperatively. There is not one clear definition of "socially owned." However, it is generally considered to be some form of ownership by the stakeholders of means of production (i.e. the workers own portions of the company they work for).

Socialist parties exist that support the economic philosophy of socialism. But, the government that implements or supports the economic system is not socialism. A government could implement socialist policies in any form, from totalitarian to democratic.

The same is true for capitalism and communism. Communism is an economic system where the means of production and assets created are NOT owned by persons or institutions (including the government), but instead are accessible to all. There are a variety of interpretations of communism, but it essentially implies the commons and community, and that assets are shared and production is maintained by communal participation. How this system is governed is a different matter.

Again, parties have claimed communism as their political identity. However, a government system is distinct from a communist economy. Is anyone confusing North Korea, officially called The Democratic People's Republic of Korea, as a democracy? This can be confusing because politics and economics are so interconnected; it is difficult to conceptually separate them.

To make more sense, look at the U.S. The government is called a democracy (although it should be called a republic), but refers to the economic system as capitalism. No one calls the government capitalist. It is important to not allow knee-jerk reactions to terms like socialism and communism to cloud our judgment, as these terms are often misused, misunderstood, and can refer to a wide range of actual circumstances.

Of course many will still disagree with these ideas automatically, without considering the possibilities, but we shouldn't allow leaders and pundits to manipulate us into being fundamentally against an idea because they align it with something it is not. To be clear, socialism and communism do not require an authoritarian government, nor do they require a central government. There just happened to be some authoritarian governments that claimed to be socialist and communist.

Finally, it is important to consider that the systems we compare all use money as the medium for exchange. The economic activity that does not involve money is left out of the equation. If we are really having a discussion on the possibilities of economic organization, we should be considering all possibilities. Ignoring the fact that these economic systems are all dominated by a single, shared trait, leads to a very narrow discussion.

Government systems and how they relate to economic systems

The countries in the Eastern Bloc claimed they were communist and socialist. This is because they promised to implement socialist and communist economies. Some schools of thought claim that a political party that represents the needs of the people should implement these economic systems. However, when we refer to government systems and economic systems as one and the same, we are ignoring the reality of the relationship between government and economic systems.

These particular parties initiated strict polices in an attempt to successfully implement the economic doctrines. Combined with the extreme levels of anti-socialist and anti-communist propaganda of the last half century, the particular methodologies of the Eastern Bloc have led most people in the west to view socialism and communism with great distain, without actually knowing what they are.

What we really learned from the Cold War is that harsh, oppressive, centralized institutions are not capable of providing a good quality of life through centrally planned economies. But what we did not get out of it is that centrally planned economies led by democratic institutions cannot provide a good quality of life. We also did not learn anything about decentralized or democratic socialism or communism. We did not learn about other schools of thought, possibilities, or combinations of political and economic systems. We did not learn anything about those because none of these possibilities existed. Somehow though, these two different scenarios have been lumped together to make everyone believe that any socialist or communist social structure is unable to provide a good quality of life. Furthermore, many people go as far as attacking any government programs that assist citizens by claiming they are socialist.

The beliefs that there are only two possibilities, free market or centrally planned economies, and that we are using the free market, are simply false. No nation uses a purely free market, or even a minimally free market, system. In a truly free market economy, for example, monopolies quickly rise and, therefore, we institute regulations to prevent that from happening. Everyone (even extreme liberals[ii] like Milton Friedman) agrees that this is necessary. But, the need for regulation goes further than that.

Most people recognize the need to prevent corporations from acting however they choose. For example, if the government did not have environmental protections in place, corporations would cause even more damage to our ecosystem than they already do. Our entire economic discourse revolves around how much government interference we want or accept, and in what aspects of the economy we will accept it.

---

ii In economics a "liberal" is someone who supports a free market with little government intervention. It is not the same as how liberal is used in American political discourse to mean the American left wing.

Assumption: A free market economy is free

Regardless of the argument above, in context of the mainstream discourse we assume we have a free market. The term "free market" is rather misleading. Unlike what we are told, capitalism is not synonymous with free market. Capitalism is a specific type of market where the means of production are privately owned. First of all, in essence, the free market left alone is no more free than the state of nature. But only in a free market, the self-interested competition that some believe is inherent to human nature is implemented as a matter of process.

The free market may be free from governmental control over enterprise; however, it is far from free. In a free market, everyone is susceptible to the brutality of other businesses. "Out-competing" does not simply mean making a better product than others; it means those who have the ability to cheat and manipulate the system will win and force the others out. Unregulated competition is like watching people play in a football league without rules.

Farming in the U.S. provides an informative example of how free markets allow multi-national corporations to crush small family-owned businesses in "competition." The number of farms in the U.S. has declined from about 6.8 million in 1935 to about 2 million today. However, the U.S. produces a greater amount of food than it did in 1935. Part of the reason is that the trend of the agriculture industry has moved away from small family farms to corporate farms owned and run by agriculture conglomerates.

These companies—ConAgra Foods, Inc., Archer Daniels Midland Corporation, Cargill, Monsanto, and others—are happy to use huge subsidies from American taxpayers to buy, undercut, and undermine small farms at every opportunity. Monsanto, for example, is notorious for harassing, threatening, and forcing hundreds of small farmers into costly, drawn-out legal battles. This was the case with Vernon Hugh Bowman, a 75-year-old soybean farmer in Indiana.

Since the beginning of agriculture, farmers have collected seeds from their annual crops to plant the following year's crops. However, when farmers like Bowman use Monsanto's Roundup

Ready seeds they are obligated to discard excess seeds so they are forced to purchase seeds from Monsanto annually. However, farmers like Bowman also buy seeds from local grain elevators, which are towers that store grain.

The problem is that once Monsanto's genetically modified seeds mix into pure crops (non-Monsanto seeds) they become contaminated with Monsanto's genetic modification and there is no way to separate them again. In fact, it is estimated that 90 percent of soybeans in Indiana now contain genes developed by Monsanto.[66] As a result of Bowman's locally purchased seeds mixing with and containing Monsanto's patented modifications, Monsanto successfully sued him for $84, 456 in the U.S. Court of Appeals for the Federal Circuit in Washington D.C., claiming intellectual property infringement.[67]

Assumptions: The American economy is a free market and, therefore, it is not planned

Of course the arguments in favor of the free market policies assumes we have a free market policies, which we do not. The idea that we have a free market is nonsense. In a free market, the market (supply and demand) determines price. Things like trade agreements and subsidies that we have for American products go against the doctrine of a free market. We discuss the limits of supply and demand later in this section, but it is important to realize that supply and demand, as a determinate of price, does not foster freedom in the manner we conceptualize it; it makes everyone susceptible to others.

The juxtaposition of a free market and a planned economy would make us believe that we do not have a planned economy. Part of the argument against planned economies is that planning cannot respond to changes fast enough. However, even a capitalist economy requires planning. How centralized the planning is in a capitalist economy is determined by how many companies there are in an industry. The current U.S. economy is highly centralized and highly planned.

Capitalism as private ownership of means of production for profits means the capitalist must plan to use his or her means of production to make as much profit as possible. Part of this entails "meeting the needs of the market." We are told that the market dictates people's actions. But success largely means controlling the market, not just being receptive to it.

What mechanisms in a capitalist society prevent planning? The government? No, the government is part of the planning. There are no mechanisms to prevent planning. Of course capitalists plan. Why wouldn't they? In fact, the mainstream model says they will.

Take Bob Sloan as an example. During the early 1980s, Bob Sloan had what might seem like a good corporate job. After earning his degree in architectural drafting and design, he spent his workdays leading a team responsible for developing and testing new customer products and designing office products like cubicles, work stations, panels, etc. He then headed a computer-aided design (CAD) training program for drafting and engineering. Instead of making a decent salary however, Mr. Sloan worked for pennies. He had been convicted of a white-collar crime in 1981 and worked for the Prison Rehabilitative Industries and Diversified Enterprises (PRIDE) while serving his time in a Florida prison.[68]

Mr. Sloan was part of a growing trend in America that allows big corporations to make huge profits by saving on the costs of labor. The market doesn't dictate the cost of prison labor; instead corporate central planning plays a large role. Not only do planners dictate the price of prison labor, they collaborate with other businesses and lawmakers to control the amount of laborers.

The American Legislative Exchange Council (ALEC) is a registered non-profit that calls itself "the largest, non-partisan, individual public-private membership association of state legislators." Actually, the group is made up of mostly wealthy corporations and Republican Congress members.

They draft hundreds of model bills in private meetings and vote on them to be brought before state congresses throughout the country. These bills attack all aspects of American life including worker rights, consumer rights, environmental regulation, public education, regulation of major industries, tax law, healthcare, social security, and voting rights to progress an extreme pro-big-corporate agenda.[69]

One of ALEC's agendas was pushed forward by the Corrections

Corporation of America (CCA). CCA could greatly increase profits by privatizing more prison systems and increasing the amount of prisoners they housed. They worked through ALEC to pass laws in states all over the country to pass tougher drug laws and make longer sentences for offenses.

In large part because of the new harsh laws, the number of incarcerated Americans rose from a half million in 1980 to 2.4 million in 2011. Many of these prisoners, incarcerated for non-violent offenses, are working for private corporations for around 20 cents an hour. Furthermore, ALEC found that other Wall Street firms, like the American Bail Coalition, could profit by charging prisoners outrageous amounts of money in bail bonds to get them released, so the cycle continues.[70]

Every aspect of the economy is planned. Marketing campaigns, advertising, price fixing (where competing companies agree on higher prices of goods so they don't have to lower prices to compete), and cartels are all examples of businesses planning and organizing to manipulate the consumers, the market, and the economic system. A planned economy and the free market are not opposites. The government not having control or say in the economy doesn't mean that it is not a planned economy in the sense that business leaders are able to get together and plan things that benefit them all.

They may want to compete by undercutting each other's prices, but they work together to out-compete smaller companies and agree to maintain higher levels of prices so they have a monopoly-esque control on price. Out-competing doesn't mean losing profits so much as it means creating partnerships that are all planned and done through negotiations. Part of planning among business leaders involves figuring out how to cut spending, including suppressing wages and controlling prices (either up or down depending on what will increase profits).

A reporter described his meeting with Marcus Agius, the chairman of Barclays from 2007-2012: "I'm not being taken to meet him or left to sit somewhere until Agius, head of one of the biggest banks in the world, is ready; instead, it's informal and personal—and thoughtful. His attire is elegant and individual. He has eschewed the uniform of the senior banker ... in favor of a designer suit and loafers. Yet he conveys authority and confidence."⁷¹

During the economic crisis, while banks collapsed around it, Barclays prospered under the guidance of Agius. However, in 2012, he resigned as chair after Barclays was fined $453 million by the U.S. and Britain for conspiring to manipulate the London Interbank Offered Rate (LIBOR), which provides the rate for trillions of dollars in transactions, in what became known as the LIBOR scandal. And Barclays is only one of many of the biggest banks in the world that participated in this scandal. The result was millions of people, towns, and cities all over the world, paid the wrong amount on their loans.⁷²

In an interview on Democracy Now, Matt Taibbi, a contributing editor for *Rolling Stone Magazine* described the LIBOR scandal:

> *Libor is basically the rate at which banks borrow from each other. It's a benchmark that sets—that a lot of international investment products are pegged to. When Libor is low, that means that the banks feel confident in each other; and when Libor is high, that means there is generally instability ... they were manipulating it both up and down in order to capitalize on particular trades, depending on what the banks were holding that day ... Basically, every city and town in America, to say nothing of the rest of the world, has investments that are pegged to Libor ... So if you live in a town that had a budget crisis, that had to lay off firemen or teachers or policemen, or couldn't provide services or textbooks in their schools, you know, that might be due to this. And remember, even the tiniest manipulation downward, when you're talking about a thing of this scale, would result in tens of trillions of dollars of losses ...*
>
> *The Libor scandal presents really the mother of all regulatory dilemmas, because this scandal could not have happened if it was just one or two or even three banks acting as rogue participants. The way Libor works is, they take a survey of 16 banks every day. They take the four highest numbers and the four lowest numbers, and they throw them out. They average out the remaining numbers. And what that means is that pretty much all the banks have to be in on it in order to move the needle in any one direction. So you're talking about 16 of the world's biggest, most powerful financial institutions. And if they're all cooperating in what essentially is a gigantic international price-fixing operation, what do regulators do?*⁷³

In this sense, we have almost no democratic control over the business leaders doing the planning, except through purchasing power. At least if the government is planning and the government is a democracy, then the people have a say in what is done.

The challenge to this argument is the claim that people "vote" with their dollars. We are told that based on what we consume and how we spend our money, we are telling businesses what we like and don't like. However, in many cases the power of this vote is rendered useless because there is a lack of options in one's purchasing. This can be because there really is no alternative company to buy from, or people in mass are largely unaware of wrongdoing by the company or that there are other options.

For example, let's say I pulled all my dollars out of Bank of America. Alone, this does not change much or have a great impact on Bank of America or its profits. This act alone would not change the way Bank of America operates, especially the banking industry. I could have expect that other people would not have pulled money out of Bank of America because I know most people do not know much about other options like credit unions.

To overcome the forces of huge banks and corporations, many people must act. In fact, chances are high that if someone doesn't like Bank of America, they would likely take their money to Chase or Citibank, that are just other bad options (or exploitative businesses). This is not meant to trivialize individual action, which is essential for many reasons, but the notion that everything we do with our money is a clear and conscious choice legitimizes a system that survives by suppressing choice. Capitalist planning mitigates the power to vote with dollars.

Voting with your dollars is not totally inaccurate, but it is a grave misrepresentation. When using dollars to voice an opinion, the analogy of voting is very misleading because when we think of voting we think one person, one vote. With dollars, there is a disproportion issue as some people have many more dollars, and, therefore, more votes. Additionally, with everyone having one vote per dollar, they vote many different ways that are often contradictory with one another so the total picture of what someone wants is not clear based on their purchases. Also, money crosses borders, so people, businesses, and governments all over the world use dollars to "vote" in the U.S. economy.

Furthermore, as mentioned above, part of business leaders' planning includes billions of dollars spent per year in marketing, public relations, and advertising industries to help control and manipulate what people think. This also hides information from consumers, which prevents them from making informed choices. This is planning. It is not seeing what people demand and responding. It is planning how to convince people to demand the goods and services business leaders produce.

As I discuss later in this chapter, for economic measures to improve, they require consumers continuously purchase new items. These models function based on the assumption that people want limitless and ever-increasing amounts of things. Instead of creating measures and policies based on how people actually live, producers use billions of dollars in advertising campaigns to manipulate demand and consumption to fit their models. Our culture and economic system motivates us to continuously buy, throw away, and buy again, not because this is necessary for a healthy economy. This is necessary for an economy that creates massive amounts of material wealth for a small percentage of people.

In capitalism, whether we lean more toward privatization and competition or communal resources and government assistance, both are based on maximizing profits. The question is who benefits from this maximizing of profits? We are told that capitalism is the best way to deal with scarcity, but we know how our version of capitalism deals with scarcity. Huge multi-national corporations tear up our planet and gamble away our money without consideration of long-term effects because they are only concerned with their short-term profits. Wealth rapidly accumulates at the top while workers' wages barely increase and jobs steadily decline. There must be a better way.

Unfortunately, almost the entire modern world has been convinced that the structure of our economy is so fundamental to human beings; it is embedded in our DNA. If we accept that we are selfish and competitive creatures that have rational capacity to pursue our selfish needs competitively, then how could we even contest a system that fosters those very qualities? The following section takes on this challenge. Beyond the philosophical debate discussed in the previous chapter, the remainder of this chapter highlights the false assumptions we have to accept as truth in order to make the mainstream, capitalism discourse make sense.

Human Nature: Just Accept It, You're Sort of a Jerk

"The irrationality of a thing is no argument against its existence, rather a condition of it." —Friedrich Nietzsche

Human nature is more than one thing. Humans have the capacity to be selfish and selfless. And even when they are selfish, the pursuit of self-interest cannot simply be narrowed down to monetary gains. Work ethic is held high as a noble trait in a capitalist society, and maybe in other societies as well. But, if a man is working hard in pursuit of self-interest and another man desires leisure time and strives for that in the name of self-interest, how different are they?

What if the leisure time was spent volunteering to coach for children? Why is one course of action nobler if they both are motivated by the same essence? Is the man that pursues leisure going against self-interest? Even if two people work hard, one may save every penny while the other may spend lavishly on useless goods. How can we judge or predict their actions in mass?

Mainstream economists argue that the total of independent actors following self-interest of monetary gain will equal a harmonious society where everyone benefits from individual gains. In this system, the mass of individual people comprises the system. The system is not a separate entity that individuals must surrender to while it governs them coercively from above. We are told it works because it correlates with human nature.

Assumption: Human nature is competitive and selfish

For this system to work, based on human nature, we must assume human nature is competitive and selfish. Human beings are so far removed from living in nature; I wonder what the relevance is. Do we really believe that there is some primitive tie to the wild embedded in our DNA? If so, does that discount the progress we have made since then? Everything we do as a society seems to be aimed at advancing ourselves further away from the state of nature; why when it comes to organizing our entire global society are we so quick to throw ourselves back into it? It is convenient for some people to attempt to determine uniformly what human nature is, but that does not make it true.

According to them, human nature is what we have always been told: we are competitive, our natural state is in a state of war, and we are subconsciously primitive beings. While there is some truth to this, it is not exclusively true. It's just a convenient piece of evidence to be used when it fits a point to be made. This is always a fall back to convince the populace that we cannot do better.

By better I mean creating a global community with understanding and shared existence. But instead, we have adopted the notion that if we try to make the world better, someone will just take advantage of us, so we might as well play the game and play to win. It is every person and every nation for themselves. Instead of working for a global community, we fight over resources and implement policy based on power and profit, ignoring the needs of the world's people.

Of course, it has been surprisingly inconvenient in our current individualistic capitalist society to point to primitive human beings' natural tribal existence. Even though tribes sometimes fought over resources (not all did, especially pre-Agricultural revolution), leadership and mainstream scholars largely ignore pointing to humans' tribal heritage when referring to our state of nature and human nature. To imply this existence as natural would suggest it is natural for us to live together, organized in a communal manner. It also illustrates that part of human nature is self-sacrifice for the benefit of others.

Ross Andrew McGinnis was born in Meadville, Pennsylvania in 1987. His childhood was similar to many other Americans: he was in the Boy Scouts of America, played soccer, baseball, and basketball, and on his 17th birthday joined the U.S. Army. In August of 2006, when Ross was only 19, his regiment was deployed to Baghdad. There he served as a gunner in a Humvee.

During an operation in Adhamiyah, a grenade was thrown in the vehicle. Ross could have jumped out of the vehicle through the gunners hatch, but instead he threw his body onto the grenade to absorb the blast. He died instantly but saved the lives of four other men in his platoon. He had only been in Iraq for six months. He was buried at Arlington Cemetery and awarded the Medal of Honor.[74] Ross is only one of several soldiers in the Iraq War who knowingly sacrificed their own lives by jumping on a grenade to save the lives of others. This is the ultimate sacrifice.

One does not have to look to soldiers who willfully give up their lives under extreme conditions to find examples of selflessness. Ordinary people make sacrifices for other people every day. Occupy Wall Street brought thousands of people together who put their bodies and livelihoods in jeopardy to help make the world a better place, and most of them were not doing it for self-interested reasons. There are famous examples of selflessness, like Gandhi or Mother Teresa, but we don't have to look beyond people in our own lives to find people who sacrifice themselves for others.

Despite this knowledge, human nature is only discussed from individualistic viewpoints in theoretical scenarios, as Hobbes and Locke analyzed it. It is common to argue that we are naturally selfish and competitive, while in the actual historical state of nature humans were largely tribal, proving the communal nature of humans. This possibility that humans are naturally communal is additional truth that is simply ignored so it never factors into debates when human nature is used to prove a point. Usually these points involve the economic structure based on competition or the necessity of war or individualism.

It is scary to leave such additional truths out of the regular discourse because when there is no other option, people will accept things that do not have to be. This is how we have fallen victim to a system that thrives on us being very individualistic.

The more we work together to find out what is really going on, the more we would work collectively in our shared interests. Usually what is in the interest of the people does not support the profit-driven goals of the system itself.

Collective interest

Everyone acting in their own best interest does not necessarily mean everyone will benefit. This mentality ignores that collective interest is often separate from individual interest. That is, there are important interests of communities that do not serve everyone's short-term individual interests. In fact, the opposite is often true. We are told, by serving self-interest we are serving the collective interest. The idea is that pursuing self-interest increases quality of life. But beyond gaining individual quality of life and access to goods and services (even if that were true), pursuing self-interest disrupts a collective interest that is separate from pursuing individual needs.

For example, extracting certain materials that will produce goods for people to buy depletes a resource which has an impact on a collective that includes those taking the resource, the person buying it, and those that have nothing to do with the transaction. Take the production of beef, for example, which requires large amounts of water to mass-produce crops to feed and provide drinking water for the cattle. As water resources diminish faster than they replenish, everyone will be impacted while only a few benefit from the beef production. There is a collective interest in conserving those resources for everyone to use. Also, such transactions do not consider long-term consequences so future generations are negatively affected and their sustainability jeopardized.

To make this idea of self-interested human nature work, we have to ignore all the aspects of humanity that we know oppose this narrow view. However, in line with the economic thought foundation, if human nature is competitive and selfish, and people do not need to be concerned with collective interests, then it follows that if humans are given an incentive to pursue, they will pursue it.

Incentives: Nothing Matters Except the Green

"Why do farmers farm, given their economic adversities on top of the many frustrations and difficulties normal to farming? And always the answer is: 'Love. They must do it for love.' Farmers farm for the love of farming." —Wendell Berry

One convincing piece of propaganda we often hear is that incentives drive the economy. They are what motivate people. They are "what get you up in the morning." Incentives in this sense, just means money and property acquired with money. Sure we can argue for a more moral stance like, "I work to give my family a better life," but that better life, in the current system, requires money. In actuality, you work to get money to provide your family with a better life.

In capitalism, the incentives are profits and private property. Since we assume humans are selfish, we assume that they will pursue property and profit incentives if they know they can keep them for themselves. Incentive structures do not actually work the way we think they do. This is because we make several inaccurate assumptions about them. We assume incentives are monetary and that pursuing monetary incentives produces desirable outcomes.

Assumption: Only measurable incentives matter (we ignore those that are not)

Since the discussion about the economy only includes things that are measurable in monetary units, we assume that only measurable incentives matter. Economics is also only concerned with external incentives like earning profit. Moral incentives are not measurable and are, therefore, ignored.

A stay-at-home dad gets up in the morning to go to work to provide his family a better life, but money is not the middleman in that equation because no one pays stay-at-home parents. Sure there is work, and lots of it, but none of that is calculated in economic factors that determine policy. Nor is it calculated when a woman goes over her friend's house on a Saturday to help him paint his house for the price of friendly conversations, and the joy of helping a loved one. Maybe we assume this doesn't matter.

Perhaps these issues are not related to the economy and should not be considered, but I implore you to consider the implications of ignoring non-monetary factors.

For example, consider the value and benefits of preserving a forest. There are many incentives to do so, but in a competitive market that only measures monetary value, there is often more incentive to destroy it for short-term profit. Furthermore, consider the value of leisure and time with family. There are strong incentives to take time off and spend time with family and friends. However, most of us cannot afford to take time off from work because we need to work a full-time schedule, if not more, to pay our bills.

Money is not the only incentive people have in life. This notion of monetary incentive ignores the creativity of people and their desires to do things. Most people love to work. Of course, they may not love their job, but people love to work. Many people make things for the sake of creating.

People have an incentive to do work when there is a need, even if it is not paid. Think of all the jobs we pay people to do, and how if there were not someone to pay, we would have incentive do those jobs ourselves without getting paid. For example, if there were not teachers, we would have incentive to teach our own children. If there were not trash disposal workers, wanting to keep our yard and community free from trash, there would be the incentive to take our own trash away. If there were not auto mechanics, we would have incentive to learn how to fix our own cars. This is not to argue that we shouldn't have people getting paid to do these service roles; my only point is to challenge the doctrine of incentive structures in our economic system.

Most people do not need unchecked accumulation of wealth to motivate them. Living a good and happy life, providing for people they love, spending time with loved ones, artistic expression, and some personal advancement is more than enough. Of course we want to make a better life for our families, but making a better life for them means more than providing them with enough money: it means spending time with them and creating a better world for them.

Assumption: Incentives lead to desirable outcomes

We assume that incentive structures produce desirable outcomes. However, because they are based on self-interest, greed, and maximizing profits, they do not usually produce desirable outcomes. There are several reasons: Incentives intended to motivate people to succeed also give them incentive to cheat. They motivate people to pay others as little as possible and withhold goods from those who need them but cannot afford them. Profit is an incentive to externalize as much cost as possible by exploiting people and the environment.

The idea that an incentive structure can be created to make human action predictable is not entirely true. Incentive structures are complicated and people who offer incentives cannot predict how humans will respond and to what degree, which results in imperfect knowledge and unintended consequences.

Pursuing maximum profits has several negative outcomes. Trying to minimize cost often leads to significant wealth gaps between owners and workers, and leads to environmental exploitation. In corporate policies, complex incentive structures intended to increase efficiency have had massive failures. Many incentives to increase efficiency and productivity simultaneously create incentives to increase destructive practices, cheat systems, and circumvent laws.

For example, CEO stock options, while providing an incentive to improve company performance, simultaneously gave CEOs incentive to increase stock prices. They could accomplish this by fabricating accounting information to give the illusion of economic success.

For example, Bruce Karatz, former Chairman and CEO of KB Homes, gained significant attention for his philanthropic efforts to help rebuild Los Angeles after the riots in 1992 and New Orleans after Hurricane Katrina.[75] These efforts put him among a small group of CEOs that are known for their focus on humanitarian efforts and not just bottom-line profits. However, he did not slack when it came to the bottom-line either. He successfully grew KB homes from $491 million in revenue in 1986 to $11 billion in 2006 and became one of the highest paid CEOs in the nation.[76]

In November 2011, Karatz was convicted of lying about his company's practice of backdating options. He was sentenced to five years probation including eight months of house arrest.[77] Companies often grant executives stock options as part of their compensation packages. Backdating practices allow executives to purchase stocks at a date where the stock price was lower, so there are profits built into the purchase making them more valuable. These purchases are an expense to shareholders so they legally must be disclosed.

These types of scandals are not uncommon. Research finds that CEOs who are compensated with stock options are more likely to make poor acquisitions, have more volatile financial results, and have more accounting irregularities.[78] Unfortunately, most scandals are never uncovered and the CEOs face little or no punishment for their actions.

Executives receive bonuses as incentives and have extreme salary increases even during significant economic downturn. Incentives in upper levels of corporations are often applied to success but not taken away in response to failure. The structure gives executives incentive to gamble with other people's money and engage in high-risk behavior. If a company loses money, why don't executives lose money or have to pay the company back? This is very different from working class people. How about the incentive is a good paying salary and when you do a good job you don't get fired, and maybe a raise once in awhile like the rest of us?

In capitalism there are owners of means of production, and workers. This owner class, pursuing its incentive to maximize profits is also fundamental to capitalism. Owners have incentive to pay as few workers as possible, as little as possible. They accumulate wealth from profits while workers' incomes remain roughly the same over time. This process leads to an extremely uneven distribution of wealth and the dependency of labor on the owner class.

Inequalities also grow because of consumer access to products. Firms will make what people are willing and able to pay for. This means products will not reach those who have a need or desire but cannot pay for them. These inequalities are not only undesirable for those on the losing end of the scale; they have negative implications for society as a whole.

In competitive markets, sellers compete to attract customers by finding the most efficient use of resources and minimizing waste costs, which drives prices down. Firms are not doing this because they love their customers; they do it because the incentive is to make a profit. Undercutting competition means more consumers buying from the firm and increasing profits, which is the goal. But when companies prioritize profits, many negative consequences result. If it is possible to out-compete other firms by lowering prices, by exploiting people and the environment, a firm will do it. The firm will put competitors out of business, and be able to raise prices to further increase profit.

In the competitive market, there is incentive to minimize cost, which means there is incentive to externalize as much cost as possible. Externalizing costs means outsourcing jobs to cheap, unregulated labor; paying workers as little as possible; replacing workers with machines whenever possible; circumventing environmental regulations; and using other destructive techniques. Firms may use child labor, destroy the environment, or do other things that consumers do not like produce what consumers want at lower costs (unless government intervenes). Unless otherwise prevented, firms will produce anything that consumers are willing to buy even if it is bad for the person, other people, and the environment.

Assumption: Profit incentives motivate firms to produce what consumers want

We assume that firms produce goods in response to consumers' desires because the firms are motivated by profit and, therefore, produce what consumers want. But companies are not innovating new products to meet consumer needs to increase profits. In fact, there is no statistical evidence connecting the number of patents issued to a business and an increase in profits.[79] Instead, firms innovate ways to sell their product by manipulating consumers.

Companies' incentive to increase profit means that they work toward making products more efficiently and market products better. There is motivation to manipulate and mislead consumers. Advertisements are not meant to provide consumers with accurate information about products so they can make calculated choices about what to buy. Advertisements are the opposite of that. Profit incentives motivate firms to sell products, and over the last century, firms have conducted more and more research on how to do that. Most of the research shows the strong impact advertising has on consumers.

Rather than make a product that consumers want to buy, firms learn how to target various groups and create advertising campaigns designed to make those groups want to purchase their product. John Kenneth Galbraith argued, "production, not only passively through emulation, but actively through advertising and related activities, creates the wants it seeks to satisfy."[80] So while we assume profit incentive is what motivates firms to make the products people want, most firms function by making people want the product they produce.

We are told that people are selfish, competitive, and rational and are, therefore, capable of making rational choices to pursue their self-interest; however, we have to accept several important, inaccurate or insufficient assumptions as truth to make theories of rational people making rational choices, make sense.

Rational Man and Rational Choice: You're Not an Animal, But a Computer

"While we are free to choose our actions, we are not free to choose the consequences of our actions." —Stephen R. Covey

Based on the theory that human nature is rational, rational choice is one of the core principles in economic theory. The model assumes that people are fully informed, rational, and act in their own best interest. However, people cannot and do not meet these criteria, as they do not continuously and rationally compute options according to economic calculations.

Assumptions: People have access to accurate information and have the capability to analyze it

We assume people have access to accurate information and have the ability to analyze that information when making a decision. This isn't true for several reasons: Full and accurate information about an economic transaction and the result of that transaction, is impossible to obtain. It is difficult to even have close-to-perfect information. Real people do not have free access to infinite information and an innate ability to instantly process such information. Beyond lack of accurate information, with so many variables it is impossible to predict the consequences of one's economic choices. And a firm acting in their own interest is likely to prevent accurate information from reaching others.

Many notable economists, including John Maynard Keynes and Thorstein Veblen, denounced the adequacy of rational choice theory. Veblen staunchly criticized the rational choice theory as susceptible to uncertainty because man is impressionable and does not always have a clear vision. He wrote:

> *The hedonistic conception of man is that of a lightning calculator of pleasures and pains who oscillates like a homogeneous globule of desire of happiness under the impulse of stimuli that shift him about the area, but leave him intact. He has neither antecedent nor consequent. He is an isolated definitive human datum, in stable equilibrium except for the buffets of the impinging forces that displace him in one direction or another. Self-imposed in elemental space, he spins symmetrically about his own spiritual axis until the parallelogram of forces bears down upon him, whereupon he follows the line of the resultant. When the force of the impact is spent, he comes to rest, a self-contained globule of desire as before.*[81]

The models we use in determining economic policy (and political participation) assume people have accurate information to make rational choice in their economic transactions. This is simply impossible. To begin with, the amount of information one needs to determine the best course of action is not available. However, even if one is capable of gathering all the current information to make the best possible choice, we do not have the capacity to process such massive amounts of information for our financial choices (even if we only considered large purchases). Furthermore, what may be a good choice in isolation may not be a good choice when the bigger picture is considered.

For example, it may make sense to purchase your fish from Fishmart because they are selling local, fresh fish at the lowest price. They can sell fish at a low price because they use state of the art technology to fish at maximum levels with very few fishermen needed to do the work. However, if everyone purchases from Fishmart, the local fishermen may go out of business. Then the profits to Fishmart leave the area, as Fishmart executives and owners are not locals, having negative impacts on other local businesses. Also, because Fishmart uses the best technology to fish at maximum levels, they deplete the local fish supply, severely damaging the local ecosystem.

There is also an inherent contradiction in the relationship between self-interest and accurate information (that is, if we are to accept these ideas as truths). Acting in one's own self-interest means not providing accurate information to the other party in a transaction. Sure, it is not that everyone always lies either, but there is a good possibility that someone acting in their own interest will not provide the whole truth to another person if they would benefit from the person not knowing the whole truth.

The structure of a corporate economy, including public relations and advertising, prevents informed interactions by consumers and producers. Even within firms, incentive structures may very well direct employees toward hiding information or outright lying.

For example, Corporation A with a profit motive produces cheap products through foreign labor, environmental degradation, etc. Employee 1, motivated by salary to perform a job, is responsible to ensure that the company continues to increase profits. With the ability to hire and fire people, this employee will ensure that the company can save as much money as possible. This includes finding the cheapest labor, laying off employees, and extracting as many resources as possible at the lowest cost, which means circumventing environmental regulations and definitely not providing more environmental protections than required.

Employee 2, in the advertising department, is responsible for increasing profits and, therefore, cannot provide consumers with full information. This employee may not know about all the destruction and harm her company is causing, because it is not her job to know. Either way, if she is to keep her job and succeed, she must create an advertising campaign that sells the product despite the negative actions of her company. Most likely the campaign will involve slogans and imagery that create an illusion of some exceptional benefit the consumer will gain from purchasing this product, while avoiding an honest disclosure about how the product is made and any negative impacts of the product.

There is also Corporation B, which is ethical and competes against Corporation A but can't keep prices as low. By paying workers fair wages and refusing to exploit the environment irresponsibly and at unsustainable rates, Corporation B cannot create the same levels of output as Corporation A. Corporation B distributes honest information with full disclosure of its products and processes. In fact, this corporation is proud of its ethical record. The problem that Corporation B faces is that most consumers do not recognize that Corporation A has such a negative record because there is no system of disclosure in place.

They also cannot reach a wide audience like Corporation A can. Corporation B's product is a lot more expensive because of lower levels of output, higher costs of production, and environmental preservation. Besides keeping costs high, this leaves very little revenue to contribute to advertising campaigns that could compete with Corporation A's campaign (or distribution levels). Without honest disclosure of Corporation A's practices, consumers do not have accurate information that would lead them away from unethical products. Many ethical companies will either collapse or be bought out by big corporations because they cannot compete.

For example, in 1968 a couple from Philadelphia left their home to pursue a simpler, more natural lifestyle in the rural town of Kennebunk, Maine. As part of their new lifestyle they consumed only natural, unprocessed foods. While they wanted to use natural healthcare products, they were unable to find them. So they did what any bold, risky, entrepreneurial American would do: they borrowed $5,000 from a friend and began their own line of personal care products. Their small start-up was called Tom's of Maine, and their products were made with all natural ingredients that do not harm the environment.[82]

In 2006, Colgate-Palmolive Company, a Fortune 500 Company with a terrible ethical and environmental record, purchased Tom's of Maine for $100 million. Most small businesses cannot and do not compete with conglomerates, and expanding is nearly impossible. When a multinational corporation approaches a small ethical business, it is an appealing prospect. Clorox bought Burt's Bees for $913 million, L'Oreal bought the Body Shop for $1.1 billion, Coca-Cola bought Odwalla for $181 million, ConAgra bought Lightlife Foods, Kellogg's bought Kashi for $32 million, Unilever bought Ben and Jerry's for $326 million, and the list goes on.

With the overwhelming challenges to expanding on one's own, it is difficult to pass up the opportunity to expand sales to a much wider demographic by selling the business to a bigger company. Tom and Kate Chappell, the owners of Tom's of Maine, said, "We chose Colgate as our partner because they have the global expertise to help take Tom's of Maine to the next level. Just as importantly, we see Colgate as an excellent fit with our cultural values."[83] Tom's traditionally promoted their fluoride-free toothpaste. But now, more of Tom's products contain fluoride and other harmful ingredients. While they seemed to have used sodium lauryl sulfate for a long time, they recently also added fluoride and zinc chloride to their products. They have also discontinued the use of their aluminum tubes in exchange for more environmentally hazardous plastic ones.

Many companies want to be honest enough to maintain a good relationship with customers, but that does not always translate to providing accurate information. On the contrary, corporations usually refuse to provide accurate information and go as far as pushing partial information as truth. Food companies have continuously lobbied Congress to remove requirements to put informative labels on food that provide consumers with information about what the product really contains. And they win these battles!

Starbucks promotes the fact that it purchases fair trade coffee so consumers feel like Starbucks is a good company. However, less than 10 percent of the coffee they purchase is fair trade and Starbucks has so far ignored demands to make more fair trade coffee available to its U.S. consumers.[84] Because Starbucks is the largest purchaser of coffee in the world, its contribution to fair trade purchases is the largest in the world. However, the information we consumers lack in this equation is that it is also by far the largest purchaser of unethical coffee in the world. Most likely, more people purchase more Starbucks coffee because of Starbucks' marketing campaigns and availability, which increases demand and perpetuates a cycle of human and environmental exploitation. But when you go to Starbucks, chances are you will not find pictures of abused and underpaid coffee farmers—you will see big signs that say "fair trade."

The constant need to increase amounts of consumption to produce growth means ever-growing amounts of want. It is beneficial for a company to hide practices from consumers. Because corporations are legally bound to shareholders to try to increase profits, and showing constant growth means attracting more investors, corporations are required to maximize profits. Increasing profits means increasing production and sales, but it also means cutting costs. Very often the practices that accomplish these goals are highly unethical.

The whole purpose of the marketing and advertisement industry is to manipulate and deceive people. Advertisements are not informative. They use false imagery and dishonesty to convince people to buy things they do not want or need. Industries conduct studies and research to figure out how to manipulate characteristics of various human groups and then they manipulate them. They increase desire and raise demand. When the sole purpose of most of the information consumers get is to trick them into making particular choices, the notion of a rational economic actor is outright ridiculous.

As described above, firms literally have an incentive *not* to provide accurate information for consumers to be able to make rational choices. They must convince them to make irrational choices. This destroys the notion of competition by better product and innovation, as most effort and investment goes into better advertising and branding to sell products. If people had accurate information, and were aware that certain choices were so destructive to the environment, they would look for other options.

Assumption: Human beings are rational actors who pursue monetary self-interest

A rational individual works to achieve specific goals at the least possible cost. Once we assume people have accurate information, we assume people rationally pursue monetary self-interest. However, the rational choice model has several inconsistencies. First, we assume the rational person knows what the rational choice is for long-term benefits; however, there are always too many unknown factors to make perfect decisions. Second, the model ignores other considerations like morals and ethics that impact people's choices. Third, the model does not determine whether these predetermined goals are rational.

There is no way to calculate the impact of changes that occur in the future that may affect one's choice. With the inability to forecast future scenarios, rational choice is based largely on short-term profit gains. An agricultural company may refuse to stop polluting within the realm of the law because it will lose profits (in fact, usually fines are so insignificant companies prefer to break the law and pay the fines). However, if the law is not strict enough to prevent water pollution, over time the water could be unsafe to nourish crops for the company. The company would lose significant profits or even go bankrupt (or switch to a new location leaving the public to suffer the consequences). Either way, rationally pursuing short-term profits can irrationally hinder long-term stability.

The rational man model also ignores moral and ethical considerations that people experience in the real world. People may weigh options against each other and select what they perceive as the best option, but different perceptions of what the best result is, will yield completely different outcomes. With diverse considerations, which would be the best scenario, rational choice to the individual could be an irrational choice to the economic man.

Among many scholars, Amartya Sen criticized the notion of rationality for individuals. One of his challenges was that rationality goes beyond selfish interests, writing, "the exclusion of any consideration other than self-interest seems to impose a wholly arbitrary limitation on the notion of rationality."[85] Sen thus argued that economic calculations must consider other influences on individuals' choices. The rational choice model focuses on extrinsic motivation. It assumes that man is seeking an individual economic reward, which ignores, or at least trivializes, non-economic motivation.

Many social scientists also challenge the validity of rational choice. Economists have shown that in some traditional societies, people's choices regarding what to produce and exchange were based on principles of reciprocity, rather than pure self-interest. Among them, Karl Polanyi showed the success of the Trobriand Islanders in Western Melanesia using a system based on reciprocity and redistribution.[86]

Furthermore, irrational behavior is typical of everyone based on the human condition. For example, habits, peer pressure, advertisement influence, hobby and leisure preferences, and relationships, can all lead to irrational behaviors. Sociological scholars highlight the limits of the model in its inability to consider preferences, which are largely determined by education, society, and outside influences.

According to rational choice theory, the rational man should be willing to pay for an item the same amount he is willing to be paid for the item if he had to give it up. However, Amos Tversky's and Daniel Kahneman's "prospect theory" found that "people under weigh outcomes that are merely probable in comparison with outcomes that are obtained with certainty ... [and] disregard components that are shared by all prospects."[87]

Essentially, losses have a greater negative value than gains have a positive value, so there are more factors in economic choices than rational calculations of monetary gain.

Assumption: Economic models can explain and predict human behavior

The fact that economists use these economic models assumes we can accurately predict the behavior of humans in mass. Rational choice theory is an unrealistic assumption used by economists to generate predictions of outcomes and probability of outcomes regarding economic trends and models. As in social science in general, these assumptions are approximations at best, and do not justify global policy.

Some economists still argue that the rational man is a practical measure of how people function in the market. Markets function in a way that makes simple cost-benefit analysis the reasonable course of action. Other economists claim that combining advanced models that factor inconsistencies into decision-making with the rational man model, provides a more accurate depiction of the market. However, these models also leave out the bulk of factors essential to the study of scarcity. Furthermore, the mainstream discourse does not reflect anything beyond rational choice.

Even economists argue over the relevance of calculating individual behaviors that do not actually exist. Some argue that it is worth analyzing purely selfish behavior just as it may be important to analyze "irrational" or selfless behavior. My concern about the discussion is not just a matter of what we analyze and consider (the more information the better). The problem is that the idea that people are rational actors with accurate information to make decisions in their own best interests, shapes policy and factors into economic models and calculations—decisions based on kindness and morals do not.

The system of deception is present throughout the whole economic foundation, so if the whole basis for the system is false, how can someone make a rational choice? Furthermore, how can we base a whole system of social order on the assumption that all actors can and will make rational, predictable choices?

If we believe the assumed truths that humans are selfish and competitive, and they rationally pursue property incentives competitively, then we may be inclined to believe that competition itself makes sense. However, there are several assumptions that would have to be true for competition to be a model that worked as an effective economic motivator.

Competition: You're Not Rich, So You Must Be Lazy

"A creative man is motivated by the desire to achieve, not by the desire to beat others."
—Ayn Rand

Competition is a revered concept in American culture. Let's be honest, it gets most of us all worked up. All a person has to do is frame an issue by dividing into sides and creating winners and losers and we line up to idolize the winners.

The problem with this admiration for winners is it misrepresents the reality of our economic system and leads us to believe things that are not true. We assume firms compete to make the best product for the lowest price, and the best firms win. To win this competition, we assume firms are constantly innovating new products and making our economy more efficient. We further assume that efficiency is positive. Unfortunately, these beliefs are not accurate.

Assumptions: Firms compete to make the best product at the lowest cost and, as a result, only the best firms succeed

We assume firms compete against each other to make the best product for the lowest cost. Based on that assumption, we further assume competition means the best people and firms succeed. However, that assumption is false. Competition does not mean that the best succeed. Most of the biggest firms do not out-compete others because they are the best; they out-compete because they cheat.

Both the government and corporations wield power over the American (and global) people, but in theory, our government has a checks and balances system that gives each of the three branches of government—legislative, judicial, and executive—enough power to limit the powers of the others. When all else fails, the people have the power to vote out any and everyone in Congress or the president as a final check of power. There are a variety of reasons why this system has not worked. Every congressperson and president has taken steps to maintain their political power, thereby increasing the power of each branch, and thereby decreasing the relative power of the people. The most overwhelming example is the solidification of the two-party system where both parties are very similar in overall philosophies and neither represents many Americans at all.

Likewise, corporations have a sort of checks and balances system. The government regulates free market conditions, at least enough to prevent monopolies; in this competitive market, corporations continually check each other by constantly undercutting each other's prices to sell more goods. Additionally, consumers hold the power of "consumer sovereignty" and they vote with their dollars. If they like what a corporation does, they will buy the corporation's products and that corporation will succeed. If consumers do not like what a corporation does, it will fail. Through competition, only the best companies will survive.

This also has not worked for a variety of reasons. One notable reason is corporate manipulations of competition through methods like forming cartels (formal or informal). These cartels make competition in an industry practically irrelevant. Advertising, public relations, and laws allow corporations to either withhold information or mislead consumers, which means consumers do not have the information they need to check the power of corporations.

Similarly, we are often told that if we do not have a job or are poor, it is our fault. We all know that any competition creates winners and losers. Very often, these roles are not dictated by skill and work ethic alone. Winning and losing can be very situational. And winners are often people (or corporations) who were willing to cheat more than the others. As we discussed earlier, incentives often motivate people and companies to use dishonest and destructive means to increase bottom lines, and not strive to be the best at what they do.

Because of our dogmatic love for competition, many of us want to say, "too bad," "life isn't always fair," and "let the best man win." But consider two things. First, what game are we playing? Markets are set up around profit and who can make the most money. We assume there is a direct link to who can make the best product. In other words, whoever makes the best product will make the most money. But this is not true.

The game is simply who can make the most money, meaning who can come up with the best business plan, create target advertising, manipulate loopholes, circumvent regulations, etc. Is this the game we all value? Second, what are the rules of the game? Is it that the best person wins, or those who are able to best cheat the system win?

Many hard working Americans succeed by out-competing others by working harder and providing a better service. Especially in our current economic model, competition like this is valuable and necessary. But do not let that fool you into thinking that because some succeed like this, everyone can. More importantly do not let it fool you into believing that most of the economy functions this way. Most big businesses succeed by avoiding competition and cheating the game. Do we not value integrity?

Walmart's Chief Executive, Mike Duke, is no dummy when it comes to the importance of integrity in business. Some might even call him inspirational. For Duke, integrity is the "foundation of the company's culture." In a 2012 letter to employees, he wrote, "as leaders, we are measured by our weakest moment, so we can't have a weak moment in the area of integrity."[88]

Perhaps, Mr. Duke was too busy focusing on his pristine integrity to respond adequately to emails he received in November 2005 from Maria Munich, then Vice President and General Counsel of Walmart International. Munich emailed Duke and other high level executives to report that Sergio Ciero Zapata, a former Walmart employee, seemed to be trying to blackmail her in exchange for keeping quiet about Walmart's illegal bribing schemes in Mexico.[89]

Duke may have also been distracted when Walmart's

123

spokesperson, David Tovar, reported that Walmart executives in the U.S. didn't know anything about the allegations. He probably learned the importance of integrity from Samuel Robson Walton, the son of Walmart's founder Sam Walton, and the chairman of Walmart. Walton proclaimed, "Let me be clear: acting with integrity is not a negotiable part of this business."[90]

Fortunately for Walmart executives, it seems everything else is negotiable including laws, environmental health, communities, and the desires of human beings. Residents that live in the area around the ancient pyramids in Teotihuacán found this out after they fought for months to ensure that Walmart could not build a store near the pyramids.

To protect their sacred land they protested, went on hunger strikes, and pleaded with Walmart. They also went through the political process of creating a community approved zoning map that would help protect the area, specifically protecting a field that Walmart wanted to build on. Walmart then paid a bribe to have the zoning map changed around the specific field so they could build a supermarket.[91]

The New York Times broke the story that showed Walmart routinely uses bribery to circumvent laws on a massive scale as a way to "build hundreds of new stores so fast that competitors would not have time to react."[92] Following the allegations, Walmart launched internal investigations where their team found "reasonable suspicion to believe that laws have been violated in Mexico and in the United States."[93] At this point, Walmart executives took extensive steps to cover up widespread bribery in Mexico.

For example, following a meeting with top-level executives to discuss the investigation around Zapata's allegations, Walmart began to transfer control of the bribery investigations to José Luis Rodríguezmacedo, the general counsel of Walmart de Mexico. Mr. Rodríguezmacedo had been identified as a key facilitator of the bribery scheme in the initial investigations.[94]

Competition leads to anti-competitive practices as a mechanism to "out-compete" others including forming cartels, pursuing predatory pricing and lending, lobbying, manipulating media and public relations, and exploiting negligible advantages. Once one firm out-competes another, it can manipulate the situation (i.e. lower price, provide free give-a-ways) to make actual competition difficult. This is not a system where the best product wins the day.

Competition does not necessitate individual competition as we are led to believe through the promotion of individualism propaganda. Everyone thinks capitalism is competitive. In reality, corporations know that if they work together they can all benefit by controlling specific sectors of the market, maintaining several large corporations in an industry to create a guise of competition. But as we discussed earlier, many large companies buy up smaller companies, form mergers, or coordinate efforts to increase all of their profits by out-competing others and manipulating market situations. It's like forming an all-star team. It is like a cartel. There clearly are not enough mechanisms against that. This is how the banks are run. This is how the cell phone companies operate. They have control over the market; the market doesn't have control over them.

This is a centrally planned system, only it is corporate leaders who are doing the planning, and the people have no say or control over what they do. There are no significant checks and balances for corporations. In many instances, there is no real choice. To make a rational choice that would drive competition there have to be different options available.

Assumptions: Firms continuously innovate and efficiency increases

Since we assume firms are competing against each other, we assume that firms continuously innovate and increase their efficiency to out-compete others. Here we are several layers deep into the deception and inaccurate information. Not only are we led to believe that competition is aligned with human nature and, therefore, the only way to drive progress, but we are also misled to believe that real competition exists and that people and corporations win by making the best product.

Once we believe that, we are also told that it produces

gains for the whole economy through efficiency, innovation, and promotion of consumer sovereignty. I discuss the fallacies behind innovation in the section below and the false notions of consumer sovereignty in the Supply and Demand Section. Here I will quickly address efficiency.

While in some circumstances it may be true that competitive practices yield high efficiency, it may also create inefficiency, overlap, and duplicate efforts that increase costs. For example, many students have spent tens of thousands of dollars on similar education when enough jobs in those fields do not exist. (Not to say education is a waste, but it has not produced the monetary results many thought it would.) Competition also leads to firms spending a lot of money on research and development to discover a new product first. However, multiple firms spend money pursuing the same thing and thus, wasting time and money (especially for the firms that do not produce the product first).

Assumption: Efficiency is good

The notion that competition increases efficiency assumes that efficiency is inherently good. The worship of the idea that competition breeds efficiency never questions the idea of efficiency itself. We need to challenge the notion that efficiency is a priority. What are we referring to when we think of efficiency? Is efficiency a good thing in and of itself?

Efficiency describes a condition where the maximum desired outcome is achieved with the least effort. It is measurable by comparing output to input. It refers specifically to short-term measurements. In a capitalist economy the desired outcome is profit and the amount of effort is cost. If we spoke of efficiency in terms of non-monetary outcomes, we would have a different discussion.

For example, if the goal was to preserve resources at sustainable rates while maintaining a healthy economy in the most efficient manner, the term efficient might not be so fraudulent. However, in capitalism, where the game is competition and the incentive is profit, there is no way to analyze "efficient" other than in terms of monetary gains. To highlight the distinction I like to think in terms of effectiveness. "Effective" is a term we do not often use in economics. Why? Because it is not measurable. Effective refers to something that produces the desired outcome. Effectiveness can be evaluated in a qualitative manner, but it is not quantifiable.

We are told that the free market drives prices up and down as dictated by supply and demand. A seller will push a price up as high as possible based on what people are willing to pay, but people will only pay up to a certain price. Goods are made at low cost because businesses are trying to find the most cost effective ways to produce. By efficiently pursuing profits (to out-compete others), corporations are forced to continuously seek ways to cut costs, which translates to suppressing wages, outsourcing jobs, replacing people with machines, and destroying the environment.

In 2010, Pittsburg Steel purchased SteelPro 1000, a robotic plasma-cutting system that does the work of seven machines and helped increase production on beams, columns, and plates by 50 percent. Each robot also replaced four human workers.[95] The process of replacing human workers with robots is highly efficient because they cost less, work faster, make fewer mistakes, and never need rest.

Most economists will argue that replacing human workers with machines fuels growth and innovation as displaced workers must find new and creative ways to make a living. However, as machines and robots creep into every industry and profits from production go to the wealthiest Americans in the owner class, it seems that rather than benefiting the whole of society, technological advances are perpetuating poverty and extreme wealth gaps.

Certainly, machines have been taking over factory jobs for a long time, but many jobs that robots will soon replace include positions that, until recently, were considered human only: pharmacists, lawyers, drivers, astronauts, store clerks, soldiers, babysitters, and reporters.[96] Robots are so cost-efficient that even Foxconn, the Chinese company known for its low-cost slave labor, that provides electronics to huge corporations like Apple, HP, Sony-Ericsson, Amazon, and Dell, is replacing one million human workers with one million robots.[97]

In the long-term and in humanness, it is effective to have people working (especially, in the current economic structure). If we measured economics in long-term considerations, we would consider the value in effectiveness. Preserving the environment and respecting humanness is effective because we would have an equitable society and healthy environment. We often hear the debate about how the government is wasteful and inefficient. This may be true, but this debate ignores the effectiveness of government. Of course the government can also be ineffective, so I'm not advocating that our current government institutions are the solution, only that the bureaucracy, while inefficient, is not inherently bad IF it is effective.

The government may take a long time to make decisions, but if that was because representatives were actually finding out what their constituents wanted and implementing those wants, then that would be effective. Effective processes take more time. Government institutions may prioritize the jobs of human beings over the increased profits created by replacing them with robots because there is value in ensuring people have jobs. Conversely, the efficiency of the private sector means prioritizing immediate profits. There is no long-term accountability so even if making a profit means harmful effects that are highly inefficient, they are not considered.

Furthermore, there is a contradiction between principles here. There is so much effort into the rhetoric around how the market loves stability. We go to war for that idea. But competition actually creates instability. Honda out-competes Ford, Ford collapses, instability. You might say, "if Honda makes a better product, that's good" but we have already shown that out-competing usually means better advertising and exploitation of workers and the environment.

Despite all the misconceptions regarding competition, we are told that it breeds innovation; however, innovation is more complex than we are told. For innovation to conceptually fit the current capitalist model, we have to assume several things about innovation to be the only truths.

Innovation: You Think, Therefore You Profit

"Governments will always play a huge part in solving big problems. They set public policy and are uniquely able to provide the resources to make sure solutions reach everyone who needs them. They also fund basic research, which is a crucial component of the innovation that improves life for everyone." —Bill Gates

Innovation is another concept we idolize in America. Innovation is creation that makes our world better. We assume capitalism drives innovation because of its incentives. We believe innovation is good because it implies progress. Also, when we think of innovation, we typically think it means creating new inventions. These beliefs are not the whole truth.

Assumption: Innovation is driven by capitalism (we ignore when it is not)

We are told that innovation is driven by capitalism. The entrepreneurial spirit thrives based on the incentive of the pursuit of profit. The evidence seems obvious. Since the rise of capitalism, the industrial nations have crafted wondrous advances in technology and quality of life has increased exponentially.

There is no doubt that capitalism has fostered amazing advances, but it is difficult to ignore some obvious questions. Is capitalism the only reason for these advances? Do we have substantial evidence that no other system provides innovation in technology? Doesn't the government drive innovation as well? Furthermore, doesn't this view ignore or trivialize all the inventing, creating, and innovation people accomplish for every other incentive besides money?

The truth is innovation is prominent without capitalism. Innovation occurs prior to capitalism, in non-capitalist societies, in capitalist societies but through the government, and for motives other than capitalist incentives.

Since the implementation and development of capitalism, humanity has made vast advances in social condition and technology. There is little doubt that capitalism at least contributed to this advancement. Many people and companies have innovated machines and processes to progress society because they saw personal, monetary gain from doing so. However, many innovations occurred prior to capitalism as well.

Glass, clocks, guns, and boats all originated prior to capitalism. In fact, they all were invented prior to mercantilism, which preceded capitalism. Consider the innovations in writing in Mesopotamia, Egypt, the Indus Valley, and China between 4000 and 3000 B.C. Mathematics also developed in this region with numeric symbols in the Cuneiform script dating back to over 35,000 years ago. Were these systems of writing created to advance one's accumulation of property? It is more likely that many advances derive simply from humans' innate curiosity and desire to explore, discover, and create.

Many other innovations developed outside of capitalist society. In modern innovations, the first vaccine for meningitis B was developed in Cuba, a so-called socialist country, in the 1980s. The first satellite to launch into space, called Sputnik, came from the Soviet Union in 1957. The United States government's Department of Defense, not a private company, quickly responded and launched its own satellite, Explorer I.

Many innovations that occur in capitalist societies occur through government assistance, not capitalist incentives. The government funds the largest portion of research and development that are then marketed in the private sector and sold for profits. This argument, in and of itself, does not hold up against the case for capitalism, in that the government funding comes from tax dollars paid in from a capitalist society. We can further say that the government, in these transactions, serves as a consumer of goods produced by private firms for profit. However, it does call many of the false notions of capitalist innovation into question.

To say the government does not have a role in innovation is false. Many argue that governments cannot innovate because there is no incentive for it to do so. Promotion of government research and development is dismissed as socialist (in a negative sense). However, some of the greatest technological advances may not have been able to get off the ground without government funding because some projects are too expensive and too risky for investors to take on. When the U.S. military was in need of a small device that could quickly calculate complex equations necessary for missile targeting, the government funded two companies working on the microchip. Without that funding, these companies, Fairchild Semiconductor and Texas Instruments, likely would not have developed.[98]

The desire to surpass the Soviet Union also spawned the Advanced Research Project Agency (ARPA). ARPA helped create ARPANET, a Wide Area Network (WAN) that connected various universities and research centers. This network was a fundamental advancement in computer technology and a precursor for what we know today as the Internet.[99]

Not only is government funding directly responsible for the research and development of many technologies, but also knowledge shared between the government and the private sector spawns more innovation. The government's and private sector's innovation are not mutually exclusive. The National Aeronautics and Space Administration (NASA) is a government-funded agency at the forefront of much technological advancement. NASA is required by law to publicize research and technology for private use. Its innovations have led to the household use of many common technologies including the global positioning systems (GPS).[100]

The truth is that we have an overwhelming amount of examples throughout history and modern times of innovation that is derived from motives beyond the monetary gains of capitalism. It is true that most modern innovations have technologically advanced the globe in a world dominated by capitalist-type systems; however, there is no significant evidence that capitalism is the only driver behind these advancements.

The asymmetry regarding innovations from capitalist nations verses other systems, only highlights that capitalism spread throughout the developed world, not that the developed world resulted from it. We cannot know what other innovations would have arisen under developed non-capitalist systems. Furthermore, this view of capitalist innovation ignores, or at least trivializes, all the inventing, creating, and innovation people accomplish for every other incentive besides money.

The logic that perpetuates the partial truth that capitalism is responsible for innovation is based on our partially correct notions of incentives and human nature as selfish, rational, and competitive. The idea that private property and profits are the only thing that foster innovation ignores a very human drive to build, create, and improve the world. Most humans are innovative beings and strive to create things and improve things for many reasons other than self-interested profit.

Leonardo Da Vinci designed a flying machine, similar to helicopters, in the 15th century. He couldn't build it and sell it. Why do people like Da Vinci invent such things? Because they imagine them, dream of them, and strive to create them. Many people simply want the satisfaction of creating. Many people want to make the world a better place. Open source technology is a prime example of people sharing ideas and creating new technology simply to make technology better and available to everyone.

We know of so many innovations and human creations prior to profit motives and capitalism, individuals' creations of technological advancements under various economic and governmental systems, and significant funding for research and development that leads to innovation from governments. Therefore, we can, at the very least, conclude that the assumption that capitalism drives innovation is only partially true. This discussion of what drives innovation begs a further question: is innovation inherently good?

Assumption: Innovation is good

Innovation is widely perceived as an inherently good thing. The capitalist system relies on innovation as its final answer to any and all questions about the natural limitations of the world. Innovation is human creativity's ability to improve the world and solve its problems. "We will innovate our way out of it" has become a sort of catch phrase to describe how humanity need not be concerned with long-term limitations or problems, like the destruction of the environment. But is all innovation good? Of course not.

We have innovated horrifying technology that has detrimental implications for the human species. The atomic bomb is one example; we innovate bombs for the purpose of destruction. We also innovate technologies with noble intentions that have negative impacts. Innovations are meant to create change; however, the effect of change is always uncertain. Innovations have unpredictable negative consequences that can destroy net value, even if the negative results are not calculated.

For example, around the 1950s and 1960s, with rising global populations and shortages of food, projections forecasted that a billion people would be at risk of starvation. The Green Revolution refers to research, development, and technological and procedural innovations that were implemented in the agricultural industry between the 1950s and 1970s and significantly multiplied global food outputs. As a result, the Green Revolution was credited with saving millions of people from starvation.

Despite the achievements of the Green Revolution, its innovations have had a wide variety of significant adverse effects on humans and the global environment. Implementing the innovations of the Green Revolution required money, which meant owners of firms and means of production accumulated profits and increased the wealth gap. New machinery put many small farmers out of work and significantly increased urbanization. The Green Revolution also required techniques of monoculture and replaced most polyculture farming techniques.

Monoculture techniques had several negative impacts. First, they led to a lack of diversity in the food supply and resulted in increases in malnutrition and death in developing countries. Monoculture crops were more susceptible to pests; therefore, pesticides were required. Pesticides have been linked to large increases in cases of cancer and to millions of poison deaths. They also had negative impacts on populations of other animals and the environment. The lack of variety in crops left soil without proper nutrients and made it inadequate at fertilizing. To supplement the loss of nutrients, farm companies used chemical fertilizers to increase production yields. This process perpetuated land degradation and soil depletion. Furthermore, it required increasing amounts of irrigation, which is still depleting global water supplies. The Green Revolution drastically altered global agriculture.

We do not know the longer-term impact of these problems,

nor is capitalism necessarily the sole cause of these problems. What is clear, however, is that innovation brings unforeseen consequences. Economist Amartya Sen found that global food shortages do not only originate from a lack of food, but also from a failed system of distribution,[101] so it is likely that the innovations of the Green Revolution were not even necessary.

Furthermore, the more society develops, the more we are exceeding the capacity of the planet. We are not just perpetuating one problem, like damaging the ozone layer, which seems to have rejuvenated itself once precautions were taken, but we are perpetuating multiple, interconnected problems that may push our planet beyond its capacity to sustain us. What is the probability that innovation is capable of coping with the rising complexity of multiple problems happening at the same time? The fact is, we do not know. And lining the pockets of the 1% is not worth the risk.

Assumption: Innovation is the creation of new products

In attempting to out-compete others, we are told that individuals and firms constantly make new and better products to meet changing needs and wants. Of course, this is only partially true. Most innovation is not the creation of new products at all. There are many different ways businesses innovate to increase profits that have nothing to do with making new stuff.

Tony Davila, Marc J. Epstein, and Robert Shelton surveyed a large number of manufacturing and services organizations. In *Making Innovation Work*, they present their findings that things like product quality improvement, expanding a product's range, creating new markets, reducing labor costs, improving production processes, reducing materials needed and energy consumption, and other efficiency improvements, account for most innovation.[102] This is in contrast to the perception that innovation is dominated by invention and production of new products.

We are told that innovation fuels supply and demand curves that drive the economy because firms respond to needs and wants of consumers and make products to meet the consumers' needs. If humans are selfish and competitive, rationally pursue property incentives, and innovate new products to out-compete others; supply and demand in a market economy will communicate messages from consumers to ensure companies are innovating appropriately to their desires. However, supply and demand is a hopelessly inaccurate model for measuring human behavior. The only reason this model is maintained as foundational to economics is because we accept several assumptions as truth.

Supply and Demand: If You Ignore Enough Factors, It Really Works!

"Rats and roaches live by competition under the laws of supply and demand; it is the privilege of human beings to live under the laws of justice and mercy." —Wendell Berry

Supply and demand is a fundamental model in economics. It is at the foundation of free market economic thought and policy, and used as justification for the way our economy functions—production, service, media, consumerism, environmental exploitation, etc. Despite its prominence, supply and demand is based on a long string of false assumptions and is completely inadequate as a prediction of human action.

The model does not apply to economic transactions that do not involve monetary exchange; therefore, anyone who cannot afford to pay for a product does not factor into the demand for it. The implications of this limitation become evident when we compare the human need for food to the economically calculable demand for food. The mathematical priority ignores human realities.

Supply and demand models also rely heavily on the false assumptions regarding rational man and rational choice, competition, and innovation. Many scholars criticize supply and demand. For example, Goodwin, Nelson, Ackerman, and Weisskopf wrote:

> *If we mistakenly confuse precision with accuracy, then we might be misled into thinking that an explanation expressed in precise mathematical or graphical terms is somehow more rigorous or useful than one that takes into account particulars of history, institutions or business strategy. This is not the case. Therefore, it is important not to put too much confidence in*

the apparent precision of supply and demand graphs. Supply and demand analysis is a useful precisely formulated conceptual tool that clever people have devised to help us gain an abstract understanding of a complex world. It does not—nor should it be expected to—give us in addition an accurate and complete description of any particular real world market.[103]

Supply and demand models may accurately portray price in the mathematical model, but this is far from the reality it aims to illustrate.

Assumption: Supply and demand dictate prices

The limitations of the supply and demand model are so significant that they cannot adequately represent reality. The supply and demand model does not accurately account for real world limitations on supplies, it does not adequately represent labor, and it does not reflect the market for money, which is the foundation for our entire system.

First, supply calculations do not accurately encompass real supplies or supply limitations. For example, primary inputs (raw materials and natural resources) in modes of production do not follow the supply and demand model as one might assume they do. To some extent, supply and demand may be calculated based on the amount of material extracted, but the process still assumes unlimited amounts available for extraction.

The total supply of raw materials is finite but that is not reflected in the price because the supply and demand curve focuses on the short-term supply. Prices in supply and demand only represent the supply in the market at the time (if they even really reflect that) and they don't take into account the limit of the resource.

For example, Lake Mead provides 90 percent of the drinking water to two million people in Las Vegas. Since 1998 the water capacity of Lake Mead has decreased by more than half with total losses above 5.6 trillion gallons.[104] Lake Mead is indicative of the greater water crisis across the U.S. and the globe. U.S. water supplies are dwindling as people typically use more than the amount that is renewable. Further compounding the problem is that we don't know exactly how much water is available in the

U.S. and how long it will last. All we know is that we are using more than is replenished by Mother Nature. Yet, water in the U.S. is virtually free, and as a result, people waste it without considering the limitations.

While the Earth is about 70 percent water, humans can only use less than 1 percent of that. In addition, large portions of useable water are becoming polluted, contaminated, or dried up. If supply and demand calculated real limitations, the price of water would be rising quickly.

Nonrenewable resources and most renewable resources that are being exploited beyond sustainability are used as inputs—as if the only limits are the limits of the day. We do not know what the full supply is. In other words, if we knew oil would run out in five years, it would be much more expensive today until we fully implemented an alternative, and then the price would be extremely low.

Supply is often controlled in ways to manage price through practices like crop burning, so the actual supply is not even considered. As we discussed earlier, business leaders often plan prices formally or informally. They manipulate demand, which is artificially inflated with marketing and advertising campaigns that perpetuate inaccurate information, impacting price. Reality is almost the opposite of what you are told: supply and demand do not determine price, but rather, price determines supply and demand.

Primary inputs are the original sources—the foundation—of the materials economy. They also have a significant impact on other sectors. For example, we use oil to make plastics and it is essential to our transportation industry. We use water to drink, but also to grow food and produce goods. If the price of water went up, the price of everything would go up. If we calculated these inputs with respect to the reality of finite-ness, the prices of goods would be much higher, consumption lower, and profits less. This may seem like a bad thing based on everything we are told about the economy; however, this would actually be extremely beneficial in terms of sustainability.

We are also told that supply and demand dictate the value of a person's work. Supply and demand let us believe that there is an equilibrium created to determine wages. If there is an abundance of jobs people could be picky and choose a job. This is because an abundance of available jobs means a relatively low supply of labor, a higher demand for that labor, and a higher price (in this case, wages). This view considers labor as the commodity, sold by the laborer.

If workers are selling their labor, they will try to get the highest price for it. However, there is never an abundance of jobs. According to the Bureau of Labor Statistics, the lowest unemployment rate in the U.S. since 1948 was 2.5 percent, which occurred for two months in 1953.[105] The average unemployment rate is much higher, around 5.7 percent annually.[106] With the current U.S. population, a 5.7 percent unemployment rate means almost 18 million Americans are without jobs at any given time.

Being that there is never an abundance of jobs, we could flip the supply and demand model around to view the labor market in a way that better represents reality. Let's say that jobs are the commodity rather than labor. With a low supply of jobs, owners of jobs (employers) can sell jobs at a lower price; the price being how much the laborer is willing to give up to get the job. For example, if your labor is worth $20 per hour, but you take a job for $12 per hour, you are buying that job slot for $8 per hour in money you are giving up, which goes toward the profit of the owner because it is money they did not spend. If you work a 40-hour week for 10 years, you are paying $166,400 to have your job. Because jobs are always in low supply, this view more accurately describes the reality of wages when using a supply and demand model.

Furthermore, we treat money as a commodity. Money is vital to our economic structure as it is the dominant medium of exchange for all measured economic transactions. However, because we treat money as a commodity in our economic system, money functions in a supply and demand model and the price of money is interest.

As with other commodities, we might assume that supply and demand dictate the price of money, but the price of money is not determined by how much consumers demand at certain interest rates. Instead, leaders in the banking industry determine the price of money. The central banks control the supply of money and determine the interest rates. In the U.S., the central bank is the Federal Reserve, a private corporation that wields power over our economy with no accountability and minimal oversight and transparency. Make no mistake; this is a centrally planned mechanism to control the economy.

Assumption: Price reflects the cost of making the product

Price is the compensation someone will pay to obtain a good or service, usually based on units of currency. We assume the price of goods and services reflects the cost of producing them with some additional charges for profits for the owner. In reality, price does not reflect the real cost of making products for several reasons: firms externalize costs of making products, disposal costs are not calculated, value of products is subjective, and we cannot accurately put a monetary cost on the environment.

In a free market, we are told that the price reflects the constant interaction of individual actors in supply and demand relations. Owners produce a certain amount of goods (supply) based on how much they can sell for profit and consumers will buy a certain amount of those goods (demand). The price fluctuates as the amount of goods made, and amount of goods purchased, changes. This continues until the price reaches equilibrium at the point where the quantity supplied meets the quantity demanded at that price. Therefore, prices should be as low as possible without producers losing money (or else they would stop making the product).

Of course, firms always try to produce the goods they make while paying the lowest cost possible to produce them, as to increase profits. They do this by externalizing the costs as much as possible. All economic transactions have consequences for other people that are not involved within the initial interaction. Economists refer to this as an externality. Externalities are the costs (not necessarily monetary) imposed on other people, who are not involved in the transactions, as the result of transactions between buyers and sellers.

These costs are often difficult to assess because they can be non-monetary, and it is difficult to ascertain their relation to the

139

transaction. Therefore, externalities are often omitted from any consideration in calculations. Because firms externalize costs, and no one calculates them, they are not paid by the producer and are not reflected in the price for consumers.

Externalities are not calculated into the production costs. When companies pollute during the production process, there is a cost associated with that pollution. For example, producing plastic requires large amounts of highly toxic chemicals like benzene and vinyl chloride. These chemicals go into the air and water supplies. They damage the ecosystems. Additionally, they are known to cause cancer and damage nervous and immune systems. How do we assess the cost of this damage? People pay hospital bills. Also, we could possibly figure out how much it costs to clean the water. But when a person gets cancer from a toxin in their water, how much would they pay to get rid of it? There is not a monetary figure that does justice to the human cost of this question.

When there is a monetary compensation associated with an externality, it is drastically insufficient to the costs people actually feel (i.e. payments for medical bills do not make up for medical suffering). Whatever these costs are, they have to be paid somehow. Someone, who has nothing to do with the economic transaction, "pays the price" in non-monetary and monetary costs. This allows the firm to sell goods much cheaper and, therefore, sell much higher quantities of them, and greatly increase profits.

Consumers purchase goods assuming that what they are paying covers the cost of producing that product, but it does not. Consumers do not pay the cost for pollution in monetary value; other people pay the cost in non-monetary ways—loss of health, loss of resources, lower wages, etc. Externalities have massive and immeasurable human costs associated with them.

Environmental damage is not calculable because every aspect of the environment has multiple values to many people and these elements impact other aspects of the environment as well. For example, water pollution might cause poor health in local people; damage to crops and food supplies; soil degradation; depletion of species of fish and birds; etc. Obviously, calculating everything affected, and the degree to which they are affected, is impossible. But the producers also do not pay any cost for polluting the environment, and do not include this cost in the price of the product. These are called externalities because they are considered external to the economically measurable; however, these costs are real and have devastating impacts on people.

For example, from 1952 to 1966 a company called Pacific Gas and Electric (PG&E) used hexavalent chromium to prevent corrosion of its cooling towers in the San Francisco Bay area. The chemical runoff from this was dumped into store ponds that were not lined properly. This chemical worked its way into the ground water, contaminating the drinking water of many of the residents of Hinkley, California and causing them to become extremely sick. The cases of illness caused by the water contamination included bloody noses, throat problems, tumors, and ovarian cancer. The case of PG&E was depicted in a 2000 movie starring Julia Roberts called "Erin Brockovich," about the law clerk who worked tirelessly to uncover the case.

In many aspects, the Hinkley case was a success—the biggest settlement for a class action lawsuit in U.S. history. Plaintiffs were awarded $333 million. However, while the movie depicts the Hinkley case as a real-life David vs. Goliath story, exploring some additional details shows that this case highlights how the companies that cause externalities never pay enough for them, if they pay at all.

The $333 million was divided among 650 Hinkley residents using an undisclosed formula that determined how much each client received. Regardless of the method, dividing up $333 million among 650 people is clearly a trivial amount of money compared to the terrible conditions the Hinkley residents suffered. No amount of money would suffice.

Additionally, while the Hinkley settlement might be unique in the large sum they received, it is not unique in that companies all over the world pollute and contaminate our environment. Many people suffer from similar illnesses and never get any compensation. Often, if cases even do go to trial or arbitration, they can be dragged out in long appeal processes that favor the corporations who can afford to keep paying for the long legal battles and do not need immediate medical attention.

The Hinkley case was also settled with arbitration so there is no public record of the litigation that occurred. Also, as Kathleen Sharp of Salon.com writes, "the Hinkley lawsuit was a case study in how the rise of private arbitration, as an alternative to costly public trials, is creating a two-tiered legal system that not only favors litigants who can afford it over those who cannot, but is open to potential conflicts of interest and cronyism."[107]

So while arbitration led to a sizeable settlement for Hinkley residents, this record-breaking settlement still does not cover the cost of suffering (of course, in some cases, no amount could) and it does not provide justice because big corporations can write a check and never face real public scrutiny.

Furthermore, the judicial process is not capable of serving justice to major corporations because the damages they cause are so vast and complicated, and impact so many people to varying degrees, that it is difficult to connect corporate actions to the effects they have. Money also cannot adequately cover the type of damage caused. Even when only the monetary costs are examined, the numbers challenge the validity of the system. In other words, even if the non-measurable factors are ignored and only the measurable factors are calculated, externality costs are so great that it would not be profitable to continue most big businesses the way they are run.

For example, a report on the impact of the coal industry in Kentucky found that coal brings in approximately $528 million in state revenue while causing approximately $643 million in state expenditures, leaving taxpayers to subsidize the difference of $115 million.[108] Even more shocking, a United Nations report that attempts to put a price on environmental damage found that the world's 3,000 biggest corporations caused $2.2 trillion of environmental damage globally in 2008. The report considers factors like water usage, greenhouse gas emissions, nuclear waste, and acid rain.[109]

In our cycle of consumerism, it is less costly for someone to constantly dispose of old products and purchase new ones, since no one actually pays the cost of disposal. If people had to pay a real cost for disposal, they would be reluctant to buy more items even at low cost. For disposable goods that we use every day, prices are driven drastically down because profits can be increased based on the quantities people buy. And since disposal costs are not paid for by the producer of a product, it doesn't affect their price.

Cheap goods make more profit than expensive goods because people will buy, throw away, and buy cheap goods again. Profit is based on how much a producer sells, not just how much they make per sale. If they sell a calculator that costs $5 to make for $10, then they will earn $5. However, if they make the calculator for $3 and sell three of them for $5 each, they earn $6.

The costs that firms externalize do not have a measurable monetary price, but they do have a value. When we think of value, we may perceive it as the worth of a good or service as determined by the market and expressed in price, based on monetary units. The notion of value may include concepts like worth or price, but value has a broader meaning as well. Value is a subjective concept. It may be relative to the perceived value of other objects. Value could also be perceived as the amount of labor one is willing to commit to obtain something. However, a real meaning of value is outside the scope of economic measurement.

Value changes over time. Is the value of a house what you bought it for, what you sold it for, or the profit you made from it? Or is the value of the house the total of the shelter, security, and memories you experienced while you lived in it? Is the value of a two-year degree the $60,000 you pay for it or the income increase received over the course of a lifetime from it? Or is it the education you received that helped you grow as a person?

Value is more than what you pay for something, or what it is monetarily worth; it is the impact on your humanness from having the item. Monetary value does not usually reflect inherent value. For example, the inherent value of a house to a family in 1950 compared to a family in 2015 would be the same because of the shelter, feeling of home, memories, etc., but the price of the same house 65 years apart is very different.

We cannot put a monetary price on nature because so many people value different elements to different degrees, and things we value are intimately connected to and depend on other things. Let's say we figured out how much the air was worth in dollar value; the same piece of air would still have value to many people whether they could afford it or not. Just because only some people have money to purchase air, does not decrease the value of air to people who do not.

You can put a container around a bottle of water and associate a value with it, but that value only represents price in terms of the amount in supply of bottled water. The total supply of water on the planet is not considered. Water has value to everyone, but the person who pays for a bottle of water does not compensate for the value that the loss of that water has to others. In other words, if we considered the limited supply of water, a bottle of water would be more expensive.

For example, a lake has a certain value to the people who live around it. It also has a value associated with it to people around the world, as it contributes to a global ecosystem. It may be a sustainable source of fish for people who live away from the lake. Birds that migrate may use it as a source of food for part of the year. Resources have a certain value when they are used for production and a different value when they are used in nature. However, the value of nature is never calculated or considered in any meaningful way.

If the lake was drained in order to water crops, it would have a value to the extent it contributed to the crops that were sold at a given price. The price of the water taken (again, a very low price) would be calculated and factored into the price of the crops when they were sold, but the value lost by depleting this resource is not included in the cost. The lake remaining in the environment provides continuous enjoyment and resources to a group of people who value it for different reasons and to varying degrees. Some people may use it as a place to swim where as other people might use it as part of their daily life or income. While the value of the lake when used for crops ends when the crops are consumed, the value of the lake in nature repeats itself every day forever.

It's not enough to say the resource could have a dollar value and to charge someone for it because the varying degrees of value make the total value immeasurable. Even if there was a way to determine actual value, the cost of taking something out of nature would be very overwhelming. Nonrenewable resources would be especially costly, as the costs would skyrocket as the resources depleted.

Being human means valuing intangible things. The value we collectively get from intangible things like health, education, and the environment, cannot be measured in monetary units. Unfortunately, because they cannot be measured, they are not even considered in the pricing of goods we purchase. Because these values are ignored, people and corporations can create huge profits by exploiting the ecosystem.

Although prices do not reflect nonmonetary costs, they are essential to earning profit and creating wealth. The idea that we can create wealth is true. We do use the human mind and creative energy to add value to natural objects thereby making them valuable to us (especially if we ignore the value lost from removing the resources from nature). We put a price on this value. However, the idea of wealth creation the way it is used in the mainstream discourse is a far stretch of this truth. We have to assume several falsehoods and partial truths as the only truth, to make the concept of wealth creation make sense in our model of capitalism.

Wealth Creation: They Don't Care About Your Drinking Water, They're Sharing Pie

"One of the things I find very interesting in our current debates is this concept of who creates wealth. That wealth is only created when it's owned privately. What would you call clean water, fresh air, a safe environment? Are they not a form of wealth? And why does it only become wealth when some entity puts a fence around it and declares it private property? Well, you know, that's not wealth creation. That's wealth usurpation." —Elaine Bernard

Wealth, an essential concept in mainstream economics, endures based on two assumptions. The first assumption is that wealth accumulation is not a zero-sum game—meaning one's gain of wealth is not another's loss of wealth. We believe this because of the second assumption, which is that unlimited wealth can be created.

Before we talk about wealth in detail, we should find some common understanding as to what wealth means. Wealth is another one of those ambiguous terms that politicians and scholars use that may mean different things to different people. We hear a lot about wealth and wealth creation in the context of economics, so we might assume that the word "wealth" has a very specific definition. However, there is no agreed upon definition of what wealth is.

Wealth in assets typically includes property, like land, and financial assets, like money and savings bonds. People also think of wealth as net worth (meaning total assets minus total liabilities). The ambiguity of value, discussed in the previous section on supply and demand, further complicates the notion of wealth because not all value is measurable. Things have different value to different people, but calculations of wealth only consider monetary value. Wealth is more of a general term, which makes it difficult to analyze and to dispute assumptions based on it.

Concepts of wealth also vary across time. With advances in technology and the driving down of costs of consumer goods, we are told that the poor have a standard of living equivalent to, if not superior to, the wealthy of the past. In terms of certain technology, this is probably true. For example, one hundred years ago, the wealthiest people in the world did not have Play Stations or even electric refrigerators. Modern labor-saving inventions have enabled the poorest sectors of today's society to enjoy a higher standard of living in this way. However, while the poor may be able to buy a cheap Play Station, use the refrigerator that comes in their rented apartment, and lease a car, the access to healthy food, higher education, and house ownership still elude them, unlike the wealthy of the past. There is a lot of ambiguity regarding the concept of wealth, yet politicians and pundits talk about wealth creation as if it could never be questioned.

Assumptions: Wealth accumulation is not a zero-sum game and, therefore, no one loses

A zero-sum game is when one person's gain is equal to another person's loss. Simple logic would suggest that if there were a finite amount of resources, and I take some for myself, that would mean there is less available for others. In a zero-sum game, the proportion of one's gain is equal to the portion of another's loss.

Economists have uncovered the solution to this would-be problem. What they find is that one person's gain does not equal another person's loss because wealth can be created. In fact, in economic transactions both parties choose the interaction because they think it is beneficial to them. If both parties are benefiting, then the transaction is a gain for both.

A couple of considerations will show that this is not the whole picture and that the mainstream view—that a zero-sum game is a fallacy—is only partially true. Several things blur the reality. First, as we have discussed before, economic transactions do not occur in isolation. The reality of connectedness between people and the ecosystem dictates a complexity of interactions. Interactions do not involve just one-to-one agreements; they impact other people that have nothing to do with the interaction. Second, resources are used at unsustainable rates for unlimited wealth creation. And third, even when both parties gain in a transaction, proportions of gain matter over time.

The model assumes that a company is an autonomous unit and that if it succeeds in creating wealth, which can be created in an infinite amount, the company's success does not mean a loss for others. Also, it assumes that the company's success has an overall positive impact. But how is wealth created?

Let's say a U.S. firm buys a large plot of land in Latin America because the land is fertile and the labor is much cheaper. Both the local landowners, who sell their land and the U.S. firm, find the exchange mutually beneficial. The amount a U.S. company is willing to pay exceeds the amount any local buyer could offer, and the fertile Latin American land guarantees the U.S. firm high levels of output with minimal labor costs. By using the land, labor, and human ingenuity to create additional output, the U.S. firm creates wealth.

This seemingly simple transaction has much deeper and complex implications that I am not going to describe here, but we can easily assess the immediate loss for others outside of that interaction. The problem is that the calculation of total wealth does not consider the net loss of the value of the resources to those that they were taken from. Calculations only consider those involved in the transaction and only the current monetary value. Therefore, future losses from not having access to the resource are not considered.

The U.S. firm must reconfigure the land to meet its needs. So, for example, if the land was a forest, the firm would cut it down to make productive farmland. If the firm wanted to transform the land to produce high yields of one crop, it would require the introduction of pesticides and chemical fertilizers. In this process, the local community loses the that value the forest provided them in quality of life that comes from being surrounded by nature, the capacity of natural ecosystems to absorb pollutants, and the replenishment of sustainable resources that untouched nature provides. The value of clean land and water is lost as chemicals work their way into the local ecosystem and naturally extend beyond the plot of land purchased by the U.S. firm.

While the U.S. firm may provide some low-paying jobs and income to local labor, locals lose the value of future prospects, as they will not be able to own the land and manage it for their own wealth creation. Once the land is no longer productive, the U.S. firm can move to another location, leaving the destroyed land behind. The expansion of negative consequences continues as the firm repeats the process in new and expanding locations.

For example, Cargill, one of America's largest food processing corporations, chose Brazil's Amazon Rainforest as a prime location to externalize huge environmental and human costs to increase their private profits. It planted over three-quarters of a million hectares of soya within Brazil's Amazon deforestation belt by 2001. Low land prices and lack of funds for government inspection made Santarem an ideal location for Cargill to build soya-handling facilities, even though building it was in violation of Brazilian law. Since the arrival of Cargill the cost of one hectare rose from about $13 to $300, deforestation of Brazil's Amazon increased 40 percent in one year, and entire communities were displaced.[110]

If we only look at Cargill and the previous landowner we might calculate a win-win transaction. But if we look at the negative impacts on all those affected by the transaction we would see a net loss of wealth.

Wealth can be created when we exclude environmental losses, but unlimited wealth creation requires unlimited resources. Ever-increasing production assumes we have infinite resources, while we live in a finite world. Most resources are finite, but we consider some renewable. We assume that a renewable resource is a resource that gets used and replenished at the same rate—you use ten trees and ten more are planted; you use water, it rains, and we get more. The reality is that renewable resources are only fully renewable if they are used at a sustainable rate, which at least for now, does not happen in our profit-based model.

We do not currently use renewable resources at sustainable rates because that slows production and slows profits. It also adds additional costs to production if companies have to fund resource replenishment, and why would they do that instead of moving to another location for less cost? Furthermore, we need to consider that most resources do not exist in a vacuum. Resources depend on full ecosystems for their health and survival. Cutting down too many trees makes soil unusable in growing more trees and makes renewal nearly impossible.

People in the business world are not oblivious to this: they know the limitations. Some of them may even be extremely concerned about the environment and try to sell the idea that a bit of environmental assistance may make the company look good to consumers and help boost sales and profits. (How else could they sell the idea to their company?) Corporations are not built to care about the environment. Their function is to make continuously increasing profits—that's it. The long-term implications of their environmental destruction do not matter when their bottom-line is being checked today.

This model does not correlate with what matters to human beings and what is necessary to respect the limitations of our earth. All of these resources have value, but when we talk about wealth, we leave out the value of the environment. If we considered the value of the loss of our environment and how many people were affected by it, recalculating the notion of gains and losses of wealth in transactions would change our perspective on zero-sum games. We would see that these transactions are not the win-win scenarios we are led to believe.

Even if we only consider the parties involved in the transaction and accept the idea that wealth is created and both parties in the transaction benefit, proportions of gain matter over time. A popular analogy for wealth is a pie. It is said that we do not have to worry about dividing the pie because we just keep making the pie bigger. Wealth creation is supposed to improve the quality of life for everyone. And in some ways, advancements in technologies do improve the lives of many people. However, our quality of life is also affected by other people.

Everyone that has a job understands that owners influence our lives. In this way, wealth accumulation matters. If the wealth pie is growing, and everyone benefits, but a small percentage of people continuously benefit more than a much larger percentage, then the wealth gap continuously grows. Growing wealth gaps have significant negative impacts on lower-income populations, even if their net income increases. The wealthy gain power over resources, politics, and labor. The control over social resources and structures leads to oppression of the poor for the purpose of creating more wealth to be accumulated by the wealthy.

The accumulation of wealth is what leads us to believe that the wealthy create jobs. However, with wealth accumulation amounting to control over jobs and resources, the wealthy only create jobs when it is in their own short-term best interests.

Assumption: The wealthy create jobs

We assume the wealthy create jobs because they need more workers to expand their businesses. As people and firms accumulate wealth from their successes, they will spend some money (helping to further fuel the economy), save some money, and most importantly, reinvest some money. Some of the accumulated wealth is reinvested back into innovation (because self-interested human nature leads to rational choices to better compete through innovation), which creates jobs. As the theory goes, private businesses that create jobs as they invest in new ventures also create revenue that is greater than the cost of the new venture. Part of the revenue gain goes into creating jobs where the new revenue made by employees is greater than the cost of their wages.

Here we come across another inherent contradiction. Investment and innovation focus on creating more products to meet demand at the lowest cost. This means innovating new technologies and processes to make products more efficiently. This means businesses are trying to cut jobs, replace people with machines, or find cheaper labor as much as possible—not create new jobs. Innovating new products is not only making new technologies to sell, but also making new technologies to replace workers because machines work for free.

The folklore inspires us. John Henry, former slave turned steel worker, who laid railroad tracks and dug tunnels, is an American legend. When the technology of the day threatened Henry's and his co-worker's jobs, he challenged the steel company owner's new steam-powered hammer to a competition of man against machine. Henry's persistence, strength, and determination proved victorious as he pounded and hammered down steel tracks at a superhuman rate, beating the steam-powered hammer and proving the dominance of man over machine. In the tragic ending to the tale, Henry collapsed to his death after winning the competition, having exerted himself beyond what his human body could handle.

While inspiring, the story sheds light on an important flaw in innovation. Technology continuously improves and has capability far beyond the human capacity. Workers are being relieved of their labor demands, but there are no mechanisms in place to sustain their livelihoods. Even in folklore, the fastest and strongest worker loses his life to narrowly beat a new machine.

The rise in technology could improve the standard of living for everyone. Technology could free humans from labor while providing them with necessities and luxuries. However, the current structure of the economy perpetuates a different result. Economist Jeremy Rifkin wrote:

> *We are being swept into a powerful new technology revolution that offers the promise of a great social transformation, unlike any other in history. The new high-technology revolution could mean fewer hours of work and greater benefits for millions. For the first time in modern history, large numbers of human beings could be liberated from long hours of labor in the formal market place, to be free to pursue leisure time activities. The same technological forces could, however, as easily lead to growing unemployment and global depression.*[111]

Even though companies will try to create more demand to make more products, which in theory would mean more work, the process still necessitates trying to accomplish the goal of creating more product with fewer and fewer labor costs, usually equaling fewer jobs. Furthermore, if it is possible to use cheap foreign labor (often including slave labor), then most companies cut costs by hiring people overseas. Companies like Apple hire workers in countries with no enforceable labor protections so workers typically work endless hours in horrifying conditions.

In *The Next Convergence*, Michael Spence unveils his research regarding which American companies created jobs between 1990 and 2008. He found that companies that operate in global markets created almost no American job growth. These industries include manufacturing, energy, finance, and banking. The firms that did contribute to job creation have a more domestic focus such as healthcare companies, government agencies, retailers, and hospitality businesses. Many of these jobs are low-paying. And even in these industries, many of the jobs created were outsourced so they did not help a lot of American citizens find work.

Economic Growth: The Fatter the Better

"An economic system which can only expand or expire must be false to all that is human." —Edward Abbey

Regardless of the environmental damage, or who gets which jobs, all of this wealth accumulation and reinvesting causes economic growth. In our current structure, economists calculate economic growth, which means firms are making goods and people are consuming them. In theory, this economic activity also means people are working. Because of all these conditions, we assume economic growth is good.

Assumption: Economic growth is good

There is a lot of debate about how to grow the economy, but we never question if growing the economy is necessary, or even a good thing. Economic growth means more products on the market at lower prices, which more people can purchase—which means quality of life is better (according to the models economists use to measure it).

We constantly hear about economic growth. We have some notion of what it means and we assume economists know when the economy is growing. Pundits, politicians, policy-makers, and scholars tell us how the economy is doing based on assessments of growth. As a result, we assume that economic growth is inherently a good thing without considering other factors like how the growth happens, who benefits from it, who could benefit from it, and who is hurt by it.

Economists measure the economy by looking for growth according to the factors they calculate: it is a circular and misleading process, which is described below in the economic measures section. According to this outlook, growth is good. We should be asking why it is good. We should define what economic growth is, how the growth is occurring, and who benefits from the growth and how much. We may expect economic growth to bring benefits to everyone. However, according to an Oxfam study, if wealth is accumulating at the top, "extreme inequalities in access to productive assets, marketing infrastructure, health and education stifles innovation and restricts opportunities for the development of markets. Seeking to build growth on the foundations of extreme inequality is not just socially unjust, it is also inefficient."[112] It is never accurate to assume a totality like "growth is good."

Economic growth also impacts quality of life, so it matters

153

who is benefiting from the growth. The Oxfam study also stated:

> *Even if it were true that economic growth raises the average income of the poor as much as the rich, policy makers with an interest in poverty reduction should be concerned with the share of the poor in national wealth. This is because for any given level of average income, the extent of poverty will depend on how income is distributed. Similarly, the distribution of any increment to growth will determine the rate at which growth is converted into poverty reduction. Highly unequal societies are bad at converting growth into poverty reduction. The rate of conversion—or 'the poverty reduction efficiency of growth'—matters because the more unequal the country, the faster the rate of growth needed to achieve any given level of poverty reduction.*[113]

It also matters how that growth is created. For example, since loss of nature isn't factored into any economic measures or considerations, long-term environmental damage is accumulating unaccounted for.

Human labor adds value to raw materials and as goods are produced they are given a monetary value that factors into the cost of wages for that labor. However, monetary value is a measure created to determine the value of things people manufacture. We do not have an accurate way to determine the value of goods in their natural environment because the concept of ownership does not apply—nature has value to everyone. There is almost no way to earn extreme fortunes without exploiting the environment, labor, or the money system. People get rich by exploiting externalities. So, we have an economic system that promotes environmental destruction and ails human beings.

It is in this context that taxes are debated. At best, having strong tax policies means keeping the destructive system in place, but requires people to share the costs of the destruction while the profit is kept by a few. They are an insufficient Band-Aid. Even if taxes were used to help repair the environment and people's health, these problems would not go away (they compound over time) and social problems like income inequality would continue to grow as well. While we may want to create economic growth, it is not worth it if we are making our future unsustainable.

Furthermore, the factors that measure economic growth are not necessary for human livelihood.

Since all this wealth is created from selfishly motivated competitive innovation, economists figured out many ways to measure economic growth by leaving out and ignoring the most important elements of human interaction. However, we assume that these measurements tell us what is important to know.

Economic Measures: Good − (-Bad) = Good

"Without measures of economic aggregates like GDP, policymakers would be adrift in a sea of unorganized data. The GDP and related data are like beacons that help policymakers steer the economy toward the key economic objectives." —Paul Samuelson

"Even if we can never quantify [satisfaction or happiness] ... as precisely as we currently quantify GNP ... perhaps it is better to be vaguely right than precisely wrong." —Herman E. Daly and Joshua Farley

Economists attempt to measure economic activity. The measures they use do not work because they determine themselves: they measure what economists consider good to determine if the economy is good while leaving out or minimizing the most essential pieces of the economy—people and nature. What economists do is measure the elements of economic transactions that can be calculated in the measures they created, ignore what cannot be, and in that context, tell us whether the economy is good or bad. Also, they do not calculate the benefits of the good work people do if it does not involve money. The result is an irrational system of study and destructive national policies.

I call economics the art of measuring the immeasurable by measuring something else and calling it what the immeasurable thing actually is. We could never calculate "standard of living" or "quality of life" in a way that any normal person would conceptualize these things. In economics, these measurements use currency (the dollar) as their unit of measure. Then, economists plug different figures into different equations that tell us a variety of allegedly accurate things.

The idea of measuring the economy is ridiculous when we

consider what the economy actually is. Economics is supposed to gauge how humans deal with scarcity. It involves calculating how all humans interact with each other. If we were to measure what the economy actually entails, we would have to consider everything, even things we do not know how to measure.

This system measures itself under the conditions that economists created—far from reality. The idea is that people constantly need new things and to fulfill these needs, things must be constantly made. However, most things people need do not have to be continuously made, as they already exist. Furthermore, many things people need do not have to be made by destroying things other people need. Because economists believe people constantly need new things, quality of life and standard of living are defined by the increase in production of more goods and services. Then economists measure them by calculating production and consumption of goods and services (that may be destroying actual quality of life), ignoring the actual human notions of these things.

If the standard of living statistic rises, which it usually does, it is promoted as the reason capitalism makes everyone better off. The notion that all boats rise with the tide refers to the idea that when the economy grows, measured by GDP, everyone is better off. The reason this does not make sense is because the standard of living is calculated using GDP. So the idea is that if GDP rises, another measure that uses the average GDP also rises, and that is supposed to tell us how good our life is.

This may seem confusing and crazy, because it is. To clarify, let me give a simple example. Let's say that Little Country had two people. The first person earns $10 per year and spends it all to survive. The second person makes $90 per year and invests whatever she doesn't spend. The annual GDP is $100 and the average GDP per capita is $50. From some good investments, our second citizen increased her annual income to $990 per year, raising annual GDP per capita to $500. Standard of living increased roughly ten times the amount. However, our poor first citizen's overall lifestyle probably got worse because of the repercussions from the drastically increasing wealth gap.

Also, measures do not calculate good things that lack monetary value (i.e. housework) and bad things that lack monetary value (i.e. environment damage). Since we assume growth is good and we measure growth by GDP, we want GDP to grow. Therefore, we have to act in ways to increase GDP, whether or not GDP measures are actually good for us.

A good economy, according to the way it is currently calculated, is based on high consumption. GDP measures consumption, so a growing GDP means a lot of people making stuff and a lot of people consuming it, which is supposedly good. The more money people spend, the better the economy is doing. But spending a lot is not enough because these calculations require constant increases. In other words, we need to keep spending more.

This of course means we need to buy, use, throw away, and re-buy for the economy to be doing well. Isn't it crazy that we have to invent our biggest industries (advertising, media, public relations) around creating wants to increase demand for things so we will consume them? So we can have increasing GDP that measures how much we consume because economists decided that was good? According to these economic calculations, a good and rising economy means an increase in quality of life for the population. This assumed truth is extremely dangerous and many of us accept it without question.

The problem is that the most valuable and scarce resources in our environment are not measurable in terms of monetary value. If we were to attempt calculating them, they would be extremely expensive. Again, one reason that full costs of externalities are not calculated is because the people who pay the costs (in loss of quality of life, environment, health, etc.) are not part of the economic transaction. Additionally, the bulk of human interaction is not measurable in terms of monetary value. (I know you think I might go into a diatribe on how you can't buy love, but I'm not even going to go there.)

Non-monetary interactions are not calculated. Consider providing shelter as a human interaction. If people and firms all over the country gave their abandoned houses to families without homes, every family in this nation would have a house to live in, and our economic measurements would plummet. Why? Because no one exchanged money in this interaction. However, all those people who finally had a roof over their head would probably argue that quality of life increased.

Maybe there is some value in measuring the economy the way that we do. But to not disclose its limitations or discuss what it actually measures regularly, loudly, and publicly, is a travesty. We need the populace to understand what these measures tell us and what they don't tell us. These measures should have very little weight in our policies and analyses.

Assumption: Economic measures present an accurate picture of economic activity (they tell us whether specific economic activity is good or bad)

Economists decide how to measure the economy. They decide what factors to measure and what factors to exclude. The major economic measurements, including GDP, only include factors that are mathematically calculable—really only those that can be counted and added. It is a quantitative measure without regard for any qualitative factors. Unfortunately, we treat these measures as if they indicate the realities of the human species and our planet.

Measures like GDP make what we consider a good economy fit to the measure itself. For example, GDP measures the total production of goods and then economists say that an increase in that measure is good, is the goal, and is a strong economy (an indicator of quality of life), while leaving out every other element of economic interactions and non-economic interactions that impact quality of life. So if the production of goods goes up, the economy is good. But depending on how goods are produced, many bad things can happen that make GDP rise.

GDP measures what makes the market good or bad and leaves out the rest. For example, a country that grew its own crops and sustained itself with handmade goods and traded by bartering would be considered to have no GDP, a weak economy, and low quality of life. On the other hand, if land was purchased and farms destroyed to build factories to make goods, which were then exchanged for money to provide the same people with food and some handmade goods, GDP would soar.

GDP counts work that produces no net change or that results from repairing harm. For example, rebuilding after a natural disaster (or war) would increase GDP as if the destruction never happened. If your house was destroyed in a storm and you had to build a new one, you're not in a better situation, and more things are destroyed than rebuilt. So why does GDP increase? The amount of work produced by the rebuilding does not outweigh the losses from the disaster.

GDP goes up when bad things happen. Increase production, increase pollution, increase inequality, and GDP will also increase. Whether the government buys bombs or pays for healthcare, GDP will rise the same.

GDP is also used to measure an economy's general monetary ability to address externalities. It is not meant to measure the actual externalities. Furthermore, GDP does not measure whether the given economy does or does not deal with externalities, but only its general ability to pay for them if it were to. Besides environmental destruction, human exploitation, and health damage, externalities include wealth distribution and non-market transactions. GDP does not represent anything done for free or things not sold for money. Additionally, old houses that are sold do not factor into GDP because GDP only calculates the monetary value of materials produced annually.

The housing market is a good example of how economic measures fail to provide an accurate picture of reality. There are enough houses in America to house all of our homeless many times over. If they all bought houses for $10,000 dollars each, the GDP would not budge, nor would the quality of life measures. However, you can imagine that the quality of life for all those families would increase exponentially. Now consider all the environmental damage caused by building new houses and the negative impacts that damage has on actual quality of life; however, new houses would increase these measures.

Economic measures leave out so many things that are not calculable like environmental and human factors. However, these factors are used in processes that are calculated in GDP—making GDP even more inaccurate. Inputs for production are positive factors in economic measurements because they are produced and sold, but there is no calculation subtracting the value of the loss of that resource. In fact, the calculation of the negative impacts would be much greater than the value of the product produced, because the product has a very short shelf life comparatively.

The resource, while still in nature, contributes value as long as it remains there. Once extracted and turned into a product it only has value because it can be sold in dollar value. (Of course, products provide value after they are purchased, but even that value is not considered beyond the monetary value.) Why don't we consider the value resources provide us in nature?

GDP only factors transactions that use money. It does not factor any goods produced that are not sold. Household work is not calculated. Free and open source software is not counted. GDP does not include leisure activity or leisure time. It does not consider human rights.

All of these human and environmental factors are left out of our economic measures, and the fact that transactions that have extremely negative impacts on people are calculated as positives simply because money was exchanged, means that these measures do not provide an accurate picture of how people are actually doing. If the economy extends beyond money exchange (and in reality it does), then these measures cannot tell us with any certainty or accuracy if the economy is doing good or bad—meaning how well the economic system is dealing with scarcity. In fact, they do the opposite: so much is left out of the calculations that GDP tells us the economy is good when we are actually destroying it.

Imagine a vast and wide pristine forest, abundant in wildlife, rivers filled with fish, trees providing the air with fresh supplies of oxygen, a constant mist, and the capacity to absorb minimal pollution from the local communities. This is the natural state of untouched land.

A private company wants to build a paper factory on the land, so they purchase the land from the state. Once the corporation owns the land, they clear a space to build their factory. They train and hire some locals to work in the factory. They clear more and more land because trees are the primary inputs to producing paper. The production process also requires the introduction of large amounts of chemicals. While the company stays within the realm of the pollution laws as much as possible, large amounts of chemicals work their way into the ground water and get into nearby rivers. The rivers unintentionally transport these chemicals to the local communities and neighboring states. Introducing these chemicals into the supplies of drinking water drastically increases the incidents of various sicknesses, including cancers, in numerous populations. While many people do not have medical insurance, and some with insurance are denied coverage by their insurance companies, payments to hospitals rise substantially.

Years pass and people begin to blame the corporation for the rise in sickness. Lawyers initiate a class action lawsuit and a long, drawn-out legal battle ensues. Meanwhile, death rates increase and families are stuck with the large costs associated with burying their loved ones. Finally, in a positive turn, the families win the class action lawsuit and the corporation is forced to pay a lump sum of money that is divided among families in the suit.

While this example is an oversimplification of actual economic interactions, consider the impact the elements of this story would have on GDP. The purchase of land, production and sale of paper, insurance policies, payment of healthcare bills from cancer treatment, legal fees, payment for funerals, and the money spent from the settlement, all boost GDP. The destruction of the forest and the chain of ecosystem damage that results from that destruction, and the suffering of families coping with disease and cancer, are not even considered. I challenge you to consider the damage that this simplistic measure perpetuates by measuring destruction as positive, or not at all.

Standard of Living: You Have 1, He Has 99, Therefore, You Each Have 50

"Like winds and sunsets, wild things were taken for granted until progress began to do away with them. Now we face the question whether a still higher 'standard of living' is worth its cost in things natural, wild and free." —Aldo Leopold

Despite all the destruction that is created by assuming falsehoods as truth and ignoring realities, we are told that all of this measured economic activity has increased our standard of living and made our quality of life better (according to the economic measures). However, we have to take several more assumptions as truth to make this belief make sense.

Assumption: Economic growth creates a better standard of living

Supposedly, more consumption means a better standard of living. We also assume that the standard of living is an indicator of how everyone is doing. The main justification for capitalism is that when everyone pursues their own best interest, it creates economic growth, which raises the standard of living for everyone. All boats rise with the rising tide, so they say. It's easy to find some truth to this statement.

Capitalism has dominated the global economy for the last century and people are typically much better off now than they were one hundred years ago. So … case closed? I'm not convinced. For example, people consume more, but what is being consumed matters. We have more access to food and meat now, but the food and meat we have access to are full of poisons and chemicals. There are many examples of how we are better off and worse off, and we cannot determine how much of human progress is because of economic growth.

Regardless of how and why people are better or worse off, there is no exact definition for the standard of living. GDP is important because, all other things equal, we think richer people are happier. The generally accepted measure for the standard of living is average real GDP per capita, which is each citizen's share of GDP if it were divided equally. High, quickly growing GDP represents lots of economic transactions that provide people with the goods and services that they desire. Higher GDP is better than lower GDP because more output produced means more goods and services purchased, and thus a higher standard of living.

If GDP per capita is rising, more goods and services are probably available and more people are able to purchase them. In addition to luxuries, this would suggest that more people's basic needs were being met. However, measures of private consumption are insufficient methods to measure standard of living for several reasons.

GDP per capita is not a measure of individual income. GDP may increase while real incomes for the majority decline. These measures are often based on national averages that do not highlight inequalities and wealth gaps, which may lower the real standard of living. More importantly, after a certain point of meeting basic needs, more consumption does not correlate with a better standard of living. Finally, as discussed earlier, methods of production used to increase GDP, may have significant negative impacts on the standard of living for certain people, for example, by destroying nature.

Furthermore, these inconsistencies apply internationally and make country comparisons faulty. Food, clothing, and shelter are calculated as basic needs; however, depending on what region of the world you live in, there may be additional needs relevant to you that are not calculated as needs.

Standard of living is measured by nations in isolation but standards of living do not change exclusive of other nations. One nation's standard of living may impact other nations' standard of living. So for example, say Nation A, a developed industrial country, increases consumption exponentially, thereby increasing the standard of living for all citizens. Massive increases in consumption produce massive increases in disposal; however, an abundance of landfills would decrease the quality of life for Nation A. Nation A pays Nation B to be the disposal site for their trash. Economists believe this interaction is a win-win because both parties agree to the transaction and find it beneficial. However, while Nation B needs the income, they will have to accept selling their land for disposal at an extremely low price. Their calculation of standard of living will increase, but their actual standard of living will decrease because of the many environmental implications associated with trash disposal.

Finally, looking at productivity as a basis for standard of living is inadequate. There is a negative relationship between increased productivity and job creation, meaning the more productive an industry, the less jobs they require proportionally. Therefore, increases in productivity slow the rate of employment growth. This is because firms continuously find ways to maintain or increase production with less labor costs. Furthermore, firms continually suppress wages and create mostly low-paying jobs leading the number of working poor to increase with more employment if there is no increase in productivity.

One report on poverty and inequality finds from "2001–2008, the same 1 percentage point increase in the growth rate of productivity resulted in a 0.54 percent decline in the growth rate of employment."[114] Furthermore, increases in productivity do not calculate negative externalities of that productivity. A loss of jobs has a negative impact on people's actual standard of living.

The problem with these assumptions is their effect on policy. If GDP measures economic growth, and increased economic growth raises the standard of living, then it follows that increases in GDP indirectly raise the standard of living, thus increasing the productivity of labor and alleviating poverty. Unfortunately, this is not true. Increasing GDP can be detrimental to people and the environment and, therefore, harmful to the standard of living. Instead, economists created formulas to measure "standard of living" that factor in consumption but do not consider environmental loss or any real factors that determine a standard of living allowing them to claim standard of living is rising when it actually is not for most people. In addition, the quality of life measure considers several qualitative factors, but as you will see, they are not adequate to measure real quality of life.

What if we applied this logic to people? When raising children we hope that they will grow to be big and strong. So we assume growth is good. How about we decide to measure growth by height (in inches X 10) plus weight? Furthermore, we will use growth as an indicator for standard of health. Now as this child grows older we measure her height and weight, which increases every year. Of course, after a certain point, this child, now a teenager, is not going to get any taller. She has reached her maximum height at 67 inches and 120 pounds. In our calculations, by 17-years-old, her growth product is 790. However, we have to keep her growing to increase her standard of health so we feed her a lot of food. At age 20, she weighs 160 pounds so her standard of health indicator is now 830. To keep her growing and make her healthier we need to fill her up with more and more food and give her some steroids. By 30, she weighs 230 pounds. Her standard of health indicator is 900! We calculate her growth rate: (900-790/790) X 100 = 13.9 percent growth rate! That's fantastic! Of course, our child is obese now, has diabetes, a heart problem, and all other types of issues, but we do not calculate those factors. To help alleviate these problems, we give her a gallon of wine and an aspirin.

Quality of Life: No, Seriously, Your Life Is Good

"By blindly pursuing economic growth, we are creating a whole set of social and environmental issues that will undermine the potential happiness and well-being of future generations." —*Nic Marks*

Assumption: Economic measures can determine people's quality of life

The entire system that assesses the U.S. and world economy is based on many insufficient calculations. For one thing, it does not take an economist to know that "quality of life" cannot be determined by a financial calculation. The quality of a person's life depends on much more.

There is no sufficient way to measure the things that make

quality of life better because to measure such a thing requires both objective and subjective indicators across many disciplines. Additionally, people value things differently and the most important factors in quality of life are not calculable. However, economists have a method that calculates what they consider quality of life.

Like the standard of living, we assume quality of life is a measure that accurately indicates how people are doing. The Economist Intelligence Unit's Quality of Life Index utilizes nine factors to determine quality of life in its reports. The factors are as follows:

(1) Material wellbeing as determined by GDP per person, at purchasing power parity according to the Economist Intelligence Unit. (2) Health as determined by life expectancy at birth in years according to the U.S. Census Bureau. (3) Political stability and security according to the Economist Intelligence Unit's political stability and security ratings. (4) Family life, which is judged by divorce rates per 1,000 people and converted into an index of 1 (lowest divorce rates) to 5 (highest) according to the UN and Euromonitor. (5) Community life, determined by using a dummy variable taking value 1 if the country has either a high rate of church attendance or trade-union membership and zero otherwise, using International Labor Organization and World Values Survey statistics. (6) Climate and geography by latitude to distinguish between warmer and colder climates according to the CIA World Factbook. (7) Job security using Economist Intelligence Unit and International Labor Organization unemployment rate statistics. (8) Political freedom by using Freedom House's data to average indices of political and civil liberties using the scale of 1 (completely free) to 7 (not free). (9) Gender equality using a ratio of average male and female earnings from the latest available UNDP Human Development Report data.

Similar to measures like GDP, quality of life leaves out so many important qualitative factors or insufficiently attempts to quantify them, that the quality of life measure becomes an arbitrary and misleading number used to justify policies that are bad for most of us.

It does not do us any good to pretend that the human existence, especially in America, has not gotten better during capitalism. There is some evidence of people's lives improving overall. But we should not let this blind us to two very important possibilities: (1) Now that we have come this far (through the capitalist system or not), we can work toward a more equitable and sustainable global society or (2), at the very least, we can get our capitalist system in check.

The argument that other economic systems do not work does not hold up very well because the global society is changing so fast that things that have not worked in the past may be able to work now through the power of the people. Furthermore, it should be obvious that our current system, with all its inaccuracies and flaws, does not work well at all.

Some scholars argue that material growth, as we have pursued it, is no longer necessary for increasing our quality of life. They write:

> *Our current socio-ecological regime and its set of interconnected worldviews, institutions, and technologies all support the goal of unlimited growth of material production and consumption as a proxy for quality of life. However, abundant evidence shows that, beyond a certain threshold, further material growth no longer significantly contributes to improvement in quality of life. Not only does further material growth not meet humanity's central goal, there is mounting evidence that it creates significant roadblocks to sustainability through increasing resource constraints.*[115]

Even if we assume as truth that our standard of living and quality of life are improving, we might still worry because we know that the earth has limited resources and we cannot continuously use these resources without limitations. Fortunately, the final assumption we have to accept as truth to make our capitalist system function, serves as a catchall to help us ignore the realities of our limitations and those of our planet.

This Economic Process Can Continue Forever! (We Assume)

"Anyone who believes that exponential growth can go on forever in a finite world is either a madman or an economist." —Kenneth Boulding

Despite all of the obvious flaws in our economic structure, we are told that this process of economic growth can continue forever. Because the creativity of the human mind is unlimited, it can create unlimited wealth. In the event we run out of resources, humans will innovate their way out of the loss. If the rationale was presented honestly, it would state: "because we haven't destroyed the planet yet, we will not destroy it."

Now you might think "I don't assume any of these things! I know this stuff isn't true!" The problem is that the people who are supposed to represent you in the government make policies that do assume everything described in this section.

We further perpetuate these ideas with extreme pro-America propaganda. Leaders convince us that we must go along with this process because if we do not, we do not love America. To question the destruction of the planet is to be a socialist, which, ironically in the land of political freedom, still carries the stigma of the McCarthy Era. Looking for alternatives to the status quo makes us traitors. This economic process, we are told, is the American way, and America is the greatest country in the world.

Chapter 7: Our Societal Structures Oppose Political and Economic Freedom, Democracy, and Humanness

"Liberty has never come from the government. Liberty has always come from the subjects of the government. The history of government is a history of resistance. The history of liberty is the history of the limitation of government, not the increase of it."
—Woodrow Wilson

"The difficulty of limiting the influence of wealth suggests that wealth itself needs to be limited. When money talks everyone else is condemned to listen. For that reason a democratic society cannot allow unlimited accumulation." —Christopher Lasch

The love of money may not be the root of all evil (Timothy 6:10), but it is clear to most of us that many people will do evil things for money. Sometimes good people in decision-making positions will do things the rest of us think are horrific because it is necessary to accomplish their profit goal. The business and economic structures allow any person or corporation to cause harm and destruction without accountability. When the social structure is problematic, you cannot easily function in the society without contributing to the problem. According to our societal structure, these negative behaviors are the righteous course of action. The perpetrators are our family, friends, and leaders. In some cases, they are us.

Academics, pundits, and business and political leaders have beaten the rhetoric of the theoretical foundation of our economic system into our minds and culture over the last century. Over and over again we hear individual pieces of the same string of thought that justifies how we make policy, structure society, and step out of the way while big businesses pillage our planet.

Intellects and others have always debated the philosophies that make up the roots of this system, but these debates are ignored and brushed aside long enough that they are forgotten. After decades of leaders touting the systemic rhetoric, ignoring dissenting voices, and implementing supporting structures, most of us just assume the rhetoric to be true. In fact, it has reached the status of "common sense."

Although there are logical holes throughout the foundation of the theory, academics brush off and marginalize flaws with terms like externalities as if they are a trivial afterthought, when in fact, they are a bigger part of our reality than all the things that we measure. Challenges and questions are answered with assumptions that have been accepted as truth.

We have seen and heard these justifications so much that no matter how much the system fails over and over again, we stand by it. It is embedded in us. We do not challenge it. We are so dependent on this system that no matter how epic the failure, no matter how devastated our society, no matter how destroyed our lives, we just call it a cycle. We repeat the mantra, "there is just no better way."

The capitalist system is the economic system that we live by. It is also the economic system dominating most developed and developing nations in the world. In its pure form, capitalism has tendencies of freedom for the market and the people functioning within it—basically all of us. It is because of these freedom traits that capitalism is closely associated with modern day democracies, but this is not the whole story. Our societal structure opposes political and economic freedom by promoting the freedom of individuals and corporations to hinder other people's freedom. It also calculates people as disposable commodities whose purpose is to produce wealth for the wealthy. Finally, the structure suppresses our humanness by leaving it out.

Unchecked freedom for individuals hinders overall freedom; it does not nurture it. It hinders freedom of the community by allowing individuals to freely exploit others and their resources. We call it choice, so we believe it is okay. But it is not. One person's choice can destroy another person's ability to choose. Capitalism has some good qualities and it benefits society in some ways, but it puts the wrong priorities forward. Pursuit of profit for individual companies outweighs serious issues that affect all of us.

Part 2 of this book has shown that our entire economic structure goes fundamentally against the notions of freedom, democracy, and humanness discussed in Part 1. The economic structure accomplishes this by discounting any notion of compassion, cooperation, and divergence among human behavior. It ignores reality. Furthermore, Part 2 highlighted how the system is justified based on inaccurate information, misconceptions, and half-truths that deceive society into assuming truths that are simply not the whole picture. By structuring our society around these falsehoods, we have created a society that pits us against each other as if we are implementing the Hobbesian state of nature and fundamentally opposes our freedom, democracy, and humanness.

There is no perfect system. What we need to consider is what the goals of our social institutions should be. Any system would probably need its national and international restrictions, but if the goals are freedom for all and self-determination, there are better ways of running an economy than capitalism, especially compared to the way the West has been doing it. But maybe a good capitalist system is possible. "Good" meaning, maybe it is possible to have restrictions on the capitalist system so that it doesn't exploit us all and plunder the environmental systems of the earth that should belong to everyone.

Promoters of the current version of capitalism, politicians and businesspeople on television, will always point out that restrictions on corporations are unjust because restrictions are against freedom. Do not be fooled. Corporations are NOT people; they do not need to have the same rules as us. In other words, we can restrict corporations without having to follow the same restrictions ourselves—taxes and tax cuts being the best examples. By allowing corporations' unchecked freedom, we allow them to steal our freedom from us and demolish our humanness!

There are elements of freedom and restrictions in every economic system. If you do not feel free, instead of blaming forged enemies of the current politicians—the opposing party, the conservatives, or the liberals—challenge the social structure. Do our economic and political structures make you feel free?

There are many people who believe that protecting the freedom to pursue profit without restriction is among the most vital freedoms. However, there is no denying that giving more freedom to the market—businesses and corporations—creates restrictions on the rest of us, for better or for worse.

The system factors in working people as part of the production process. Like any other part, we are exploited as much as possible for the profit of others. Most of us "average Americans" are poor, maybe not based in poverty, but poor: we struggle to find work, make ends meet, and survive. In spite of rhetoric that the average American lays in the middle of the socioeconomic spectrum, most of us are poor. This is the result of the economic disparity in the country. Most of the money, property, and wealth are owned by one percent of the people. The 1% owns around 40 percent of the wealth. The next highest 20 percent own approximately 50 percent of the wealth. The bottom 80 percent of the country shares the remaining 10 percent of the wealth.

Think about that: the bottom 80 percent of the people in the wealthiest, freest, greatest country in the world, share only 10 percent of the nation's wealth. The remaining material wealth leaves the large majority of us poor, some even homeless (while the American landscape remains flooded with empty, unused houses).

Has this gap in the distribution of material wealth occurred because the "free market" has allowed everyone a fair shot and those who worked harder—those, according to the rules of the system, with motivation to acquire profit—succeeded more than the rest of us? Did they succeed because they earned it? Are poor people lazy? Is 80 percent of the U.S. population *lazy*? Low-wage labor jobs are the most work and the least paid. I think most working Americans would probably agree with that. What do you believe?

I believe that those who deny the effects of history have not studied it long enough. There are causes for the current structure of the economy to be the way it is. There were purposeful choices made by our leadership that accomplished and maintained their intended goals. For example, there is an obvious relationship between race and income. Why are a high percentage of blacks poor? Slavery DID exist. That is, African human beings were sold to Americans to slave under horrible conditions for little or no wages.

The Thirteenth Amendment abolished slavery on December 6, 1865, almost a century and a half ago. Or should I say *only* a century and a half ago. It was almost another century of fighting before the people succeeded in a civil rights movement that lawmakers could no longer ignore. These decisions revolve around making and increasing monetary profits as much as possible. When it was profitable to keep slaves, people kept slaves. When it was profitable to let blacks into the labor force, they were given low wages. And when it was profitable to incarcerate mass amounts of blacks, laws were enacted and enforced at rates that would fill the privately owned prison system.

Corporations like Corrections Corporation of America (CCA) and the American Legislative Exchange Council (ALEC) lobby Congress to write increasingly stricter laws to increase incarceration rates. The prison corporations then take millions of dollars per year in taxpayer money to manage the prisons. These policies never prioritized or acknowledged humanness.

Today, racism still exists and the history of slavery has had lasting effects on our society. The system, that is the economic system of capitalism, is not inherently racist. But it perpetuates racism and other divisive ideologies by dehumanizing people by keeping poor people poor. The economic system does not care about color, gender, or religion. It is based on the goal of the fastest pursuit of maximum profit gains. That goal alone structures a system that keeps the cost of commodities, including labor of people, as low as possible.

The system is structured to keep poor working people at as low of a cost as possible to maximize immediate profit. As the old saying goes: "the poor stay poor, while the rich get richer." Within the capitalist system, the people are a commodity. We are laborers and consumers. Our function is to produce and purchase. This profit-driven system has created a multitude of social problems.

The structure suppresses our humanness. Society consists of groups of people who are interconnected through their political, economic, and cultural institutions, relationships, and expectations. If as Americans we value freedom for all, we must recognize the necessity of balancing between freedom and restrictions because there is no escaping the interconnectedness of individuals and groups in a society. Once we acknowledge this condition of freedom, then it becomes clear that real freedom in a society necessitates real democracy, which must respect the diversity of behaviors, habits, and choices that are part of our humanness.

The notion that human nature is fixed, self-interested, rational, and competitive, ignores our human capacity for compassion, empathy, emotion, morality, and cooperation. These traits are not simply fringe elements of our nature. These are every bit as prevalent and relevant as our rational, selfish competitiveness. Part of being human is satisfying our inherent desire to have valuable relationships with other humans. The economic structure opposes this quality and continuously brings people further away from others in their communities by perpetuating individualism, commodifying people, and preventing true democracy.

The notion of monetary incentive devalues our capacity

to enhance our community. We are communal, moral, creative, social, working beings who aspire to contribute to the betterment of others, our community, and our planet. As spiritual beings, we feel inherently connected to our species and our environment. While the desire to create may not be enough of a driving force to perpetuate exponential economic growth according to mainstream measurements, the justification that monetary incentives are the only practical motivator to get people to work overlooks our inherent desire to create and improve. It disregards our capacity to collectively create mechanisms to ensure our survival for its own sake and because of our compassion for our families, communities, and others.

Economic measures ignore human suffering, environmental destruction, and other externalities when calculating economic growth, thereby disregarding the realities of our physical humanness, which is dependent on the earth for our nourishment and survival. Our collective relationship with the earth should be the most valuable dynamic of our existence because our humanness depends on it. Instead, our economic structure has no consideration for this need and is stripping away the very resources our lives depend on. This is not freedom. By disregarding the majority of our humanness, this economic structure does not perpetuate freedom—it oppresses our freedom.

There are poor, hungry people in the U.S. Opportunity in this country is far from equal; the lack of healthcare and education is unacceptable in a modern society. We are forced to choose between two political parties that do not represent us, making ends meet on our income is becoming more and more hopeless, and we could go on and on about the struggles we face.

The problems are complex and the solutions may seem even more complicated. However, there is an easy path to perpetuating political and economic freedom for the whole of our society: we must acknowledge and respect our humanness. The reality is no one, not even the small group of people who lead the masses, has the answers; the answers require all of us. This book is not about my answers, but it is about finding our answers. Finding solutions requires everyone.

Freedom in an economic system must respect our humanness and, similarly, we need real democracy in our political structure if we hope to achieve actual freedom. There are many ways we can accomplish this type of freedom. And with advances in technology, humans have even more capacity than any other time in history to implement processes that enhance freedom, ensure everyone's health and happiness, and stop exceeding the sustainability of the earth's resources. Mainstream economists, media pundits, and political leadership tell us that this is not possible, but they are mistaken.

There is an interesting contradiction in the rhetoric that leaders, pundits, and economists do not talk about. We are told that given an incentive, the human entrepreneurial spirit can create the technological means to meet any challenge. We can explore the greatest depths of the ocean, reach the highest mountain, and even put people on the moon. The human mind and labor can create anything. They are so confident in our ability to innovate, to defy any limitation, that they tell us to ignore the destruction of our own planet because they think we will figure out a way to survive.

Despite this belief in a divine ability to transcend the limits of the physical world, we are convinced that we cannot find a better way to structure our society than one based on plundering the earth as fast as possible to accumulate unusable amounts of wealth for a small number of people by coercing the bulk of people into slaving endlessly and buying the junk being made. Really? That's the best we can do?

We no longer believe the rhetoric. We know we can create a better way. Social movements like Occupy Wall Street and others are creating socio-political space in a way that has never been done on this large of a scale. But now we must go beyond using only social movements as vehicles of change. By fostering principles of humanness and implementing processes for democratic societies, people are building alternatives to the current oppressive, economic and political structures. For real change, we must all create societies of humanness in our own communities. This is the only way that we can help achieve the goals of freedom: by empowering EVERYONE to use their voice.

Part 3: Creating a New Society of Humanness

"Another world is not only possible, she is on her way." —Arundhati Roy

Part 1 and Part 2 highlight some of our deepest social problems and expose that the root cause of these problems is our lack of recognition of humanness in our political and economic structures. The way we rectify these problems is by focusing on our humanness Part 3 offers a new path for social, political, and economic organization based on humanness. It argues that when people come together with open minds and recognize humanness, they can form organized communities that are the best vehicles for creating a new society.

Chapter 8 uses Occupy Wall Street and the 99% Movement as examples of social movements that correlate with humanness. By revisiting the start of Occupy it is clear that the social conditions that led to it are the result of the political and economic inadequacies outlined in Part 1 and 2. Chapter 8 discusses the messages of the 99% to show that they resonate with most Americans (similar to many Tea Party messages). What separates us is how the media frames these messages to polarize the populace.

Chapter 9 seeks to get beyond these divides by focusing on the principles of humanness. These principles are critical because to create a new society we must shed the social conditioning that has led us away from treating each other like human beings. This list is not exhaustive; rather it is a starting point. If these principles are implemented in communities, they will be transformative.

Chapter 10 outlines methods to help create practices of humanness in our communities. This chapter provides ideas and examples of organizing for humanness but the techniques are by no means a panacea. While these methods will not work for everyone, they are laid out here to provide some ideas to help people get started organizing in their own communities.

Chapter 11 then focuses on what individuals can do to organize in their own neighborhoods and communities. This chapter breaks down the different levels of social organization—individual, small group, local area, and community—in simple terms and offers some steps people can take to organize at each level. It also discusses how creating a network among these communities will provide a vehicle to spawn broader change that prioritizes humanness and our planet. These small steps can create a new way of interacting with others to initiate the local changes that will create a new world for us all!

Chapter 8: American Revolution 2.0

"I believe that there will be a clash between those who want freedom, justice and equality for everyone and those who want to continue the system of exploitation. I believe that there will be that kind of clash, but I don't think it will be based on the color of the skin." —Malcolm X

A Seed Was Planted

"All the forces in the world are not so powerful as an idea whose time has come." —Victor Hugo

There is a general, underlying current of disenfranchisement in the country. For example, the Pew Research Center finds Americans' trust of their government is consistently low, but has steadily declined since the period immediately following 9-11, based on several factors: "The forces contributing to the current wave of public distrust include an uncertain economic environment, overwhelming discontent with Congress and elected officials, and a more partisan environment."[116] However, as Part 1 and 2 illustrate, the roots of these problems run deep into the fabric of our society and culture. With an abundance of consumerism and materialism in our country coupled with a lack of capacity of individuals to significantly affect the quality of their existence in a meaningful way, our society has systematically suppressed itself from what it really means to be human. It has marginalized our humanness.

Our political structure should be the vehicle for our enfranchisement; however, the political and economic structures are pretty much exactly as you think they are. You have said things like, "it's all about oil," "you can't trust the government," "you can't trust the banks," or "my vote doesn't count anyway," etc. There is a class of people that run the world economy (and, therefore, much of the political system). They willfully exploit people, resources, and circumstances for their own benefit. They function in a system that rewards such behavior. Furthermore, these people —political and business leaders—help each other advance and maintain power and wealth because they know they will also benefit from such arrangements.

It is a "one hand washes the other" world. It's not a big boardroom full of conspirators planning world domination—it doesn't have to be. The global economic system, led by the United States and its allies, is set up that way. The system functions by allowing the exploitation of resources, including people, in the name of profit. The reach of this system is so vast that individuals have almost no ability to impact their own existence in a meaningful way.

The inability to affect our own existence in a significant way means that in human interactions our decisions and choices—political, economic, social, and/or personal—do not dictate the outcome of our lives. Based on our discussion on freedom in Part 1, we realize that it is impossible to dictate such an outcome because other people's choices naturally affect us and the outcome of our situations. But instead of a system that fosters self-determination for hard-working people who are making a positive impact on their community, overpowering far-off systems predominately determine our reality. We have very little choice in the matter, or better yet we have a lot of choice in the matter (like what brand and flavor of toothpaste we want) but none of our choices make much difference. This is why we feel a significant lack of self-determination, despite the fact that we are constantly told that we control our own destiny and "the harder you work, the better off you'll be."

A married couple who desires to raise a family wishes to bear children who they will then love, nurture, raise, educate, support, and spend time with. They make this choice—this is their self-determination—which was a common one only a generation or two ago. Most families could have one parent stay home all day and the working parent was home early enough to be with the family in the evening and on weekends. However, reality today for most families is that both parents have to work at least forty hours per week, likely more, just to financially support the family.

Because of the significant rise in prices and the decline in real wages, both outside the control of the family, this couple will fall far short of their desire to fully commit to and engage with their children. Like most families, they will do the best they can and they will "get by." They will work as much as possible and pay for daycare and babysitters because they need to work. Their diets will suffer and so will their health because they will have less time to prepare nutritious food and exercise. If they do buy nutritious food, they probably don't know it is laced with chemicals, contains pesticides, and is genetically modified. Their children's education will suffer because they will have less time to read to the kids and help them with homework.

Most likely you are part of a hard working family that is struggling so I don't need to convince you that hard work does not usually equal significant advancement the way we are supposed to believe—not to suggest that no one advances in our society. People can succeed against the odds and some do. And those examples are touted as the propaganda that keeps the rest of us going day in and day out at meaningless jobs that we loathe. Those success stories are the exception, not the rule.

Most of us will work hard all our life and never be any better off. In our capitalist society, money and wealth supersede all else. Why is a choice, like spending most of your time with your children, that is so common throughout the world and in our recent past, so far out of reach for most Americans? It doesn't need to be but we have prioritized monetary gains over humanness. Part 2 highlights systematic flaws like how our need for perpetual growth to increase measures of GDP bleeds us of human and environmental resources. Meanwhile, innovation replaces the need for human workers and the profits are passed up to the wealthiest Americans.

Human interactions occur on different levels and have many different forms. In our modern culture, these interactions are dominated by economic transactions, with money as the common dominator. Needs, wants, and relations have moved further from communication and understanding. Society is commodified.

Once society was convinced of the infallibility of self-interested pursuit of profit, the chase was on. People began to find ways to put a price on everything.[iii] Things that have not been

---

[iii] We have to wonder, are those in power convinced that this pursuit of unlimited wealth creates a better society, or did they figure out that they had to convince the rest of us it works because for them to benefit, the rest of us must participate?

commodified simply have not been sucked in yet, but this is the transition period. The strategy is to commodify everything, which entails dividing, compartmentalizing, and quantifying human and environmental elements that are deeper than any price tag.

As this system barreled forward, expanding the realm of profit driven social organization, it devoured everything it could grasp and commodified it. To constantly increase profits, it is necessary to continuously bring more and more things under the umbrella of price. This system has attached arbitrary monetary value to nature; water, air, seeds, and soil are not the only things being sold. Schools, students, prisons, and police are all being taken over by private corporations for their profit. It has put a dollar value on a human's labor and even put a price tag on human life—whether a human being lives or dies is determined by how much money they have. Commodification has stripped away our self-determination. It has washed away our humanness.

There is no way to make the perpetrators fix this problem. Voting alone will not fix this because elected officials are not the main problem. They are commodities as well; they make decisions for a price. We cannot rely on them. They are part of the system, which is the problem. We must make these changes for ourselves. The people of any country have the right to and the responsibility of self-determination. Most of us just do not realize this. There is power in numbers and citizens always outnumber governments and big businesses. But we have to use the power we have.

In 2011 a seed was planted. There were many inspirations: the anti-globalization movement; the Arab Spring uprisings in Tunisia and Egypt, that quickly spread through the Middle East; and mass protests in Spain and Greece. However, nothing will inspire uprising more than oppression.

Back in 2008, an invigorated nation was putting an abundance of trust and hope in their newly elected president, Barack Obama who promised change. After years of war, the stripping of civil liberties, and extreme polarized discourse, a divided populace saw the opportunity for a transformation. Simultaneously, the economic collapse of 2008 engulfed the livelihoods of millions of people from around the country.

Americans lost their savings, pensions, and their homes. The collapse left people looking for answers. There was a spotlight on the economy's systematic traits that accumulate mass amounts of wealth in the hands of a small few. Meanwhile, their civil rights continued to be stripped away. And as ordinary Americans fought tooth and nail to survive and feed their families, they helplessly stood by and watched politicians stab them in the back for big corporate interests. Only five months after President G.W. Bush signed the Emergency Economic Stabilization Act of 2008, which gave over 700 billion dollars of American's tax money to the biggest banks and corporate institutions, President Obama was already pushing for another 750 billion.

The current economic and political institutions (and the people running them) that we trusted to govern our society, have failed us miserably. They have robbed us of our freedom and of our self-determination on almost every level. The government and economic systems do not represent us. The model of corporate capitalism and its financial markets suppress realistic and meaningful livelihoods for us including fair political and economic participation.

While unemployment is the highest it has been since the Great Depression, ordinary people, who struggle to find or keep their jobs to barely make ends meet, listen to headline after headline about record breaking corporate profits, executive bonuses, and unpunished banking scandals. To top it all off we are still coping with the bitterness of our government representatives funneling our tax dollars to these same corporations. The leaders in the corporate world were so greedy that they tanked the entire economy to increase quarterly profits for their own firms.

We should not have been surprised. A system that functions solely on earning a profit obviously seeks to minimize costs as much as possible. Machine labor over people labor, cheap foreign workers over domestic American workers, and if big business leaders must hire Americans they pay them as little as possible and cut their benefits. These are all choices that maximize profits.

Minimum wage does not meet a living wage in many areas across the country. Meanwhile, CEO salaries have increased by 300 percent since 1990. Average hourly earnings for workers have not increased in over fifty years and CEOs are making 350 times what an average worker earns. Taxes on the rich are the lowest they have ever been. The richest one percent of Americans own and control more than every other American combined. The wealthiest 5 percent of Americans hold more than 70 percent of the wealth. Income disparity in the U.S. is worse than in India, China, and Iran. Economic inequality in America is similar to some of the poorest countries in the Western Hemisphere.[117]

Accessibility to quality education has declined while education costs and student debt have reached all-time highs. Unemployment and under-employment remain steadily high as companies become more "efficient" and workers become more disposable. The majority of jobs available are overseas where laws do not protect workers and their wages are extremely low. Many jobs available in the U.S. are also low paying. With a lack a financial stability, mortgages and credit card debt pile up and foreclosures and homelessness increasingly become a reality to more families.

Pundits and politicians scramble to find solutions without giving up the power structure, but the structure is the problem. There are many solutions to different pieces of the problem. For example, we could end the FED, stop corporate personhood, end corporate welfare, get money out of politics, get help for the working class, tax the rich, create jobs, provide healthcare, increase access to education, provide debt relief, reform banking, make government smaller, and many others. However, any solutions that do not transform the political, economic, and cultural structures of oppression are insufficient to meet the needs of our collective ideals.

We want to prioritize people before profit and we want our humanness recognized. We want a just society. We want our voices heard and we want them to be valued. We want freedom for all and we want our socio-economic structures to align with humanness. And we know we need to create these structures ourselves.

Our political representatives have failed us because they became commodified as well. To keep their jobs and hold their power, they bow down to the almighty dollars. Less than one percent of the population reaps the benefits of this power and wealth on a grand scale. The people and institutions that make up the 1% control our political and economic landscape. As long as the abundance of wealth and power remain accumulated in less than one percent of the population, and in these large, undemocratic institutions, genuine freedom for all will remain elusive. The world does not have to be this way. Everyone has an interest in returning the power of self-determination to the people; well, 99 percent of us do.

In that environment, all it took was a seed ... an idea. On July 13, 2011, the online activist group, Adbusters, posted a call for action to flood lower Manhattan and occupy Wall Street to inspire the restoration of democracy for the people in America. The original goal was to gather 20,000 people to occupy Wall Street on September 17 for two months and come up with one common demand.[118]

The idea was to replicate a model based on other movements using nonviolence, persistence, and people's assemblies. As people continued to gather at Liberty Square (a small park near Wall Street called Zuccotti Park by the private owners) and Occupys popped up all over the country and in many cities abroad, we witnessed the growth of the seed into something we could not have imagined. Using tools to promote horizontal democracy, the leaderless movement has transformed beyond simply a protest to demand change, and has also become a mechanism for change. There is no doubt; the time was ripe for a social movement unlike any other we have witnessed.

In the face of vast deprivation, oppression, and exploitation in the name of unchecked wealth accumulation, people united under the idea that human beings matter more than profits. Wall Street is the essential site of intervention because it is the symbolic center of the global capitalism we are fighting and it stretches into every corner of America. This is why we Occupy Wall Street.

Occupying Wall Street

"The only thing necessary for the triumph of evil is for the good [people] to do nothing."
—Edmund Burke

Occupy Wall Street was a crucial step toward building a new society. At its core, Occupy Wall Street was a democratic awakening: it was the American Spring. It grew into a movement by the people and for the people that exists to express grievances through non-violent dissent while simultaneously rectifying them on our own. What was different about Occupy was that its purpose was to include ALL voices. While the media pinned Occupy as left wing, it also constituted conservative voices including people who were in the Tea Party Movement. This philosophy of all people working together to achieve change is essential to building a new society in our communities.

Occupy began in the fall of 2011 when thousands of activists gathered at Liberty Square in lower Manhattan about two blocks from Wall Street. Activists camped out in the park for months, partaking in two or more marches per day to express disdain for the current state of affairs. Soon similar movements began popping up all over the nation and abroad.

As more and more people came together, shared stories and ideas, and rediscovered faith in the ability of society to self-govern, Occupy Wall Street quickly took on a new shape and a life of its own. The original call for action entailed collectively coming up with:

> *Something profound, yet so specific and doable that it is impossible for President Obama to ignore ... something that spotlights Wall Street's financial capture of the U.S. political system and confronts it with a pragmatic solution ... like the reinstatement of the Glass-Steagall Act ... or a 1% tax on financial transactions ... or an independent investigation by the U.S. Department of Justice into the corporate corruption of our representatives in Washington ... or another equally creative but downright practical demand that will emerge from the people's assemblies held during the occupation.*[119]

The use of space manifested in the actual occupations, specifically by the people who lived and worked in the parks. These fulltime occupations had several functions, but one purpose was a protest. Occupying public space in and of itself is a direct action. People being there was a statement. The message was (something like) "we are so fed up with the status quo, we are willing to be here, showing our dissatisfaction, all the time." This protest element was also to raise awareness of the general discontent, anger, disenfranchisement, and common desire for change. Whatever the effect or implications, agreements and disagreements, this protest let people know we were there. Even though it was heavily distorted in the media, this awareness is crucial to creating change together.

The Occupy Movement has gone far beyond the original call to demand one thing from President Obama. By demanding something you are essentially telling someone else to give you what you want. Occupy Wall Street is about creating alternatives. This is the fundamental difference between a sole protest and a movement.

With a stand-alone protest, there is a demand, or an end attached to it. You protest against the war, and when the war ends, you don't protest it anymore. A movement is different. Movements consist of groups of people who want to move society in a different direction. Success does not mean an end, because even as change is created, people will continue living the change; they are never static. Occupy Wall Street was a sort of microcosm of a democratically functioning community. It modeled ways in which society can transform itself to a place where self-determination, sustainability, and humanness are actually realized.

Occupy Wall Street grew around the idea of itself as a "leaderless resistance movement with people of many colors, genders, and political persuasions. The one thing we all have in common is that We Are the 99% that will no longer tolerate the greed and corruption of the 1%. We are using the revolutionary Arab Spring tactic to achieve our ends and encourage the use of nonviolence to maximize the safety of all participants."[120]

Occupying and living in public spaces raised awareness about the causes of social justice and inspired people to act. These open spaces served as anchors for the larger movement. People in these parks inspired each other and the group as a whole inspired everyone. People outside the movement, who could see past the media lies, were also inspired by the dedication and persistence of participants. When the conversation changed and people started talking about issues that really matter, they began to realize that their opinions were not as different from everyone else's as they thought. They began to speak up and speak out and that led them to want to act. And because there were so many occupations around the country, they had a place to go. Where there were no occupations, people felt empowered to start their own because they saw what others were doing.

The occupations in the parks also served as microcosms of egalitarian and humanness-based communities. When we gathered in parks, the occupations served an immediate need, which was providing people with services. We provided food, healthcare, education, and met other human needs for each other. All of these were provided for free which also created outlets to explore alternatives to the capitalist (mixed economy) method of delivering these services through private institutions and government programs.

As riot-gear clad police forcefully evicted citizens from public spaces across the country, Occupy Wall Street grew into a network of activists and organizers passionately collaborating for social justice in many different forms. The media wants people to believe that Occupy is dead but it's growing into a real movement of the 99%. It is evolving and blending with other movements. Now people are organizing in their own neighborhoods and building communities. This is how the message of the 99% will take root.

The Message of the 99%

The message of the 99% is a complex one and it doesn't meet the standards of the neat little bullet point messages we are accustomed to. First and foremost, no message represents ALL of the 99%. To understand the message you must accept the notion of humanness and how people function in a society when they are interacting open-mindedly.

Occupy claims to represent the 99%, but as this movement continues to progress, it will eventually represent 100 percent of the people because if everyone participates, they will represent themselves. Everything that every person in the movement says obviously does not represent 99 percent of the population. We are all different, individual humans.

The 99% name is based on a statistic of wealth inequality. One percent of the people control 42 percent of the wealth in the country and they maintain the asymmetrical power by exploiting the 99%. It is this systematic inequality we are against—not one percent of people. Chants like "banks got bailed out, we got sold out," represent a genuine frustration of people toward the system that allows and perpetuates such massive inequality. Even though the movement is comprised of many beliefs, there are commonalities along the lines of discontent. What the 99% have in common is that they are not in that 1% who has way too much wealth and power and exploit the people and planet.

The 99%'s message is complex but it's really not that confusing. To understand the message, you must consider it in relation to humanness. Is it hard to believe that a large group of people facing global political, economic, and environmental problems has different opinions on them? Is it so hard to believe that people are passionate about different issues? Is it crazy to believe that different, specific messages may be small pieces of much bigger ideals or beliefs? And should we be beside ourselves to imagine a world in which these people want to hear the opinions of others and work together to find mutually beneficial solutions to common problems? We shouldn't be. This is how people function. This is part of our humanness.

When considering humanness, it is obvious that the messages must be broad for any large group. Every message or idea that includes whole societies is going to be broad. The mainstream media frame messages in simple, black and white sound bites that seem to include large groups of people, but this is an illusion. For the most part, people emotionally respond to such messages and they agree or disagree with them, but the actual messages are never as simple as they are presented and neither are the person's beliefs that responded to them.

There probably isn't any statement anyone can make that would represent 99 percent of the population (aside from extremely vague and inclusive statements). The 99% and Occupy Wall Street Movements have every type of person you can imagine: the unemployed and fully employed, homeless and well-off, and people who left their jobs to commit all their time to the movement. It has lawyers, business owners, police officers, firefighters, soldiers, teachers, and people from every other occupation. There are people from the left and right sides of the political spectrum. It is a gathering of people, all with different ideas on how to create the changes we want. It is not a structured organization with a mission statement that everyone must follow. We have different wants and needs, different views and beliefs among us.

While there are differences, there are some very obvious collective messages that run through all of Occupy Wall Street. Many of them are similar to the message of the Tea Party.[iv] We are fed up with the way our political system functions. We elect politicians over and over. Whichever party is currently in the majority stays if things are going okay, or we vote in the other party if things are not going so well. Usually we determine if things are going good or bad based on media spin and by our personal economic situations; but our reality never really changes. Either way, we know that these politicians do not represent their constituency: us. There is plenty of common ground the 99% (including you) can agree on.

If you believe we need to end corporate personhood; and/or we need to end corporate lobbying of political representation; and/or we need equal political representation, open sources, and transparency in government and policy; and/or we need to stop environmental degradation and exploitation and hold violators

---

iv The Tea Party attracted many Americans at a grassroots level who were fed up with the overspending and unaccountability of the government (among other complaints). This message is extremely similar to Occupy Wall Street, but the media focused on outrageous behavior and incidents of racism by some participants, rather than the messages that were bringing them out to rallies. Since the Tea Party promoted a message of fiscal conservatism, the Republican Party co-opted the movement and promoted it as the polar opposite of Occupy Wall Street. Sure there are differences among the dominant messages, but they are not opposing viewpoints; they are not even very different.

accountable for their destruction; and/or we need diverse political representation, not just two very similar choices; and/or every gender, race, religion, and people deserve respect and equality; and/or the mainstream, corporate media is incapable of fulfilling the mission of a free press; and/or Americans are capable of self-determination; and/or the current political and economic structures are not working for the people ... then you are the 99%.

While almost all Americans fit under the umbrella of wanting change toward more self-determination, false messages from media and leadership cripple any efforts of unity. The challenge in gaining agreement among the 99% is that the 1% and their corporate media outlets falsify our messages and skew reporting to keep the people divided among the usual lines. The corporate media is not capable of projecting reality. Of course, people who have to rely on corporate media are going to have a difficult time understanding our message. It does not fit into the sound bite model the media relies on. Reality is complex. It's not possible to sum up anyone's beliefs in a sound bite, never mind an entire group of people's beliefs.

Additionally, the corporate media will not give an accurate picture of Occupy (or the Tea Party or any activists) because they represent the 1%. It is not in their interest to provide an accurate picture. The media needs to polarize the conversation. FOX News is going to paint Occupy as a bunch of lazy, entitled liberals so any right leaning, conservative American will automatically discount Occupy. MSNBC will support Occupy but bash the Tea Party even though both movements argue against the federal government. These institutions do not want common discourse and conversation. If we were having these discussions we would soon be tuning them out and their ratings would drop along with their billions of dollars in income from advertising agencies. Their model is no longer capable of producing honest dialogue because their function is to create profit. They cater to the 1%, not the 99%.

Framing Occupy Wall Street as a capitalism verse socialism debate is a drastic oversimplification. In the U.S., we debate regulation and deregulation, the degree of taxes, and what to do with tax revenues as if these are debates on capitalism verse socialism. However, anyone who has a basic understanding of these theories knows these debates are not about socialism. Rather, these are discussions about how to use wealth, accumulated by capitalism.

These debates also occur within social movements like Occupy Wall Street. People have all kinds of ideas. You wouldn't know it from watching the news, but there are many people in Occupy who consider themselves pro-capitalism. There are people who want a more socialist type of economic organization. There are people who believe in anarchist and libertarian models and many others. Of course, most people do not fit into one specific category because they are human beings.

Whatever your position on these ideologies, the movement is not against American values. What people share in the movement is their willingness to open up to each other's beliefs and ideas. It promotes American values such as free speech and equal voices, democracy, and freedom, among many others.

People are not generally opposed to someone who is working hard to get ahead and achieves a little more than others. However, most people are concerned with the degree of inequality and how the political and economic systems create that inequality. I haven't heard anyone say a small businessperson who works hard and makes a good living should be taxed on principle. It is more the extreme profits from unethical activity that people oppose. There are also people who believe most things can be communally divided. All the varying opinions represent one opinion in a group of many opinions. This is the beauty of the movement of the 99%.

It's unfair when the media categorizes Occupy as a group where "everyone wants a hand out." Being angry about student loans, predatory lending, healthcare, and most importantly, so much tax money going to bailout big banks and war, does not mean people want handouts. Wanting education, medical, and food costs to be fair is not the same as wanting a handout. A handout implies people are not willing to work for what they want instead of simply wanting what they deserve in return for their work and sacrifice.

The media pigeonholed Occupy as a crazy left movement and, as a result, people who do not associate themselves with "the left" avoided these spaces where all voices are welcome. There cannot be adequate solutions if there are not people sharing different ideas from all perspectives. This is not a left or right issue. And, in fact, these terms are insufficient at describing most sociopolitical and economic opinions in the U.S. They are corporate media categories that are used to manipulate and divide a nation.

Politicians and pundits tout the phrases "American principles" and "American values" to create divisions among us. Anytime anyone has a different view or challenges the status quo, they are deemed as un-American. Real American principles and values allow for a wide range of ideas and beliefs. The founding documents protect fundamental freedoms, like speech and press, create a system of checks and balances for governance, and give ultimate power to the people through voting so everyone has a say. While some things are difficult to change, our system is literally set up to allow change.

American values include many things and there can be many interpretations of them but they are based on freedom and self-determination. People must be allowed to voice their opinions and work toward the changes they desire. Other people have the right to voice different opinions and stand against change.

America was founded on dissent: the Declaration of Independence explicitly states that it is the right of the people to alter or abolish the government if it no longer represents them. Not that everyone in this movement is advocating abolishing the government, but the founding documents, structure and organization of the government and political system, and the history and progression of our country are all set up to allow people to work toward changes. When people argue that change (or challenging the system) is "un-American," they are ignoring the historical facts that the founders set the structure up to allow for change. It really isn't change people are against; they just don't want the perceived "other side" to achieve changes.

We all know change is needed. Our current political system provides us with no outlet for self-determination, thereby depriving us of our humanness. Our culture comes mostly from corporate advertisements. We are told what we want, how we are supposed to live, and how we are supposed to look. Advertisements foster our self-image and our image of others. To live up to these images we have to fall in line, buy what we are supposed to buy, and our money continuously flows to the wealthy that maintain control of our representatives. We are supposed to play the game and follow the rules. We did this, even though we knew the game was fixed against us.

American citizens reject the current approaches to and of government, financial institutions, and corporate institutions—the 1%. None of this should be shocking. I've spoken to many people who have worked on Wall Street for years that believe Occupy Wall Street is absolutely necessary. Wall Street gambles with our livelihoods and keeps losing, yet its profits continually soar. Nothing can expand forever; the current system is not sustainable. If you get past the media lies and look at Occupy for what it actually is, almost no one would disagree with it. I mean, except maybe 1% would, but that's all; the 99% will agree.

Most people have the same fundamental belief that the current government and economic systems do not represent us. The current model of corporate capitalism and its financial markets suppress realistic and meaningful livelihoods for the people, including fair political and economic participation. That said, people within movements like Occupy have very different opinions among each other as to what another world should look like and how to get there. So you may very well disagree completely with various peoples' opinions at Occupy, but you would definitely agree with others.

The only way to find solutions to the overwhelming failings in our society that would reconcile the differing opinions, beliefs, and values, is to do it collectively. We have common problems, common concerns, and common needs. We have answers, but we do not have THE answer (because there is no single answer). We work together to figure out ways in which everyone's humanness can be realized and valued. It will take a lot of work, but it is very possible.

The simplest way I am able to boil down the message of the 99% is to say we want three things: (1) An economic shift. We want a more equitable society. Again, how we get there is undetermined (there are many possibilities) but we must create and expand space for the discussion—we want our economy to align with our humanness. (2) A change in political representation. We are trying to expand and get more and more people involved to have their voices heard and then they can decide how they want to be represented. Maybe the current system would stay even in a new society, but, if it does, people will have more influence on their representatives because many more people will be participating. They will be empowered, informed, open-minded, and will speak collectively. We want our political system to mirror our humanness. (3) A cultural shift. We want people to interact in a way that correlates with humanness and to participate in the political discourse beyond just voting and acting out on what they are against. If we succeed in fostering this cultural shift, then social organization and interactions will function in a way that promotes freedom for all in political and economic engagements.

Our society's debates are largely framed by nonsense passed down from the corporate elites who own the media or the politicians that cater to them. For example, we may argue over healthcare, but we ultimately want the same type of results. We all want people to be healthy, cared for, and get the services they need. We may even go further and fight over how much the government should or should not be involved. And then how much in taxes we should or should not pay to accomplish such a goal. At the root of such a debate, we would all prefer to have everyone's needs met and not have a huge government with high tax rates.

The conversation is really about how to accomplish a better society. Instead of pitting two ideas against each other, or putting up one idea and voting for or against it, we need to figure out a better way to combine ideas. For example, what if we had a system of coordinated volunteers to provide healthcare to those that couldn't afford it? We could coordinate these efforts through local instead of federal governments and we could do it with a substantially lower cost. Maybe this doesn't sound feasible, but once I raise the issue, other people in my community say, "that won't work because ..." We address the "because" and so on and so forth until we arrive at a collective solution. If experts and people were having this discussion publicly, I doubt we would continue with the current healthcare system. And the problem is not only about Obamacare: this is about healthcare as a big business where every service is outrageously overpriced.

Like the rest of the 99%, I want something different and better. I define "better" as a system that is more equitable for people and respects the ecological limitations of the planet. How we accomplish that should be a combination of many ideas. There are no cookie-cutter panaceas; most solutions will be highly localized. Most people are open and interested in hearing a variety of opinions once you engage them. We must engage each other and develop our own local solutions. And for those that are closed off and ignorant (left, right, or whatever), there are enough reasonable voices to represent different sides to all perspectives.

Creating a new world requires that we organize against the current structures of oppression—the government, big banks, and oversized corporations. The rich and powerful expect our silent complacency and exploit our apathetic acceptance of the status quo. They use propaganda and the perpetuation of assumed truths to impose their will onto the masses for their own benefit. Dissent must battle the overwhelming corporate public relations and advertising industry. So it is crucial that everyone add their voice to the 99% to help make it louder.

We can confront and transform a society that prioritizes material wealth over human life and establish a society of cooperation, community, and humanness. The powers that be and the brain-washed mainstream will tell you this world is not possible. They will say it has been tried before and it has failed. Others will say that this type of change is not possible because they have been convinced of their own insignificance. But these arguments are fully flawed.

They are the product of social structures that reward those who are morally unopposed to the exploitation of human life and the environment that nourishes us. These are not facts; these are fallible opinions of the beneficiaries of the status quo. These are the messages of the 1% and they oppose the message of the 99%. We need to remind them that we are not commodities that can be calculated. People are still human beings.

Those who have decided to commit to building a new society are choosing to have their voices heard. We want freedom for ALL people, not the illusion of freedom covered by a minimalist and marginalizing electoral process and the propaganda of the powerful few. The freedom we speak of, that is self-determination for all, has never been.

The freedoms we have achieved are being gradually stripped away from us. These are government granted freedoms, still controlled by the government, and the government is still controlled by corporations. It is an easy trail to follow. Private, unaccountable institutions have bought out the people we have empowered to represent us. This is not a new phenomenon. It is an old tradition that has continuously grown, expanded, and progressed despite its ups and downs. Not only are haves and have-nots essential to this system, the growing divergence between them is a natural progression of it.

We need major changes like election reform, the Federal Reserve to be transparent and accountable (if not abolished), and an end to corporate personhood. But these are simply examples of corporate power being used to exploit people and resources unchecked by affected people in the name of freedom. Economic, political, and social powers are not separate, mutually exclusive relationships. They are intimately connected and even if we "take the money out of politics" and "end corporate personhood" the political and economic systems will still exploit people and the planet to accumulate wealth for the elite.

What most people overlooked when Occupy Wall Street was on the national stage was the way people organized democratically and cared for each other based on humanness. This IS the message for a new society. We cannot simply demand it from the government or corporate leaders: we must live this change for ourselves. This is essential for the 99%, social change movements, and every community across the globe that desires a new and better world.

The American political system is not a democracy in the way most people conceptualize it. We need to show political and business leaders who wield massive power that we believe there is a better way to experience democracy and achieve freedom, that the current political and economic systems deny us. We must gather as communities because we believe that through the power of the people we can achieve a new society. We want self-determination and must implement processes of direct democracy among ourselves to explore ways to attain it.

Occupy Wall Street brought to the forefront something we all probably already knew: that big banks and corporations have control over our lives. They manipulate us, try to own us, and destroy our planet to line the pockets of the 1%. This capitalist system has commodified us for over 200 years and it has forced us to compete over jobs and to fight over table scraps. The time for the rich to run rampant is over. We want to create a livelihood for our families, have a home, live in a clean environment, and possess the ability to express ourselves. We want economic and social justice.

No true democracy is attainable when it is determined by economic power, especially in an economic system that creates extreme asymmetry in power. We cannot demand the world we want from the 1%. We must make the world we want on our own. We do not ask for our freedom. We live freely together. We do not ask for our democracy. We build our own democracy together. People are beginning to come together and discuss the issues that affect them and matter to them. They are the ones who will find solutions to their problems.

The way to further build the message of the 99% is with a model that allows and includes all voices. To speak on behalf of other people without having heard their voices would be unreasonable. We must create more open spaces and show people the value of gathering and talking to each other. Everyone should voice their opinions in public discourse. That is what represents the 99%.

We know another world is possible. We will accomplish a new world by committing to the principles that recognize humanness and the social organization of human beings. These principles, described in the following chapter, inform the processes that allow us to function together in ways that correlate with our humanness and can guide our new society.

Chapter 9: Principles of Humanness

"A people that values its privileges above its principles soon loses both." —Dwight D. Eisenhower

Guiding Principles for a New Society

"Man must evolve for all human conflict a method which rejects revenge, aggression and retaliation. The foundation of such a method is love." —Martin Luther King, Jr.

Movements for social change are not perfect. They include the Tea Party, Occupy Wall Street, Idle No More, Environmental Justice, and many more. They can be messy and somewhat confusing because a lot of individual people are doing a lot of different things at the same time. They are hard to keep track of, and it is impossible to calculate their impact. However, they usually align with humanness.

When people criticize activists they often repeat the unfounded media pundit attack, "get a job!" Most activists have full time jobs. Additionally, everyone working for social change is busy on a project or a campaign. These usually do not pay in dollars. But, employed or not, we work countless hours and sleepless nights for no extra money. We are servants. We all serve each other, our friends and families, and our communities. We help meet each other's needs but we also serve everyone by working to make the world better. We are motivated by notions of justice, fairness, and compassion. The result is a movement of millions of activists, all working on different projects and different goals.

This arrangement is a little chaotic, so many people argue that movements for social change are not working. But how do we define "working?" Part 2 highlighted step-by-step how the current economic structure does not align with humanness—humanness is not easily defined and compartmentalized in neat little boxes. It is not measurable, and it is not always as "efficient" as possible.

Social movements align with humanness because of their vague and universal inclusivity. They are a manifestation of collective existence—meaning the totality of individuals working together for the good of everyone. We are people living and working and being. If you look past measures that calculate the fastest and most cost effective ways to accumulate massive amounts of wealth regardless of the consequences, then it is obvious that the humanness of social movements works: it just has different goals than we are used to.

A lot of work is directed at recognizing that we are physical beings and respecting the implications of that. We are part of a physical world of air, water, and earth that we interact with to nourish and maintain our bodies. We appreciate our dependence on one another and our environment.

Most of us are curious. We research. We think. We solve problems. We logically pursue what seems like the best course of action. We make mistakes because we overthink problems. Many of us also respond emotionally and impulsively at times. We often make mistakes because we do not always think things through before we act.

We are moral. We recognize a consciousness of something greater than ourselves, and even those of us who are not religious, form bonds with others simply because we identify with each other—we recognize the value of the collective. We practice yoga, meditation, prayer, and other spiritual exercises together.

We make things and we express ourselves through our creativity. We share our art, poetry, and stories. We sing, dance, and play instruments we created. We act freely and interact with others to exchange, share, and co-exist, creating a sense of commonality and connectedness. We learn to interact without hierarchy and authority. We live and work as a community. We create relationships of trust, justice, equality, respect, and solidarity. We also nurture our individuality.

We interact this way because we believe that self-determination is achievable. We believe there is a better way to pursue democracy and freedom than the current political and economic systems that govern us. We are willing to put in the time and effort to discover how to achieve it. In our efforts to try to find true freedom and real democracy, we are living them.

In order for this collection of people and their actions to function in a way that respects humanness, they require a foundation based on principles of humanness. Many of these principles became prominent during the Occupy Wall Street encampments partly because the movement was based on small communities of activists living in camps and working together around the clock every day. Also, since one of the main goals of Occupy Wall Street was to foster direct democracy, principles of humanness were essential.

However, principles of humanness in social movements are not enough. Social movements often focus on specific issues and one movement may counter another. So we need to apply the principles of humanness in communities across the country where people have strong common interests despite differences of opinions. If we can all approach our communities with principles of humanness, we can alter the way society functions and create a new world.

The principles of humanness in social organization combine individual freedom and autonomy with collective consciousness. These principles include empowering every individual with an equal voice through direct and transparent horizontal democracy; creating social change with non-violent resistance; building solidarity based on mutual respect, love, and acceptance; and exercising personal and collective responsibility. This model simultaneously emphasizes individualism and collectivism, which are not mutually exclusive ideas as we are often told. Respect for individuality allows every person to pursue and develop their own interests, skills, and talents. Collectivity brings them together.

It is difficult to separate these principles because they are all intertwined. However, the remainder of this chapter explores the principles of humanness that guide social organization and make organizing social structures based on humanness possible. These principles are not only necessary for social change movements, they are essential to all people, groups, and communities that want to create a new and better world for us all.

Horizontalism

When it comes to social change, the single most fundamental

principle of humanness is horizontalism. Horizontalism is an approach to social interaction that empowers everyone who wants to participate in the community, dialogue, or decisions with an equal voice. This is not the same as freedom of speech. Freedom of speech protects people from persecution for what they say in public. Freedom of speech is essential to democracy but it does not allow everyone to participate equally in political processes.

Horizontalism also is not the same as electoral politics where everyone gets one vote. As all Americans are well aware, the voting system does not equalize voices; instead it strengthens voices of those with enough money to buy television advertisements, hire lobbyists, and payoff politicians. It breeds corruption. Horizontalism, on the other hand, means every person has access to speaking with an equal voice in dialogue and participating with equal value in action.

One tool we use to promote horizontalism at Occupy is the general assembly (GA). Technically, a general assembly implies a legislative body, but we use it as a people's assembly that is open to the general public. No one is excluded. At a general assembly a culture of horizontalism is built by utilizing direct democracy to move collective agendas forward. Participants embrace the idea of horizontalism and apply it to other meetings, groups, and areas of their lives.

Methods to achieve horizontalism are discussed in Chapter 10. Horizontalism allows other principles of humanness to be realized in social change, or is a means to achieve them. Horizontal social organization is the opposite of traditional, vertical forms of organization, or hierarchies. A horizontal society encompasses all of the principles discussed in this section, but its foundation requires three essential principles: inclusion, equality, and empowerment.

Inclusion

To have horizontal social organization, all affected people must be included in the group. Anyone is welcome to opt-out by making the conscious choice not to participate, but true horizontalism requires that everyone affected at least be made aware of the group acting on their behalf. If a group of people is making decisions for another person without their consent, this is oppression and is not aligned with horizontalism.

Inclusion is the most difficult task that any horizontal organization faces. When we refer to inclusion we are not only talking about allowing anyone to participate. Inclusion is an intentional process. Groups and communities must make sincere efforts to open all meetings and projects to anyone who wants to participate. But once at these meetings, everyone should feel welcome and empowered.

Inclusion also requires massive outreach. As I have said previously, if we intend to represent the 99%, we need to hear the voices of the 99%. For example, the main issues of economic equality and political marginalization that Occupy Wall Street targets impact poor communities of color the most. Proceeding without significant participation from these communities is problematic. However, there are still many challenges to overcome when reaching out to any community including lack of trust, oppression (no community wants outsiders coming in and telling them what to do), not believing this type of change is possible, impatience with slow processes of change, and the media constructed image of activists.

Despite these difficulties, an inclusive environment helps increase diversity, which makes a stronger, more versatile, educated, cultured, and enhanced community. Diversity results from inclusivity and is a necessary principle of humanness.

Diversity

By organizing the community through horizontalism, groups can attract a diverse population. As discussed earlier, people from many different types of jobs and social classes participate in social change movements. Political and economic beliefs range the full spectrum. Different ethnicities, races, nationalities, genders, sexual orientations, cultures, and ages all participate.

Including people for the sake of diversity is not enough. In most organizations, diversity means bringing different people into the group and coercing them to meld into the homogenous group. Instead, everyone must recognize the value of extensively bringing diversity to the group with the intention of those people altering the dynamics of the group—not conforming to it. No social movement or inclusive groups have perfected this yet. There is still a lot of work to do.

Increasing diversity generally increases instances of oppression, which are contradictory to principles of humanness. Therefore, anti-oppression is a vital principle of humanness.

Anti-oppression

Oppression is ingrained in most aspects of our society and culture. Prejudice, racism, sexism, ageism, ableism, classism, and other types of oppression can be so subtle that many people do not realize when they are engaging in oppressive behaviors. Both personal forms of oppression (such as hate speech) and structural forms of oppression (such as Stop and Frisk policies or the economic structure) dehumanize people and perpetuate divisions among people and communities.

In modern society we fail to recognize the significance of oppression. Battles for legislation that legally make everyone equal are still being fought, yet many Americans think that oppression is a thing of the past. Pundits openly challenge anti-oppressive efforts like "political correctness" as insignificant issues being driven by weak people.

Oppressive language is often touted as courageous and tough, backed by rantings of freedom of speech and derogatory comments about people who confront this type of ignorance. The majority of such ignorance emanates from people in communities of privilege who do not have the capacity to comprehend what it is like being a person who is traditionally and continuously oppressed. Nor do they have the ability to understand the impacts of their actions on the humanness of others.

Anti-oppression is a necessary and conscious effort to recognize and deconstruct all forms of oppression with the intended goal of eradicating them. At Occupy, we recognize that oppression exists and that it is detrimental to our notions of horizontalism and community, as well as to our common goals of social and economic justice. But again, we still have a lot to learn.

Oppression does not have to be as obvious as hate speech. It can be as subtle as dismissing or trivializing someone's opinion based on one's own privilege or cultural values. We must educate each other about oppression and openly share when we feel oppressed. The courage and willingness to call out instances of oppression and share feelings about it are irreplaceable tools to helping everyone understand oppression as much as possible.

At Occupy we use a concept called "step up, step back." This concept is used to ensure individuals check their privilege and step back to encourage those who have been silenced all their lives to step up. Essentially, individuals are encouraged to recognize why they may feel empowered to speak up often, or over others, and why they may feel they should "take charge."

It also means those who have spoken a lot at the meeting recognize that and step back while encouraging those who have not spoken to step up. In these instances, they should give pause to speech or action as to allow someone else, who may not feel emboldened to speak, the space to step up and speak. Likewise, those who are traditionally marginalized or encouraged to remain silent are encouraged to step up and embrace their own voice and power. For example, women are typically rewarded in our society when they speak less.[121] As a result, they may be culturally conditioned to speak less around groups of men.[122] We want to actively change this patriarchal condition.

We must also use such tools to try to understand the impacts that privilege has and the barriers it creates to engaging in a community. The more we can understand the dynamics of privilege and oppression, the more able we will be to eliminate dehumanizing behaviors that are harmful to our growth as a society.

Equality

Once people start participating in a group, they must have the option to participate with a voice equal to everyone else.

Equality is not always a simple concept because people are not made equal at everything—meaning some people are better at certain things than others, due to natural factors and/or societal factors. But vertical organizations of any kind do not value all contributions and, as shown in Part 2, do not even promote the most qualified people. We must recognize the value of every individual and work together to make sure everyone has the opportunity to say what they need to say and contribute what they want to contribute. Like Gandhi said, "Everyone holds a piece of the truth."

It is not important that every person articulates the most well educated point at any given time. What we need is to hear everyone's perspective because no matter how formally educated a person is, they do not have the capacity to experience issues from another person's perspective. Formal education does not automatically lead to wisdom: life experiences build wisdom. As much as governments, academics, NGOs, and other organizations have tried to ignore them, the opinions of all affected people, regardless of their education level, race, gender, and social status, are essential to decision-making processes.

To foster horizontal social organization, we must create spaces and processes for all voices to be heard on equal footing. (This is discussed further in Chapters 10 and 11.) There are also processes that attempt to reconcile all voices and opinions in a way that mutually satisfies everyone. This mutual satisfaction is what attracted so many people to the Occupy encampments and continues to bring people into the Occupy Movement.

Empowerment

Creating a new society will require helping people empower themselves with confidence. Instead of creating institutions with power, we must use processes to facilitate power among individuals within the collective. As more and more people participate in their community, they will feel included, see others are included, and recognize we are all working on equal footing. Hopefully, through the processes and interaction with others, they will understand that the barriers of disempowerment are removed and they will feel empowered to say and do what they believe is right.

Empowerment is not a process that gives power to people; rather it is the removal of barriers that oppress their existing power. An empowered people have accepted their own strength and ability because they have seen their power's fruition. Empowered people are leaders, and by empowering everyone, everyone will be a leader.

Leaderlessness, Leaderfullness

People cannot be empowered to participate in something that is already predetermined or decided on. When people realize they are empowered in their community they find that it takes on a particular meaning: empowerment means anyone can take ownership of any aspect of their community as they see fit. If they are interested in something that already exists, they participate in it equally to everyone else and help shape it. If they find a need that is not being met, they can start something to fill that need—a new group, or action, or service—whatever it may be.

Everyone who wants to lead in an area that they feel passionate about, simply does so. People often work in groups to accomplish mutual goals and make decisions collectively. In this way we must challenge traditional hierarchies. This is why Occupy used to be called a "leaderless movement" (with no single person or small group being in charge). But because everyone in Occupy takes ownership over the projects they are involved with, it is considered a "leaderfull movement."

Confronting hierarchy in this way does not mean we are eradicating power. It means we are dispersing it and embracing our own individual and collective power. Disproving the popular belief that any socio-economic structure other than free market capitalism means central state power, we must create and implement methods that not only disperse centralized state power, but also centralized economic power.

Traditional leadership and experts can be harmful to the empowerment of individuals because their presence encourages others to step back and let them take over. "I don't know enough about it to say anything" shouldn't be a common phrase. People tend to be more passive when one person seems like they have everything under control: "Why should I help if the guy who knows what he's doing is already working on this?"

It is essential to incorporate all people's ideas because no single person has the answer for everyone; rather everyone has a piece of the answers for all of us. Our ideas and the sharing of ideas correlate with humanness. The purpose is in the process not only the result. We need to be mindful of the benefit of experts to the collective, while not minimizing our own wisdom and talent and those of others.

Leaderfullness means that everyone can be a leader. It requires three other principles of humanness: participation, autonomy, and personal responsibility.

Participation

Participation is key to true democracy and it is the only way to have self-determination as an individual who is part of society. By participating, people represent their own political voice. Horizontalism means that everyone participates to the extent they desire.

During the time we spent in Liberty Square, many occupiers only wanted to occupy space in the park and nothing more. They were perfectly content to simply live there with each other and mind their own business. Being that our park occupations relied heavily on our commitment to public ownership of public spaces, people who were willing to put their bodies on the line against the constant threat of police violence to simply occupy public space were invaluable.

Many artists are perfectly content to come to events and perform—drumming, singing, painting, etc. Others combine art and political action. Many activists who have jobs or other commitments are happy to show up to events and demonstrations and participate in whatever others have planned. And many more see some need in the community or the movement and initiate a solution. Everyone participates to the degree that suits them, and no one is coerced into something they do not want to do.

Participation is essential because it is what gives everyone a voice and empowers them in horizontalism. By participating in something, you can be a custodian of it; you are a leader of it.

Autonomy

When people choose how they participate in the community, they do so autonomously. The only way this participatory form of social organization succeeds is by everyone recognizing and valuing the principle of autonomy, which continues to be fundamental to humanness. Autonomy simply means that everyone has the power to voice and implement their own ideas and make their own choices and decisions. Anyone else who wants to support their ideas does so, and those that do not, abstain.

As simple as this concept is, it is extremely important. People are socially conditioned to be governed. People want to know what they can or cannot do and what they should or should not be doing. To create a new society we must attempt to dismantle power structures. Group decisions do not have power over the individuals in the group. These individuals freely choose if they want to go along with the group's decision or not.

Autonomous actions can be done collectively by groups or by individuals. In social movements the term "action" is broadly defined. Actions include protests, marches, civil disobediences, political art, speak-outs, and others. Everyone has autonomy to organize and execute actions that represent their voice. We can use public spaces and gatherings so individual people or groups can share specific messages and organize actions around issues. This way they can gain support of other people who share similar sentiments and make their voices louder.

Personal Responsibility

Because people function with individual autonomy, personal responsibility is an essential principle of humanness in a society.

The people who choose to take responsibility for any part of their group or community are the custodians of it. If individuals stopped taking responsibility for the work that needs to be done, we cannot create a new society. There will not be a small group of leaders to conduct the direction of the society by passing down a list of commands or controlling our resources from afar—we already know that hasn't worked. So without the initiative of thousands of participants, a new society cannot emerge.

When someone becomes part of a group, they form relationships and trust with the people they are working with. Organizers take personal responsibility for certain tasks or projects and report back to the group at different times to discuss what has been done and what still needs to be done. Most organizers are extremely passionate about the work and refuse to disappoint the community they work in. Feeling personally accountable for the work we do is one of the benefits of working as a community. This is an example of the non-monetary incentives that align with humanness.

Mutual Respect

Horizontalism equates to a large amount of participants, including an expansive variety of voices, who are empowered to take on leadership roles. But there is no way to prevent divisive infighting with an abundance of different people, personalities, opinions, beliefs, and approaches. We could easily fall into the dysfunctional, detrimental, polarized fighting that our mainstream politics resort to. We must mitigate this problem by fostering a culture based on the principle of mutual respect.

Mutual respect means we find value in each other. Of course not everyone likes everyone and everyone will not want to work with everyone else, but they do not have to. We can only try to maintain respect for each other and be conscious of doing so.

We must try to find ways to alleviate and deal with conflicts such as people using oppressive speech that causes tension. When people use oppressive speech, they are not utilizing the principles that allow other voices to be heard. How can we value a voice that is being used to oppress other voices? Oppressive speech is fundamentally opposed to the values of humanness. However, we still need to develop creative ways to deal with such conflicts. We must educate each other, remove hate speech and oppressive language, and continue to engage in productive dialogue.

When people come together with the understanding of mutual respect and the group holds them accountable for their behavior and actions, we must aim to keep our communication non-aggressive. We should be conscious of using inclusive, respectful, positive speech and avoid negativity.

Mutual respect means we value individuality, cooperate with each other, and take responsibility collectively.

Individuality

Modern society has been so drastically individualized that it is difficult for most people to even feel a sense of community. Individualism pushes the agenda of the capitalist system and in turn capitalism perpetuates individualism. Individualism helps mold you into a consumer: you watch more TV so you see more advertisements and you share less so you buy more. The sense of community is sucked out of us, thereby degenerating essential components of our humanness.

To build a new society, we must focus a great deal on community. Almost everything we do, we will do with others. We will work together, share food, and entertain each other. Many of us will live together, and care for each other. For many people, when they first engage their community, it takes getting used to. It's a different lifestyle. Our society is conditioned to do things alone, argue with others, and not trust others. The alternative is much better. We can cherish individual personalities and differences because we know the value every individual has to the group.

You might think that community organizing is the total opposite of the individualism we have all grown so accustomed to, but this is not the whole truth. Communities are made up of individual people. The culture of any group must respect individual people and differences. As much as we work as a community, we must work just as hard to honor and value individual needs and wishes.

Cooperation

When people mutually respect each other's individuality they are more likely to cooperate with each other. In some ways we must choose to cooperate with each other as an intentional opposite of individual competition. While cooperation may not always be as time-efficient, it is much more effective in terms of humanness. We recognize the immeasurable value of cooperation—by working together everyone adds value to projects and everyone learns from each other.

While humans may be competitive in many situations, cooperation applies to almost every aspect of daily life. Cooperation aligns more closely with humanness than competition does. Even in the most competitive situations, we cooperate with others to compete. When we cooperate we are enhancing relationships with other humans, thereby nurturing our humanness. It is an essential principle of humanness because the purpose of our work is to realize everyone's self-determination. This can only happen when all participants work together.

Collectivism (Collective Thinking and Responsibility)

When groups of people are engaged in a culture that respects and empowers individuality and encourages cooperation, a natural collectivism will emerge. This may seem counterintuitive, and in fact, it goes against traditional definitions of individualism and collectivism, which consider these philosophies to be opposite.

Instead, individualism exists within and makes up the collective. The idea is that, within the collective, understanding and feelings of individual members of the group are interconnected and interdependent. We must balance individuality with collective responsibility and accountability. By doing this we are empowering each other, thereby strengthening our collective energy. We value sharing resources. We work to collectively meet everyone's right to safe shelter, food, health, space, education, and sanitation. We also think and work collectively to achieve common goals for the betterment of everyone.

Collective thinking is the process of constructing ideas together. Instead of arguing against ideas with the intention of proving each other wrong or "agreeing to disagree," people take truths from various ideas, thoughts, experiences, and beliefs and build a new idea that includes all the pieces. This new idea could not have been envisioned without the synergy of ideas.

Many, who have not experienced this, will think it is not possible. However, that is the beauty behind outdoor gatherings. Parks offer public spaces for anyone to come, participate in processes and discussions, and experience collective thinking and decision-making. By engaging in collective processes people learn how to interact and communicate with each other in a whole new way. We should actively listen to others and respond thoughtfully. Through the principles of mutual respect, solidarity, and horizontalism, people care for and support each other in just and humane ways, even when they disagree.

This is not to romanticize the notion of collectivism. Working collectively in a large group of people has many challenges. Understanding each other, holding collective discussions, and making decisions take a lot of time. In any large group there will always be conflicting personalities and some people are more disruptive and aggressive than others. We will still harbor our human emotions, but we are more conscious of them, and the group keeps us aware of our impact on others and holds us accountable.

Of course, conflicts still arise. We must approach conflict differently than the societal norm. We must make it a point to know each other's boundaries and respect them. We should all attempt to mediate for each other. When conflict arises we must try not to turn against those that we disagree with. Instead, we can engage them in dialogue through what will be revolutionary tactics of collective responsibility.

Solidarity

Solidarity is another crucial (and often contentious) principle of humanness for social change. Solidarity is the recognition that everyone working for social and economic justice is interconnected. It means that we stand together and support each other no matter what because we are all fighting in the same struggle. Even though we may be in drastically different situations, we have common bonds.

The "no matter what" is where solidarity gets contentious, as many activists are unwilling to support other activists who use tactics that they view as detrimental to others and in opposition to their values. This manifested in Occupy in a widespread conversation about diversity of tactics: what is violent and non-violent, can non-violence include property destruction, can we support others who use tactics we do not agree with, what does it mean to support those we are in solidarity with, and many other complex considerations.

Regardless of where people stand on these debates, everyone fighting for social and economic justice understands there is at least some level of solidarity among all of us. We can empathize with people we have never met and we hope for their success because they are in the struggle with us. We can create actions around showing our solidarity with others so they feel our support. In these ways we inspire each other from all over the globe.

Fluidity and Flexibility

It's important to note that fluidity and flexibility are necessary principles in any horizontal democracy. As groups grow or change, group dynamics will change. We must have processes in place to ensure that new people arriving to our groups are not confined to decisions of the past. The ability to fluidly and flexibly change as life and circumstances change is completely in line with the realities of humanness.

Transparency and Accountability

Good governance requires transparency and accountability. In a horizontal democracy the people are the governance. Essentially, transparency means that information is visible and accessible. Transparency is essential to the principle of horizontalism because if everyone does not have access to the information they need to make informed choices, then they cannot participate successfully or meaningfully.

Likewise, accountability is essential. In hortizontalism, people are held accountable to the group for their actions. But accountability is difficult to determine—there is no boss to reprimand you when you make a mistake. However, as a starting point, openness and transparency allows everyone to be aware of each other's actions. Most people will be deterred from acting maliciously simply by knowing that the whole group will know about their actions.

Unlike politicians who remain removed from their constituents, safe from shame, we will interact with each other in our communities every day, so we will care what the group thinks about us. We do not want to disappoint our friends and comrades. We are accountable based on our human relationships and our desire to maintain them.

Humanness

These principles are not only part of humanness; they are essential components of a new society based on humanness. We cannot continue blindly pursuing our own personal interests. We must acknowledge and respect the natural limitations of coexisting in a society with other people and create a community based on liberty. We must prioritize human beings above monetary gains and initiate revolutionary tactics of collectivism that will transform our communities across the nation—thereby changing the world as we know it.

Chapter 10: Methodology of Humanness in Social Movements

"Laws alone can not secure freedom of expression; in order that every [person] present [their] views without penalty there must be spirit of tolerance in the entire population."
—Albert Einstein

A new society does not just happen—people must create it. To achieve a society based on the principles of humanness discussed in the previous chapter, we have to implement methods that foster change. Most of these methods have been used by activists and have emerged from the long lineage of global social justice movements. They are constantly developing and adapting from a continuous influx of creative synergy that different people bring as they gather. But they are not only useful for social movements; they are essential to creating communities based on humanness. These methods include how we utilize actual space, execute direct actions, use and develop technology, implement working groups, practice direct democracy, hold general assemblies, make decisions with consensus processes, and interact as communities.

Actual Space: Utilize and Democratize the Commons

"Since loving is about knowing, we have more meaningful love relationships when we know each other and it takes time to know each other." —Bell Hooks

Most people were aware of the nationwide police crackdown on Occupy camps. But only those who are involved in Occupy Wall Street or follow it closely would know that the confrontations with police are constant. The police block legal marches and gatherings protected under the first amendment rights and demand that participants follow orders to walk in the directions police choose or disperse when they say. When these American citizens do not obey, the police arrest them, often violently.

But this is not new. Police take their orders from politicians and politicians take their orders from corporations. Anyone who opposes the power of corporations is going to be targeted by police and painted as a deviant in the media. Stopping this attack on our constitutional right to assemble is crucial for America because if we cannot gather in large groups and exercise our political voice, then we will not see change. We need space to work together.

This is not simply the need for any space; it is the type of space that is important. Using public, outdoor space is essential to the new direction of democratic social interaction and is fundamentally different than indoor private space. Large, public outdoor space does not have the hierarchy associated with private space. It helps cultivate a synergy that is conducive to the humanness of democratic discussions, and it has a logistical capacity that most indoor space lacks.

Relying on private space creates a dependency and a division between those with and those without. Coming together in public space to engage in meaningful dialogue about the issues that matter most to us is how we can be truly democratic. Outdoor, public space is shared by the people; therefore, there is no ownership-driven hierarchy. No one person or group is in control of the space and, therefore, no person or group has leverage over the larger group. In privately owned space, the owner can charge fees, impose restrictions, and have the group removed at anytime.

This is not to condemn all forms of private space or ownership; instead we should condemn the idolizing of it. We must not let discussions of the impacts of ownership remain taboo and divisive. There are many people who have made a lot of money in the current capitalist system, but believe in creating a new society. Almost everyone stands against the massive accumulation of wealth through the exploitation of people and resources, but there are many different views regarding wealth accumulation and private property.

Occupy engages in foreclosure protections and home defenses that are some of the best actions aimed at helping victims of the housing crisis. But we must recognize that these actions are still fundamentally about protecting private property. Whether we like it or not, private property is an element of Wall Street. It is absolutely essential to liberate public space even if it is done in conjunction with protecting private property for individuals' shelter and safety.

The liberation and synergy created from engaging in outdoor, open, public space is not something that can be replicated elsewhere. Indoor rooms have walls, are closed off, and closed in. There is a different energy in closed rooms, there is less fresh air, and there is no contact with the land and environment.

Outdoor public spaces can serve as the perfect community platform for participation in democratic conversations. They create a unique dynamic where one feels obligated to participate as a U.S. citizen, the same way they do to vote. In that environment, we have more resources available to amplify our voices and listen to others. It is a platform where everyone's voices can be heard.

There are also simple logistical issues that make outdoor space necessary to participatory democracy. Outdoor public space is open to the public and, therefore, discussions and decisions are accessible to everyone. Anyone can join and participate. Meeting in public spaces where anyone can see what is happening also means there is exponentially more transparency and people are more accountable for their actions. Also, vast, outdoor public spaces are among the only spaces equipped to handle regular large and continuously expanding gatherings.

Of course, there are many logistical difficulties that come with working in outdoor spaces—like battling the weather—but the benefits far outweigh the costs. Furthermore, it is not necessary that everyone, everywhere interact outdoors at all times, but this type of engagement should be utilized whenever possible.

The public, using public space to benefit the public, is actually a radical concept. Liberating these spaces by taking them from the state for our own use and actively engaging in public discourse, even if it is only temporary, is a remarkable achievement. How we go about using space is simple. We coordinate with other people, go to the space, and whatever activity we are choosing to do, we do it in that space. We liberate public spaces by occupying and reclaiming their use for the people.

Parks and outdoor spaces serve as places to work on the issues that matter to us. People can come to a park to get information, share information, and work together. They are places where we can hold our general assemblies to coordinate our work, engage in political discourse, and make collective decisions. By talking to other people and groups who do different types of work, it is easy to find ways to contribute, coordinate, and collaborate. The work and communication can also happen online and in community spaces like churches and schools so it will be accessible to more people.

Using public space and building communities of people working toward social change is transformative. Occupy Wall Street took public spaces all over the nation, made them their own, and used them to care for each other. With the brutal police crackdowns on encampments making sustainable outdoor space difficult and unsafe, we need to keep being creative at finding new spaces and utilizing spaces in new ways.

People seeking change can use parks legally and temporarily for events, meetings, and assemblies. Groups like Occupy Town Square made park occupations mobile by setting up in different parks throughout New York City one day at a time. Other groups are making use of various indoor and community spaces as well as online spaces. (There are some resources for utilizing and organizing outdoor spaces available in the Appendix.) All it takes is a little organizing, planning, and creativity. We have a right and an obligation to utilize public spaces. They are vital tools for creating democratic communities based on humanness.

Direct Actions: They Speak Louder Than Words

"Power concedes nothing without a demand. It never did and it never will."
—Frederick Douglass

Actions for economic and social justice are usually protests or awareness-raising events. They can be marches, civil disobediences, artistic performances, information campaigns, and many other things. However, in the context of economic and social oppression in a capitalist system, simple humane actions that put humanness before profit, like providing each other with healthcare or education, can be direct actions as well—they can be revolutionary.

Work can be coordinated through the GA or online, or people can just do it. This may seem chaotic, but it aligns closely with humanness. People do work they feel passionate about. People share their voice through their actions. This is the most powerful part of direct democracy. The sum of all actions paints a clearer picture of the will of the people than any other form of governance.

Technology: The Great Equalizer

"A popular government without popular information, or the means of acquiring it, is but a prologue to a farce or a tragedy, or perhaps both." —James Madison

Advances in technology have made it easier than ever for people to stay in close contact with each other across large distances. Cell phones are the new weapons of choice for revolutions around the world. Nothing was more powerful during the Iranian uprising in 2009 than thousands of brave activists recording images and videos of government atrocities and uploading them to be broadcasted before the eyes of the world. A YouTube video uploaded by a young brave female activist in Egypt called for the January 25th protest in 2011 that sparked the revolution that took down the dictator, Hosni Mubarak.

We can all use technology to our advantage in organizing in the community and networking nationwide. People must use their knowledge and skills to create things that are beneficial and accessible to the whole group. We can use Twitter, Facebook, Riseup email and listservs, and Livestream to coordinate and communicate with each other. We can also use these tools to send our messages out to a larger world audience.

In Liberty Square, the tech and media teams created amazing tools (some using open source technology) that were essential to our coordinating efforts and helping to make the movement more accessible, transparent, and successful (see Appendix).

Working Groups: People Get It Done Together

Most of the work that was carried out in Occupy Wall Street was done by "working groups." These are groups of people that coordinate efforts around specific elements of the movement. At first, whenever someone wanted to start a working group they simply announced it at the GA and whoever wanted to participate in the group went to the meetings. Later, mostly because of funding, the GA decided to approve working groups before they were recognized by the assembly and able to access funding. This became a very contentious process.

Some working groups focused on logistical needs like Kitchen and Medical and others focused on creative elements like Arts and Culture and Vision and Goals. Direct Action Working Group organized daily marches and Facilitation Working Group organized and assisted the GAs. Soon there were over a hundred working groups focusing on various elements of the movement. Other groups and caucuses formed based on common identity, for example, Women Occupying Wall Street and the People Of Color Caucus. Additionally, groups of friends or affiliates and individuals carried out necessary work autonomously.

The structure of working groups in Occupy and other movements might not be the best course in every community. However, working in groups of some kind will be critical for creating a new society. People often like to work in groups so, in line with the principles of humanness, people can start their own groups and work toward a common goal.

Direct Democracy: Anything Else is Not Democracy

"There can be no daily democracy without daily citizenship." —Ralph Nader

Living in a society means that one persons actions impact the freedom and livelihood of others. Therefore, it is necessary to have community discussions and make some decisions collectively. Our current system of political debate, juxtaposition of parties and voting, illuminates differences, encourages disputes, and institutionalizes hierarchy. Horizontal direct democracy, on the other hand, is a type of social organization where there is no hierarchy. It works to give everyone an equal voice and fosters self-determination if everyone follows a democratic process. This does not mean democracy as in "majority rules" and it does not mean process as in voting.

The democratic process explained in this section aims to give everyone a meaningful say in their own self-determination—true democracy. The process requires patience and mutual respect for all opinions but the benefits are immeasurable. Remember, freedom for all requires finding trade-offs and balance so there must be a process to achieve it. It is how we can experience humanness in political participation and discourse—true self-expression in politics and society (something we currently lack).

Instead of following the decisions of leaders, or relying on representatives that at best are doing only what some of their constituents want, direct democracy is a way for groups of people to come to decisions collectively. By following processes that give everyone an equal voice and prioritizing principles of mutual respect, direct democracy can empower all participants and ensure no one is coerced into doing anything they have not agreed to.

Everyone must approach all other participants as well intentioned, honest, and principled. We are challenging the current system where everyone is expected to look at others with suspicion. You will find that most people won't disappoint you when you engage them with humanness—especially when the elements of capitalism, like cutthroat competition, are removed.

Horizontal direct democracy means participants consciously acknowledge the value of everyone's contributions to discussions as they develop on equal footing. By conditioning ourselves to interact in this new way, we are working on a conscious shift in cultural norms that will bring us closer to our humanness. We must denounce the established hierarchies and patriarchies that people traditionally function under where public conversations are led by those in positions of power and the loudest and crudest are the ones heard the most.

Direct democracy does not only refer to the decision-making processes, but it also means that everyone should be continuously part of the conversation. We can use collective discussions for information sharing and collective thinking. We can construct ideas together through small intimate conversations and large collective discussions. Collective discussions are typically meetings or general assemblies, but they can be informal as well. Additional methods, like open space, are explained later in this chapter (see Appendix for additional tools).

Collective discussions are difficult to comprehend and incorporate because they are drastically different than the current processes of public dialogue. We are conditioned to think that people who have different opinions cannot find common solutions. We defend our opinions against those who disagree without ever acknowledging both ideas could be true. We try to convince others to agree with our opinions until we succeed or just accept that we do not agree.

In decision-making in our current systems, the best-case scenario is a compromise where opposing sides both give up part of what they want. Conversely, by constructing ideas together, no one loses—everyone wins. Instead of compromising you learn from others and build new ideas that appeal to everyone involved. Collectively constructing ideas takes time, willingness to value different opinions, and a commitment to democratic processes.

To make sure everyone has an equal voice, collective discussions are often facilitated by teams of volunteers from the group committed to ensuring the discussion flows smoothly. The facilitation team works to help support and moderate a general assembly, meeting, or open space dialogue by utilizing various mediation tools and concepts. Facilitation roles are leadership roles but that does not mean that anyone on the team is the "leader." The leadership aspects do not go beyond the realm of the meeting itself—they are temporary roles, specific to the meeting. The team should be accountable to the participants and can be removed if needed.

The job of the facilitator is only to ensure participants follow the process that allows everyone to speak in turn. They are simply there to keep the meeting on track and ensure people are being respected. It is best, as a facilitator, to remain neutral and unbiased. Furthermore, anyone can be on the facilitation team. Participants who are uncomfortable with the facilitation team or process are encouraged to get involved to help improve it.

Finally, there are different degrees to which discussions can be facilitated. Some groups are small enough that making sure everyone's voice is heard is as simple as someone in the group being conscious of speakers and pointing out when someone is talking too much compared to others. They make sure those who are not speaking much are not being overlooked. The degree to which discussions are facilitated is up to the group. Also, large groups can be divided into smaller groups to promote deeper, more fulfilling discussions. These groups create ideas and then share them with the larger group.

When a large discussion is facilitated, it helps to have someone to fill all the important roles. These roles were used during the GAs and other meetings at Occupy. They are helpful to guide conversations but they must be flexible, fluid, and non-oppressive. In most group settings, facilitators should be extremely light, letting conversations develop naturally. Facilitators will remind participants about mutual respect so everyone can comfortably share their thoughts; take note of group dynamics like stress levels and time constraints; and summarize conversations and goals to ensure the group is moving in a direction they are happy with.

Facilitation Team Roles:[123]

Here are some roles that are helpful on a facilitation team:

Co-facilitators – Facilitators manage meetings to ensure everyone's voice is being heard and that the meeting stays on task. This is the verbal component of the facilitation team. Generally these roles should include all genders and ethnicities on a rotating basis whenever possible. It is important for the co-facilitators to be precise and clear as they help support the discussions. Co-facilitators should never interrupt speakers or ignore individual needs, but instead, politely and actively engage with individuals on a personal level to ensure process is respected and the discussion isn't derailed.

Stack Taker – This person keeps a speaking order list for each item on the agenda and ensures everyone is heard. People who want to speak raise their hand and the stack taker writes their name down.

Stack Greeter – This role is to help the flow of people who want to speak. The greeter receives individuals who would like to be on stack and then relays the information to the stack taker. They should inform the person who wishes to speak about the process and how much time they have. Also, the stack greeter reminds them about the specific topic being addressed and that they should remain factual, specific, and brief. If the participant wants to share an opinion or discuss a different topic, the stack greeter can inform them about the proper time or format for that discussion.

Minutes Taker – This is the record keeper. They write or type the dialogue of the meetings. Also, they ensure that the minutes are given to the proper person to post them online. When taking minutes, it is not important to type every word that is said, but simply to ensure all-important information is accurately included in the record.

Time Keeper – They make sure everyone stays within time limits and ensures the meetings stay on schedule. Each item on the agenda is allotted a specific amount of time based on it's perceived importance by the group and the time keeper should let speakers and facilitators know if they are running over. It is best for the time keeper to have a hand signal that tells the speaker (in a respectful way) that they have to wrap up what they are saying.

Vibes Checker – The individual in this role should be on the look out for how participants are feeling. If needed, the vibes checker can ask for a temperature check to gage the crowd. This is communicated by using the hand signals (outlined below). For example, the vibes checker might ask, "How are you feeling about staying on this topic?" and the crowd would use a hand signal to show if they feel good about the topic or they do not. If needed, the vibes checker can ask for a short break so everyone can relax, talk, and regroup.

Point of Process Person – This person lets people know when they are out of process or off topic. For example, if we are deciding on a proposal and someone on stack begins to talk about their event next week, the point of process person puts up the hand signal (described below) to let the speaker know they are breaking the process.

When the signal is given, the speaker should stop and the point of process person will explain what the group is currently working on, when the speaker's comment should be addressed, and bring the group back to the topic. The point of process person must focus on respect and compassion, and inform the participant of the appropriate time for their comment/question, as to not silence their voice indefinitely. This is only to allow everyone the chance to speak on topic, and to allow the other speaker to be heard in another, appropriate format.

Human Mic – On occasion a facilitator may call for volunteers to act as a human mic. The volunteers should stand in various positions, spread out around the assembly, and amplify the voices of the speakers outward by repeating what the speakers say.

Hand Signals:[124]

At Occupy we use hand signals (inspired by other social movements) to help facilitate conversations and ensure everyone's voice is being heard. These are used as a method of non-verbal communication to ensure everyone can express their opinions without interrupting the speaker and that everyone is respected. Hand signals are useful for large groups to share their general feelings on a topic without taking much time. However, all over the world people are using different ways to engage in collective discussions and direct democracy. Everyone interested in direct democracy should explore different methods and use what works best for their groups.

Agree – Hand up in the air, wiggle fingers (called "up-twinkles"), or fist up means, "I like this," or "I feel good." It can also mean, "I agree."

Unsure – Hands out flat wiggling fingers means, "I am unsure," "I am on the fence," or "I don't know."

Disagree – Hands down, wiggling fingers (called "down-twinkles") means, "I don't like this" or "I don't feel good." It can also mean, "I disagree."

Point of Process – A diamond shape with one's hands means the process has been derailed, or what is being said is off topic. When this occurs, the group should pause, explain why what happened was off process, and get back on topic.

Point of Information – One finger in the air means, "I have pertinent information about what was just said." It is not a question or a concern: it is merely information. For example, if someone announced a march would be held tomorrow at 2pm, but you knew the march was actually at 3pm, you would raise a point of information and correct the mistake.

Speak Up – Pointer finger pointing up while moving your arm up and down repeatedly means you cannot hear the speaker.

Clarification – Forming the hand into a 'C' shape means you need some clarification on what is being discussed.

These facilitation roles, hand signals, and concepts are enough to get any group through most collective discussions. A general assembly though, is a unique type of collective discussion. It is held regularly and is a good format for decision-making on items that impact the whole community. It uses similar processes; however, achieving consensus on proposals at the GA is a bit more complicated and difficult.

The General Assembly and Imperfect Processes

A general assembly (GA) is a gathering where fluid processes are implemented to create a platform for anyone who chooses to engage in horizontal democracy. GAs facilitate communication among empowered individuals. Like any collective discussion, it can be used for information sharing and collective thinking; but the GA is also used for decision-making.

Participants may come to the GA to share information of mutual interest. When sharing information there is no need for the group to debate the content of the information. Groups or individuals simply announce something that will happen or report back on something that already happened. This can include information about local groups, actions, meetings, events, updates, or topics of interest, etc. This is one of the many ways we can help coordinate efforts. Participants can come to the GA to find out details about groups that are meeting, actions taking place, and anything else going on and then they can join whatever they are interested in.

The GA is also a good place for collective thinking, which occurs when the group jointly thinks through an issue or problem. This is often used as a precursor to decision-making. Information and opinions are given by anyone in the group and discussed, but there is no need for an immediate decision. The group collectively works through a problem to gather enough information and ideas that could be the basis for a proposal or would improve the community.

In Occupy we often split up into small breakout groups to have these discussions and ensure everyone is getting their voice heard. These small breakout groups can report back to the larger group so that everyone is aware of what was discussed. Even when the group is not working toward a decision, this is extremely valuable for educating each other, building relationships, and fostering community values.

The GA is a format for everyone to have a political voice. To ensure this, the GA cannot be a place to soapbox, make political speeches, or rant. Everyone has valid opinions and knowledge to share. However, the purpose of the assembly is to address specific issues collectively. No one, including the facilitation team, should make grandiose speeches, as there is not enough time for everyone to do so. However, other formats should meet this need. For example, the NYC GA established a nightly soapbox immediately following the GA.

Also, to ensure that everyone has space to use their voice, when speaking during the GA, people must be as brief as possible to allow time for a variety of voices. Those who have spoken should step back and allow others to speak. When people step back, someone else usually offers the same information or opinion anyway. Being patient is worth empowering others to speak. Also, it's good to avoid repeating what others have already stated. Participants can show support for comments by using hand signals, but should avoid wasting time by repeating comments.

Most of the interactions at the assembly are information sharing and discussion. The GA does not try to prevent autonomous actions—there are a lot of people and groups working on many issues in different ways. However, at times, there are issues that impact the whole group and decisions should be made together.

When collective decisions must be made, a **consensus process** can be used so everyone's voice is heard and respected. Unlike voting, the consensus process does not disadvantage people who disagree with the majority. People gather at the general assemblies, devoted to making decisions based on consensus. Usually a person or group will make a proposal to be decided on, which will then go through the consensus process before it can go into effect. Anyone is free to propose an idea or share their thoughts about the proposal and have their voice heard.

At Liberty Square, the GA used the consensus process to make decisions on how to spend the money that people donated to us. This turned out to be a very contentious process. Beyond finances, the GA made decisions about statements that represented the movement in NYC and about actions the group endorsed.

However, keep in mind the principle of autonomy when holding a GA. Not everything has to be decided on, as most things do not require consensus of the whole group. Decision-making with consensus is a long and arduous process so groups should be extremely particular about what they require consensus on. This long consensus process should discourage people and groups from bringing proposals to the group when no collective decision is needed. Decisions only need to be made when the outcome will impact the whole group. The GA is not another type of hierarchical governing body. People and groups can plan and execute actions as they choose; they just should be conscious of their impact on the larger group.

When the GA, made up of all individuals, makes decisions, the decisions are valid for the group. But individuals only follow the decisions to the extent they agree with them. For example, if the group decides on an endorsed action that will represent all of them, someone may not feel strong enough against it to block it, but they may choose to not participate in it and, if they want, they can speak out against it.

The processes and procedures we use to interact in the GA context are simply what have emerged thus far. Many GAs around New York, around the country, and in other movements around the world use different procedures and variations. Many people also challenge the notions of the GA, strict processes, and consensus as the best ways to implement non-oppressive democracy and freedom. Thus, inherent to the process is fluidity and flexibility. The more we engage, the more we find impasses and hindrances that necessitate a change in our processes. These processes must be changeable and adaptable.

Decision-making with Consensus

When GAs or other groups want to make a collective decision, consensus is a process that can help guide the group to a decision that satisfies everyone affected by it. Although the GA can serve as a collective decision-making body for the group, the group is only made up of members who choose to participate in it. Those who do not choose to participate are not bound by the decisions of the GA. Furthermore, participants can opt out of decisions during the process.

The assembly makes decisions that reflect the group in the present and near future. As the group changes, there must be processes to change past decisions. These decisions also coincide with autonomous actions, which are encouraged by all group members. These actions express the decisions of the individuals who participate in them, but do not reflect the whole group.

Because humanness entails so many different things, the totality of collective actions and autonomous actions of individuals create a society that better reflects it—both individual and collective. People act collectively to represent their human connection to the larger group and individually to represent their own unique humanness.

Using the consensus process is fundamentally different than the electoral politics we are used to. Our election system is based on political campaigns and majority rule voting, which polarize people. Campaign teams and the corporate media create, fabricate, and emphasize every minor difference in candidates to create an illusion of separate choices (this has the additional effect of silencing opinions outside of the narrow debate). Candidates usually do not represent even those citizens that vote for them. Participating in consensus means respecting and valuing differences of all opinions and every individual getting to represent themselves.

Voting fosters unnecessary competition where cooperation is needed. It creates a drastic oversimplification of beliefs and a situation where people either win or lose by choosing one option, an option they often do not fully agree with and what people usually refer to as "the lesser of two evils." The voting system doesn't seek alternatives that may satisfy all participants' needs, and minority voices are easily marginalized. Laws that govern our lives are put in front of representatives (that do not actually represent us) for a yes or no tally, with very little collective discussion or mutually reached agreements.

As we have seen in the U.S., this polarization creates unnecessary tensions among large groups. The manufactured divide between some liberals and some conservatives is appalling. People are led to hate other people they don't even know and discount their beliefs and ideas, simply because they hold some different political beliefs.

In actuality, people we call "conservatives" and "liberals" can agree on most things, but in the public discourse these invented categories of people hate each other. Consensus processes work to combine differing opinions or ideas—not pit them against each other. It is fundamentally different from voting in this way.

Voting minimizes people's participation. The voting process does not account for individuals' needs or ideas. Therefore, citizens do not feel very compelled to engage when all they can do is choose between two similar people once every two or four years. They have very little, if any, say in the discussion. We can write letters and protest, but representatives ignore us as long as they have a base to support them and financial backing from corporate donors.

In contrast to humanness, which necessitates self-determination, electoral politics do not empower people to achieve self-determination. Individuals vote for someone they hope will best represent some of their needs, but they are not empowered to voice those needs in a meaningful way.

Direct democracy is based on the consent of empowered individuals within a larger group on every decision that affects them. Consensus is an inclusive process where participants think and feel collectively to reach mutually beneficial decisions about issues that impact them. The result is that individuals are empowered to achieve self-determination by letting their voices be heard, impacting the decision-making process, and committing to decisions they support.

To get consensus, a person or group presents a proposal. Proposals, which can be presented by anyone, will usually come out of earlier collective thinking. The proposal will likely be adjusted during the consensus process as more people in the assembly weigh in on it. If it still does not pass consensus, the proposer can adjust it and resubmit it at a later date. An example of a consensus process, following a proposal, is laid out below. This is similar to the process used in Liberty Square.

Process: The Steps to Consensus[125]

For the consensus process, we can use the same hand signals described above, plus an additional hand signal called the block.

Block – Arms crossed in an 'X' is only used in consensus. It is used to prevent a decision when an individual believes the decision goes against the fundamental purpose of the group, and negatively affects everyone. When a person blocks a proposal it signifies that they feel so strongly against it that if it were to pass, they would walk away from the group. Blocks are a contentious part of the consensus process because they can be abused and give power over the group to one person. Each group must find creative ways to manage this problem.

The consensus process is aided by the facilitation team. Here are the basic steps to achieving consensus:

1. Proposal is Presented to the Group
2. Clarifying Questions
   - Temperature Check: "Does everyone here understand what is being proposed?"
   - A stack is followed for clarifying questions; not opinions and not concerns
3. Proposers Answer Clarifying Questions
   - It is essential that everyone is clear about what is being said
4. Concerns
   - A stack is followed to present concerns
   - Hear all concerns first, without response
   - If the concerns seem numerous or serious, the presenters may wish to withdraw the proposal and rework it for a future assembly
5. Proposers Address Concerns
6. Friendly Amendments
   - A stack is followed to propose amendments that address individual and group concerns
7. Restate Proposal With Amendments (if they were accepted)
8. Call for Outstanding Concerns or Reservations
   - A stack is followed if necessary
9. Call for Stand Asides
   - Ask if participants who do not support the proposal will stand aside and not block the proposal—the person standing aside is basically saying, "you cannot count on me to work on this but I don't disagree with it enough to prevent it."
   - The option of standing aside ensures that blocks very rarely happen

- If a lot of people are choosing to stand aside the facilitation team should recommend the proposers consider withdrawing and revising the proposal
10. Call for Blocks—a blocker believes that the proposal goes against the group as a whole. Some groups find ways to challenge whether a block is based on principle (whether the blocker is genuinely ethically or morally opposed to the proposal), or if the person is blocking to sabotage the group, as misuse of the block can derail the entire process.
11. If there are no blocks ... You reached CONSENSUS!!

The process of reaching consensus is essential to forming the idea that is agreed upon. Rather than one person or a small group presenting an idea to be voted on, when a proposal reaches consensus it is the sum of all the individual knowledge and ideas. Someone initiates the conversation with a proposal, but the final outcome is based on common interests and is a construction of the entire group. It is a collective and cooperative approach to building ideas. It empowers participants to help shape ideas and make decisions based on them. Individuals must participate by sharing their opinions, and everyone must listen to and respect each other's views. Participants can voice their concerns to the group and the group alters the idea to satisfy them.

By hearing individual voices, the group continuously changes proposals until everyone is satisfied enough to consent to them. This way people are invested in carrying out the work needed to realize the visions decided on. When groups generate consensus, everyone knows that they are part of a larger whole. As a group, we can consider all opinions and focus on what unites us rather than what separates us. The process itself is a powerful expression of humanness.

Consensus relies on a variety of perspectives. Because participants hope to find a decision that satisfies the needs of everyone, diversity of opinions is valued. It broadens the process and makes it more appealing to more people. Everyone having the power to block ensures that the decisions of the group will never contradict the principles of any individual without their okay. But it is the responsibility of every individual to let their dissenting opinion be known to the group so the group can alter the proposal. When the group reaches consensus, it means everyone in the group is accepting the decision.

Everyone does not have to agree with each other for this to work. Participants, approaching each other with mutual respect, are willing to make trade-offs to find balance in the group. They also do not have to agree with every decision made by the group and can choose to not partake in it. Social organization like this ensures that no individual is obligated to submit to something that they do not believe in. This type of social organization is sustainable because participants only agree to decisions they support.

Consensus is a fluid, organic process. It is constantly developing and adapting to the group's needs. Many Occupys and other groups around the world use different methods of direct, participatory democracy and processes for consensus. Nothing said here is set in stone; it is merely a starting point to help people interact on equal ground. Every community will find different methods that work for them. We will improve the process together as we work to hear each other's voices.

Beyond Consensus

It is important to point out that the consensus process caused a lot of problems in Occupy. There are many reasons for this. First, there are natural flaws in the consensus process. For example, someone can put forward a proposal that is the opposite of what they want and then they can have someone else block the proposal, thereby single-handedly passing what a small group actually wants. Second, consensus does not work for random, unaffiliated groups. Participants must have a stake in the decisions being made. When people who do not have a stake in the decision, participate in the decision-making process, they are holding power over others without conceding their own power to the group. In this way, they shift the power dynamic of the group and corrupt the process.

While the consensus process should prevent the group from

oppressing any individual, it inadvertently allows individuals to oppress the group by blocking something everyone else supports. These and other problems make consensus difficult. However, if used properly, it can be a powerful tool for collective decision-making. Structure-less decision-making can have oppressive qualities as well, because if one small group acts autonomously, their decisions and actions may impact a larger group who had no say in what was done. Communities and groups must figure out ways to conquer such flaws and problems in ways that makes sense for them.

There are many ways people engage in collective dialogue without GAs or consensus. Various methods involve new technologies and online resources that are quickly making open discussions and political participation more accessible and democratic.

One alternative method of naturally organizing groups of people for productive dialogue is called open space. During one Occupy event, Spring Awakening 2012, we used an open space format to organize over 500 hundred participants in Central Park into self-selecting groups. This event helped revitalize and inspire Occupy activists who had been struggling against harsh and sustained police oppression.

To accomplish this, we made a huge chart with time slots and location details. Any participant who wanted to hold a discussion or event could post it in a block on the chart. Participants who wished to attend the events could find the information for it on the chart. This turned out to be a beautiful way to foster conversations among a large group of people.

Additional ways of engaging people in collective dialogue include appreciative inquiry, circle discussions, and the World Café. Appreciative inquiry is a strategy for change that focuses on things that are working for the group, rather than the problems, to move toward greater possibilities.

Circle discussions work well with small groups who gather in good faith. They include a method that allows participants to speak in turn and listen when someone else is speaking. Participants openly discuss issues in an egalitarian manner. These work well as a way to get information out to everyone. For example, circles are used at the beginning and end of large events so participants can share information and reflect on experiences.

The World Café uses face-to-face and online communities to create a network of collective dialogue. It involves several table discussions where participants engage in multiple rounds of conversation, each focused on different sets of questions. Participants can move around to different tables after each round. A host will stay at each table to share ideas and information with participants as they move around and answer questions. Each host collects the information relevant to their topic to share online. These, and other methods for collective dialogue, can be implemented in communities to engage people and keep them connected.

If possible, hosts of these discussions should either inform participants of some goals before the event or inform them that creating goals is part of the agenda for the gathering. To make these dialogues more effective, it is a good idea to collect information into a document or visual aid that is made accessible to an even wider audience. Also, information should be organized and reflected on, as many topics will continually reoccur at such meetings.

By participating in open discussions and forming strong ties in the community, people will realize that the need to use consensus is minimal. Most problems in communities do not require consensus because they will be addressed through a variety of actions that do not impose on others in the community and, therefore, do not require their consent.

For example, if people in the community are having difficulty affording daycare, a small group can offer daycare to several families. Other groups can choose to start daycare groups as well, but either way, the small groups' decision to help address the problem doesn't require everyone to consent to it.

There are many resources available online and many organizers and activists dedicated to guiding groups in using the tools and processes to foster open dialogue (see Appendix for additional resources). As more groups begin to engage and actively seek out tools to foster democracy and self-determination, the processes will spread to communities all over the country. The first step toward creating another world starts with you.

Chapter 11: Bringing It On Home: How Engaging in Your Community Will Change the World

"The ultimate end of all revolutionary social change is to establish the sanctity of human life, the dignity of man, the right of every human being to liberty and well-being." —Emma Goldman

    The Tea Party Movement emerged because Americans were fed up with the government being overblown, unaccountable, and too powerful. A few years later, the Occupy Wall Street Movement grew from the general desire to transform the current political and economic system into a society that values humanness over mass wealth accumulation for the 1%. The occupation on Wall Street and in other public spaces across America, persistent protests against the 1%, and the overwhelming focus of activists on simply and practically helping the victims of these systems invigorated the nation.

    The new social change movement is one that focuses on people, relationships, and community; not just issues. It includes Occupy Wall Street, Idle No More, Occupy Sandy, the 350 Movement, and many more that are part of a long lineage of struggle. The goal of this movement is to create a society that organizes in ways, both politically and economically, that value humanness and our finite planet, respect freedom for all, and foster self-determination.

    To accomplish this we must pull our money away from big banks and multinational corporations and take back power from our political structures. We must focus on our communities and, in doing so, we can make big business and big government irrelevant. The new drive to social change cannot just come from political movements; it must be embedded in communities all over the country. This transformation must prioritize humanness and it must start with you.

    This book is not attempting to provide the answers for you. It is not a call for you to join social movements or protests you see on the news. Rather, the premise of this book is that only when people come together in their own communities, with accurate information obtained through a network of communities, they will determine and create their own solutions. This section is about how you can organize in your community and how your community can network with other organized communities across the country. This network can be the agent of a global social shift toward humanness and the method of maintaining such a society.

Creating a drastic social and cultural shift such as this requires that individuals all around the country begin to implement principles and methods of humanness in their own communities. As groups of self-organized humans grow, they will work with other groups in various communities across the nation doing similar work. With a strong network of self-organized people working together toward common goals, the people will have the capacity to pull money from the overblown multi-national corporations and financial institutions of the 1% and funnel it into their own communities and local businesses. Likewise, they can accumulate enough political power to remove legitimacy from their local political structures and funnel it into the hands of the people.

As communities of humanness begin to develop throughout the country, its essential that we maintain a strong network of organized groups. What is even more important is that people everywhere, in all facets of American life, organize in their own communities. Organizing must not only be directed at specific issues, but rather the focus should be creating space to give everyone a political voice. Once everyone feels empowered to use their voice, we can collectively work on the issues at hand, and build our own political and economic networks that disperse power horizontally to all people.

While the mainstream media was all too eager to proclaim the end of Occupy Wall Street, those of us on the ground were continuing our work around the clock, focusing on different issues, and bringing the culture of humanness back to our communities. Because of our involvement in the Occupy Movement, we are forever connected to each other, aware of each other's work, and ready to mobilize in a moment's notice. Essentially, occupiers and participants of other social movements are dispersing and planting the seeds of humanness throughout the country to grow into local, organic, and sustainable communities. But creating a new society based on humanness requires that more people start organizing in their own communities. We must all create a global network of community-based groupings of politically and economically empowered humans.

It sounds a lot more complicated than it actually is. If we are to create real change, people everywhere in the country need to start building their own principled communities, in their own areas, grounded in the unique dynamics of their areas. Global networks of community groups are already active on the Internet, open-source online tools, and face-to-face networks. People who organize all over the world are aware of each other and, in some cases, are in contact. People simply need to organize and tap in.

Shortly after Occupy Wall Street began, Occupy Sunset Park, Occupy Queens, Occupy West Harlem, and many other groups, started to form. Occupys started popping up all over the country with people organizing around similar principles of humanness. Soon after, Occupy Sandy developed in response to the devastating hurricane in New York City, and Idle No More grew from indigenous people in Canada defending their rights to their land. You can organize in your community too. It only takes one small step. You don't have to be in New York City to find Wall Street. You can just go to the square closest to you. You will find the 1% there. The 1% is everywhere. It's at your doorstep. If you want to see change in the world, that's where you should start.

Make a Difference Starting Now

"If you assume that there is no hope, you guarantee that there will be no hope. If you assume that there is an instinct for freedom, there are opportunities to change things, etc., there's a chance to contribute to the making of a better world. That's your choice."
—*Noam Chomsky*

For a democratic society to function properly, it is crucial that people participate on multiple fronts. The most effective way for people to participate in a democratic society is to organize in small, local and community groups. These groups will be connected to a global network of community groups. Our humanness suggests that our greatest impact will be around those closest to us in proximity. At each level, however, citizens need to be active in several key areas and roles. For example, you should look for ways to be actively democratically organizing in the community where you live, in your place of work, and in your social circles. On a broader level, everyone must be horizontally and democratically active in city, state, regional, and national politics, economics, and business.

Leveled Horizontal Organizing

"In every community, there is work to be done. In every nation, there are wounds to heal. In every heart, there is the power to do it." —Marianne Williamson

The problems we face appear too big, overwhelming, and hopeless. But in reality, everyone can make a difference. Change is possible. Leveled horizontal organizing is a way to wrap your head around the idea of organizing a global movement from the perspective of one person. It is also a way to practically activate your self-determination in all of your roles as a global citizen.

Levels are essentially the groups of humans you share factors of self-determination with at increasing proximity or population (i.e. your neighborhood, city, and county). As human beings, existing on a planet full of other human beings, we have different levels of connectedness with others. At each level, the processes of interacting and making decisions (like those discussed in Section 3:3) must be horizontal and based on the principles of humanness (discussed in Section 3:2) in order to achieve true democracy, self-determination, and freedom. The goal for all of us is to disperse power among people by taking political legitimacy away from the current government structure, money away from the current financial institutions, and business away from multinational corporations in a way that correlates with humanness.

At the first level, you are an individual human being empowered with your own self-determination. At the second level, you make up small groups with people you closely associate with for political, economic, and cultural reasons. These are typically your friends and family. They are people you associate with at work, in your leisure activities, in your place of worship, and in your neighborhood. The third level is locality. This might be a collection of different, smaller groups throughout your neighborhood. At work, this may be all of your co-workers (depending on the structure of your job). (The third and fourth levels may be very similar depending on the size and population of your neighborhood.) The fourth level is your community.

This community is a larger group that is made up of many groups from different neighborhoods or areas. People in the community share common bonds because they share resources, schools, space, government, and many other elements. These four levels make up the central body of social organization for creating and maintaining our new society.

Although levels of organizing continue to expand (i.e. from town to state or region to country, etc.), the levels that make up the community (self, group, local, and community) are the most important. Our purpose in organizing is to create a new society by developing our political and economic organization based on humanness. A reality of humanness is that we are more closely interconnected to the people we live near. Focusing most of our organizing efforts around our own communities will ensure we are maximizing our freedom and self-determination as well as our survival based on environmental sustainability.

Each level is made up of smaller groups from the level before it and levels expand based on considerations of self-determination in given areas. In other words, when an issue in a given area impacts an individual, the individual should have a voice at that level. Currently, America is subdivided into geographical regions like states, counties, cities, communities, etc. In this structure an individual might organize using these perimeters.

For example, an individual citizen from Cranston, Rhode Island has a small group of people she works with and spends time with. These people are close friends that have common beliefs. That they work together to accomplish these beliefs on all levels. They live together, share many aspects of daily life, and help shape each other as people.

She also lives in a neighborhood that has its own political representation, so she starts an organization of neighbors that she and her group spend time with to work on local issues. She is also a member of the community. She and other members of her neighborhood organization work with other neighborhood organizations on community issues that may involve schools, education, healthcare, and other things.

She is also a citizen of the city of Cranston and the State of Rhode Island. Her community group will network with other communities in Cranston to impact decisions that affect the whole city. Her Cranston group will network with other city and town groups on issues that impact the whole state.

This pattern continues to the region, the country, and the world. While this may seem like a lot of work, much of the work at each level can happen simultaneously—many issues that impact the community also impact city, state, region, country, and world issues at the same time. Furthermore, the work is divided among many people. And by working together, other aspects of our lives become easier, so we can achieve a balance.

If government structures shift and break down, the focus of each level would also shift. For example, if the Rhode Island State Government became so weak that it was obsolete, there may not be any reason to work on a level that impacts the state of Rhode Island. However, the people that live in the area of Rhode Island and the surrounding states would still share various bodies of water, economic connections, and a plethora of other factors that would make coordination necessary. The levels would, therefore, come to be based on these types of factors.

Self-organizing for Social Change

"Walker, there is no path; the path is made by walking." —Antonio Machado

The first level of organizing for social change is self-organization. For the purpose of this explanation, you are represented by a circle. You are an individual. You are a complete, closed, and perfect entity in and of yourself. You are a human being. Every human being is unique. Your natural inclinations toward individuality and community make you the building block of human social organization.

one individual human being (H)

Too many of us are defining ourselves through things that do not actually matter. We are victims of a consumer culture. It is important to educate ourselves (as well as each other). To realistically control our democracy, we need to get and maintain access to truthful and relevant information. We cannot just accept what we see on the news or read in the newspaper. To find out what is really going on we must seek out alternative sources of news. And we cannot only focus on state and national issues. You can start in your own community where you can easily find and validate information that is relevant to you. Subscribe to the local papers, newsletters, and alternative sources of information and share this information with others.

The problems we face are so big and overwhelming that people often feel as though they cannot change anything. "What can I do?" you ask. The question you should ask yourself is, "What do I do?"

Do What You Do

To take hold of social change in your community and build a new world based on humanness you must look at what roles you play in society. We all fill many roles in society: we are customers, employers, circulators of currency, parents, and students. In all of the roles that you fill, are you contributing to the society you want to live in or the society corporate institutions have created for you?

In their society, you are first and foremost a consumer. Your role is to buy what they produce blindly, faithfully, and continuously. Secondly, you are a worker. Your job is to help create wealth through your labor. But all the wealth you create is funneled to the 1% and they give you a small portion so you will continue to work and continue to buy.

First, start to reign in consumer spending to whatever level makes sense to you. Buy as little new stuff as possible. Start by looking for alternatives and support local, ethical, and environmentally friendly businesses. Also, whenever possible, encourage businesses in your community to take on more local products, implement ethical business practices, and be involved in the community.

Pressure local businesses into being transparent, and when they are not being ethical and supporting the community, ask them to change with the promise of more loyal business. Keep a list of the local and ethical merchants you buy from and share that information with your friends. Encourage the local stores to purchase local goods and help them market these goods in your community.

Your local shoe store probably doesn't buy from any local shoemakers, because there probably aren't any. Encourage workers there to look into making their own shoes and starting their own clothing line, or any business for that matter.

Electronics are highly unethical products but we all rely so heavily on them. Companies make them by using labor in countries with no enforceable protections for workers. This modern-day slave labor allows products to be sold so cheaply that it is now more cost effective to throw away your television and purchase a new one, instead of having it repaired.

Perhaps someone in your community is savvy with electronics and would be willing to teach people how to fix their own computers, televisions, and other electronics. Perhaps some people in the community can build their own electronic devices and sell them to people in the community. The more ways you can help pull people away from the capitalist elite, the more we can spread a culture of sustainability and equitability. We can do this without sacrificing the "entrepreneurial spirit" so dear to American culture.

You can start a business making goods using local products and services. It doesn't matter what it is. Do whatever you're into and you can do it without leaving your current job if you are already employed. Start small and in your free time. Find other locals in similar fields who might be interested in a similar project. If you don't have a specific interest in something you want to make, look into your local economy, find resources from your area and use them in a creative way to produce something new. You could look at the products that big businesses are selling in your community and create a local, ethical alternative.

Avoid big companies like Walmart. My brother always said that they make their products so cheap you can't afford to shop anywhere else and he's right—in monetary terms. People do not make enough money to buy the same goods for 50 percent more somewhere else. But the actual cost of buying Walmart goods is much greater. We can't afford to give all our wealth and resources over to Walmart.

Companies like Walmart are directly responsible for driving wages down and outsourcing jobs so that we can't afford to buy ethical goods. Such companies cause environmental degradation and the exploitation of human beings. They are the drivers of the economic model that destroys humanness. We must work in our communities to take our humanness back. The main way to accomplish this is through a major shift in our economic organization—one that is highly localized.

You should purchase local food from local organic farmers as much as possible. But you can also find ways to grow your own food. Even in the city, people keep finding new and sustainable ways to produce food, using areas like rooftops and community gardens. Whenever you can buy used goods, do so. Visit your local thrift stores often. You can donate stuff you no longer want or buy something you need. Stop throwing everything away. You can swap goods or give things away using online resources like Craigslist or local papers and magazines. Also, recycle goods whenever possible.

Recycling is more than sorting papers, plastic, and glass for the city to pick up. You can make all kinds of products from old materials. There are many organizations that specialize in this type of production; perhaps they would be willing to teach members of the community what they can make with recycled materials.

Learn to barter for goods as much as possible. Build a network of people who can provide you with goods and services in exchange for goods and services you can provide them.

It is best to buy predominately from local businesses because you will get to know the people you are buying from and form relationships with them. They will have a vested interest in you, your family, and your community (especially since they are part of the community). You will find value in these relationships that is not measurable in the current economy, and they will make your life better. You will be more to them than a dollar sign, and that is important for your humanness and theirs.

Furthermore, by keeping your money out of the hands of big businesses, and in the hands of your own community, you are helping take power and wealth from the 1% and distributing it to the 99%. You are thereby shifting away from the current, destructive economic structure.

Finally, this model is much more sustainable than allowing huge, multi-national corporations to plunder the earth for their own personal gain. When you shift away from the current destructive economic structure successfully, you will find you can easily help other people and groups do the same at all levels of social organization.

As a parent you can organize to meet the needs of your children: food, shelter, education, healthcare, daycare, and quality of life. You can organize with other parents to influence school boards and politicians and you can work together to care for each other's children. For example, you can provide each other with daycare on a rotating basis to meet everyone's needs.

Students organizing for a new society will be forced to tackle deep social issues embedded in our educational institutions. Education in the current system is largely for the privileged in society. However, you will likely start by organizing to influence the immediate needs of your campus: costs, services, and transparency, among others. You will want to make sure your school, whether it is an elementary school or university, ethically fulfills students' needs.

You will also want to find ways to provide services to other students for free: book shares, art classes, healthcare, etc. You can share your education with others in the community by offering free university classes in the local parks, for example.

You will want to create strong networks and relationships that will keep you connected when you leave school and settle in different communities. Finally, you will challenge the system of education in this country that perpetuates wealth and class inequalities, and sentences our youth to a life of debt.

As a business owner you can focus your business toward meeting the needs of the community. Perhaps you will want to give your employees a share in the business, use locally produced goods, provide jobs to people in the community, and/or help others start their own businesses. In turn, you will benefit because the members of the community will support your business and you will be advancing your community.

Organizing as a worker must go beyond union membership. Workers can organize to gain influence in their workplaces— higher wages, better conditions, etc.—but, whenever possible, workers should start to organize to gain ownership of their workplaces. Maybe this will involve creating a worker ownership program where each worker owns a certain amount of shares in the business or consist of creating an alternative by starting your own business cooperative together. Over time, organized workers will gain influence over their workplaces or create new ones.

There are countless ways to organize yourself for social justice and to work toward political, economic, and cultural shifts by simply doing what you do with new purpose. You can find ways in every aspect of your life: family, friends, work, religion, hobbies, passions, and others.

What are you good at? Better yet, what do you like to do? And what do you want to do? All too often we limit ourselves by thinking we are incapable. For example, one may say, "I am not a writer." But passion can trump skill. Anyone can learn to write. Start a blog for your community. Let your love for humanity and need for change drive you. Research. Think. Write. Talk. Teach. Speak. Sing. Film. Photograph. Paint. Dance. Perform. Most importantly, organize!

Extend from Home: Organizing with a Small Group of People Around You

"There is no doubt that it is around the family and the home that all the greatest virtues, the most dominating virtues of human society, are created, strengthened and maintained." —*Winston Churchill*

The greatest work you can do starts at home. Unfortunately, the powers we are up against reach way beyond local communities. The externalities and negative impacts of their actions affect the world and all its people, so while we must start our work at home, we must do so with the aim of extending our reach beyond our own homes.

This doesn't mean that a few ambitious people will rise up and seize power from the 1%. It would be self-defeating to challenge the power of the few elite by consenting to the power of a new few. Rather, you can organize with a small group of people to work toward similar goals of helping organize and empower others in the community.

Human beings are social creatures. Individual human beings make up groups. The group is the second level of social organization. We gather in groups for many different reasons: we are families, we share similar interests, we live in the same area, we share similar beliefs, we work in the same place, etc. What is important to realize, and is represented in the diagram below by the small circles, is that even in groups, individuals maintain their own separate human identity. Furthermore, each individual human being has their own connection or relationship to other individuals that is separate from the whole group, but is also part of the group. While this may seem contradictory, by looking at the chart you can understand how human relationships form groups as a natural part of human existence.

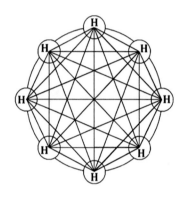

an organized small group, comprised of several individual human beings (H)

Your group will be one of many groups that continually work to help mobilize and organize others in direct democracy; influence the current government, financial, and corporate institutions; and create alternatives to the current social structures that will provide a sustainable and wonderful quality of life for all people. The group that you start with is probably a few people who live on your block, or close by, and who share similar beliefs and goals with you regarding social change. They are your core group because, not only do you have similar beliefs, but also you share the same living or work space. The people in this group will likely be (or become) close friends of yours. The natural process in which we form group friendships is applicable to organization for social change because the root of social organization is human relationships.

When we expand our influence by interacting with others, we legitimize the power we have by extending it to other people.

We thereby empower them to participate in an ever-growing network of groups and communities that claim power over that, which is under the scope of their own self-determination. In other words, people everywhere should have a say in things that impact them directly. Problems that impact one city block should be decided on by the inhabitants of that block. Problems that impact a community should be decided on by the inhabitants of that community. And the citizens of a nation should determine national issues.

Form Your Group: Meeting Your Partners for Change

"Never doubt that a small group of thoughtful, committed citizens can change the world; indeed, it's the only thing that ever has." —Margaret Mead

You need to start with a core group of somewhat like-minded people. But how do you find them? What is important to you and how can you create an outward expression of it? How should you engage people? How can you reach out to people in your community? What's the best way to talk to people in your neighborhood?

You will probably want to meet people by holding some type of event. Since you are the one organizing the first event, you should consider what type of setting will be most effective for meeting and talking to people.

It may be best to have an outdoor event in a public place or a place visibly accessible to the public, like your front lawn. Your first event could be a block party without a political agenda. It is a good idea to get people in your area out together to talk and meet each other. You can organize some games and music and advertise it as a potluck dinner where everyone brings some food and drinks to share. During the party you can casually talk about your desire to get some people together in the community to start organizing democratic processes.

However, if this is not possible, you might organize an indoor event in a community center, hall, or your living room. You might feel more comfortable having an intimate meeting with people who are interested in organizing in the community. You will want to advertise this meeting with a specific message about the goal, which at this stage will be creating spaces and processes to foster a democratic community group.

As described above, the long-term goals include harnessing enough power among the people that you will collectively control your government or, even better, be an alternative governing structure based on true democracy. Also, long-term goals include taking economic power back to your community by using your labor and spending power in your own community and avoiding giving your money to big banks and corporations.

Depending on the area that you want to reach, you can advertise by posting fliers in local bookstores, libraries, coffee shops, community centers, places of worship, schools, and other central locations. Advertise with keeping in mind your goal of targeting a small, local group of people. Start a conversation with neighbors, friends, and community members about politics or the economy. Write an Op-ed or a Letter to the Editor. Host a teach-in or use social media. Post an event on meetup.com or hold a sign that says, "I'm sick of the current economic and political structure! Let's talk about it" on the corner of your street. The best methods may be as simple as putting fliers on your neighbors' doors or you can go door-to-door, meet people, and talk to them.

You only need to start out with a few people and an idea. Try to inform and mobilize people in the community about what is really happening around them. Try to meet once or twice a week. You can start by going to each other's houses for dinner. Each person gathers some information to bring for discussion. Here you exchange information and sources. Bring newspapers, documentaries, and books.

You could start with a few friends and family members who have an interest in politics or in the neighborhood itself. We usually know who these people are. They complain about their situation, their job, the news, and other things. They are mindful of the world around them and the problems we all face.

People in your group don't have to agree with you on all issues, but they do need to be open-minded and willing to work with others who think differently than they do. Many of them probably don't realize that they can affect the situations they are complaining about. However you decide to initiate the conversation, your goal is to start working with a small group of people to organize others in your community and the communities around you.

Build a Local Base: The Redistribution of Power

"If you have knowledge, let others light their candles in it." —Margaret Fuller

Once you have a group of people working together, you will want to establish a local base. This is the third level of horizontal organizing. Depending on where you live, your local area and community may be the same and, therefore, one level. I separate them here because I think the vision of various groups coming together periodically is a worthy visual of social organization and is practical for urban and suburban areas.

The local base is a network of small groups living or working in the same area or neighborhood. This level of social organization is made up of small groups and also individuals who have relationships with each other.

Once you have a local base, explore what types of activism are already taking place in your neighborhood. Get familiar with people and how their groups function. Ultimately as the base grows, it will be essential for participants to split up and also organize smaller groups in their own areas. It is important to keep in touch with people you meet and get to know new people doing similar work near you. You will find that you will be working with them and they will make up your larger groups, assemblies, and networks.

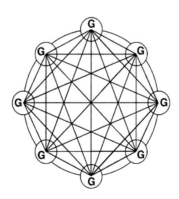

an organized, local group, comprised of several smaller groups of people (G)

While activism will likely be a large part of what your group does, organizing in your local area and community is not the same as activism. So simply finding activists isn't going to be enough. Activism essentially consists of actions that are aimed at changing a social condition or raising awareness about it: letter writing, protests, marches, boycotts, among many other things. Organizing is work aimed at bringing people together and building relationships.

For your local group, you want to find people who are interested in organizing and facilitating general assemblies and collectively fulfilling needs in the community. While you will likely find people who are already activists, you may want to begin by focusing on people who are not activists but have a significant stake in the community. These are people who have lived in the community for a long time or plan to. They are people who are raising a family there or own a local business.

While at first, you may be inclined to seek out activists right away because of their skills, experience, and networks, there are several reasons I suggest you do not start out this way. Activists are already doing the work they are passionate about. At the earliest stages of organizing your community, you will not have the foundation that is necessary to help this type of work in a way that ensures your goals are represented. Seasoned activists are going to be doing the work with or without you, so you can join them on issues once you are better organized. They also usually have specific issues they focus on.

Conversely, your goal in organizing is not to focus on a specific issue or campaign. For example, if your group starts off by focusing on environmental actions, you will marginalize a lot of people. Not everyone is passionate about one issue like defending the environment, no matter how crucial the issue is. Instead, build a community of concerned citizens and educate and politicize each other. Then people will work on issues like saving the environment either because they learned more about them and care more, or because they care about you and you are working on them.

You do not want specific issues to detract from your mission: creating methods and space for real democracy and self-determination in your community. So focus your attention on getting people to engage, who may not otherwise. Help empower them by giving them a platform and method to express and act on their beliefs.

People who are not used to actively engaging their community can be quickly turned off or burnt out by an overly opinionated and ambitious activist. People who are new to participating in this type of democracy and community organizing can also get distracted by activist leaders' charisma and knowledge about specific issues. In participatory democracy, we need to ensure that everyone's voice is considered valid and know that everyone's knowledge is essential. As important as expert knowledge is, you do not want others to stop organizing because they are intimidated or feel that someone more qualified is already working on the pertinent issues.

Activists often have strong and well-developed opinions and are comfortable jumping into leadership roles. The purpose of organizing a community is to empower every participant to lend their voice to the group, help form the messages, and act in a way that represents their beliefs.

It is important that a culture of empowerment is built and that those who participate are not simply following the leader, as that method is not sustainable. Everyone has to be able to be a leader; that's what self-determination is. As your local group gets more experience with democratic organizing, you will naturally work side-by-side with seasoned activists. They will be embedded in your groups and you will be collectively working on many specific issues.

Ultimately, this focus is just a suggestion, because you know your local area and community best. You have to decide the best course of action. I do not suggest alienating anyone. If activists are involved from the beginning, then run with it. Everyone should just be clear on the purpose and principles of organizing. And no one should control the message of the group; the group must decide its course together. These activists are part of your community and will, therefore, be part of your group even if not during the initial stages. They will be essential to the work you are doing.

Most importantly, you will be hosting conversations that

build community and empower individuals to act based on personal beliefs. It will be a work in progress, but it is a real chance to build a new democratic society. We need to bring in the rest of the 99% and that means that everyone must act in all corners of the country.

Everyone must have space to have their voices heard. You have to figure out the best way to get to know the people who live immediately around you to help create that space for you and them. Be sure to engage traditionally marginalized voices in your area. You are trying to represent the people of your neighborhood (and your community), so be certain to include voices from all races, religions, genders, sexual orientations, cultural affiliations, and classes—include everyone. Make a plan and implement it.

You are going to be looking for people who are also interested in transforming the community into a principled and democratic society. Whatever your method, you should start with a specific message that outlines your purpose and what you are asking people to do if they decide to meet with you.

What you are looking to do is get people to engage and talk with you; and your goal is to have the conversation be ongoing in order to create change.

For Your First Meeting

At first you will want to establish the purpose of your group. Those who are not interested in the same purpose of openness, democratic process, collective organizing, and self-determination should not participate. Instead they should join a group or start a group that meets their desires. Don't be afraid to be honest about your group's intentions and let them make informed decisions about whether they want to participate in it.

At the first meeting you must be clear about the principles and purposes of the gathering. Participants who are interested in controlling the message of the group should be informed that these meetings are not outlets for personal agendas. Everyone's opinion must be heard, valued, and empowered by the group. Therefore, no one should be disempowering others by trying to control the course of the meeting. This is extremely difficult to accomplish and will be a continual learning process, but it is imperative that the group remains mindful of it.

In the initial stages it will be important to gather, share ideas with, and hear from more people in the community about common struggles, desires for the community, and resources. You will also want to lay out some processes to help guide the meetings in a democratic process (you may choose to use the guidelines and tools in the previous section). Remember, these processes are meant to let everyone have a voice—not to silence people. The process can also be very difficult and will require a lot of trial, error, dialogue, flexibility, and creativity.

Once you have laid out the processes for an effective democratic discussion, you can spend some time gathering and sharing information. Here you want to find out the needs of the community, the problems people are facing, possible solutions (temporary and long term), and what people need to keep them coming to meetings and participating (i.e. daycare or tutoring services during meetings, community dinners, alternative meeting times, or ways to participate).

People may be frustrated and want immediate solutions. While the group may be able to address some immediate concerns, it is important to realize that creating the type of change that will last is a long process. The foundation for a new humanness-based society is relationships, and they take time to build.

Just by getting people talking you will discover that people will be able to offer solutions to each other. For example, someone may need work done while someone else is looking for work. This will take some time and maybe several meetings, but it is probably best to divide the time up between gathering information and discussing solutions.

Before the end of the meeting, you should decide what you will do in the next meeting, or you can decide on a facilitation team to work on the agenda for next time. It is also important to have sign up sheets to collect contact information for all members. You will want names, phone numbers, and email addresses. You can use riseup.net, which provides secure tools for communication to people working on promoting liberty and social change. They provide email accounts and listservs so you can create the means for everyone in the group to send messages to the rest of the group (see Appendix for resources).

Be mindful of everyone's feelings about what you are doing. While there will be many emotions of excitement, hope, and joy, it is likely going to be an overwhelming experience as well. People are not used to interacting in this way and it can be confusing and frustrating. There are many ups and downs. The group must create a culture of mutual support. You will gather people who are interested in the same purpose, but you will determine additional aims as the group grows and new voices are added.

Once You Have a Few People

In New York City, when general assemblies were popping up rapidly, we were advertising them using social media tools like Twitter, Facebook, and Livestream. These tools are helpful in organizing big events and reaching large amounts of people. For organizing a small, local area, they may be more detrimental than helpful. You want to focus on reaching people in the area, not simply getting anyone to show up.

With the resources you have and the goal of getting more people involved, you will want to collectively determine the best course. One purpose of your group will be helping other groups start up in their local areas and forming a larger community group. Perhaps you will organize a larger meeting or party. Perhaps you will start doing community outreach, talking to businesses, visiting more public places, and knocking on doors as a group.

If it makes sense for your goals, you can start seeking out existing community based organizations, places of worship, co-ops, tenant housing groups, and school and parent associations. You will need to find space—outdoor and indoor and online—lots of it. Seek out many different spaces and network with people who have access to those spaces.

You could also conduct outreach to the community by offering a service. One of the reasons that people who desire social change do not act on it is that they are too busy trying to survive and make a better life for their families. If your small local group can fulfill some of their needs, more people will be able to attend meetings, organize plans, participate in actions, and create alternatives to our dysfunctional society. Events like food drives, teach-ins, tutoring sessions, potluck meals, or events focused on children, give you an easy opportunity to attract people who are invested in the community, offer you a chance to talk to them, and allow you to show that you are a force for positive change. Social change is reciprocal, but the reciprocity fosters a synergy greater than the sum of its individual parts.

For example, if you add up all the human labor hours that individual people commit to feeding their families in your community, it would be a lot of hours. Many families cut this time down by purchasing cheap and unhealthy fast food. Instead, a small group of people can cook large amounts of food to meet the needs of the community. The food will be healthier and it will free up a lot of hours many families might spend cooking. Cooking in bulk is also cheaper, so many families could save money by pitching into the group meals. Families can then use this free time to invest more into their community.

You can use such incentives to bring people in the community to the table. However, the greatest perk in community meals is in the sharing of food. In every culture people bond over food, but in the U.S. we have diminished the experience of food sharing. Most of us do not even eat with our families on a daily basis. We are all caught up in our busy schedules and working in various shifts. Who has time for scheduled meals? We also want to eat in front of the television so we don't miss our favorite shows. But while sharing food, we are sharing experiences with our family, friends, and neighbors.

Sharing food touches on several elements of humanness we have long neglected. By eating with others, we recognize and share the reality that we are physical and dependent creatures. People engage in conversation over food because we are social and communal beings. We share stories and connect with each other. We build trust. We learn from each other. We engage in open, political dialogue.

Whatever course you choose, you will want to conduct outreach to people with information specific to your group and to them. Again, tell them your specific purpose and how it can help them. Parents are concerned about quality education for their children and the price of higher education. Students are concerned about debt and getting jobs when they graduate. Elderly folks might be concerned about medical costs, caregiver services, and their family's well-being. Everyone is concerned about these issues and more, but you have to reach out to people in a way that touches them.

In West Harlem we targeted people with specific questions. For example, when we handed out fliers to parents, the big bold line at the top asked: "Has your son been stopped and frisked yet today?" Stop and Frisk is an issue that significantly impacts people of color in West Harlem. Parents, who naturally want to protect their children, are extremely concerned about changing this racist and dangerous policy, so messages like this grabbed their attention.

In addition to the person-to-person network you will create and the face-to-face methods you'll use, you can utilize your social media, like Facebook and Twitter, to keep your group members and allies updated.

Once you have a local group of people, I will repeat: Passion can trump skill. Let your love for humanity and need for change drive you. Research. Think. Write. Talk. Teach. Speak. Sing. Film. Photograph. Paint. Dance. Perform. Most importantly, organize!

Community: The Building Blocks of a New World

"If we have no peace, it is because we have forgotten that we belong to each other."
—Mother Teresa

To transform the world, we must start in our own communities. These are the places we know the best and where we have the most humanness invested. We know other people, we buy from nearby businesses, we utilize the community centers, and we follow the politicians. In our own communities, we know the land. Most importantly, we know, feel, and experience the intrinsic values of the things that cannot be measured in mathematical equations: space, people, relationships, and history.

There are a lot of organizations in the community that are

worth participating in. Volunteering at organizations like Little League, community groups, and homeless shelters, and participating in any other community service activities are crucial to living in a good community. However, these groups alone do not meet the goals of a democratic and equitable society.

Participating in these types of groups is not enough. The main purpose of your community organizing will be attaining a democratic society. The goals to accomplish this type of democracy should have something to do with the people obtaining control of local media sources, local elections and government, local businesses and economics, community enhancement programs, and space.

Of course, no single one of these goals is an easy task. To accomplish all would be an amazing feat, but the more people involved in your local group, the more impact they will have on the community.

Local organized groups come together and make up the community. This is the essential unit of organizing for social change. The community is small enough where many people will know each other—relationships are strong and deep, and people have common interests based on shared experiences. People also have common resources and services. But the community is also big enough that its people can collectively take control of the institutions that impact it: schools, banks, corporations, businesses, government, and others. In addition to the local groups having relationships, individuals in the community have many different relationships, both as part of a group and as distinct human beings.

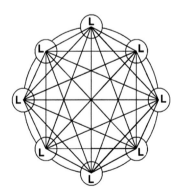

an organized community, comprised of several smaller groups of locally organized people (L)

In practice, your organizing won't be so neat and clean. For one thing, you may find that you are forming a core group of people who are spread out across the community—no problem. You will help each other build your local groups and you will already have your connections throughout the community to tie those groups together to make up the community organization. Also, this model is a simplified, geometric version of reality. Of course, human relationships are not this calculated and neat.

We all have a variety of relationships to many people across different distances and they vary in strength and value. However, the pattern of the graphs represents the different levels that human beings and groups of human beings relate. And it provides a conceptual model for how we can accomplish global social organization through focused community organizing and networks of those communities.

Because we are organizing based on principles that correlate with humanness, it doesn't matter that reality isn't so calculated. Unlike economic models, we are not using these to create policies or calculate things that can't be calculated. Our model recognizes that humanness cannot be graphed or calculated. A drawing of the links between people in a community would more closely resemble a random jumble of lines with multiple links between people and groups of varying sizes:

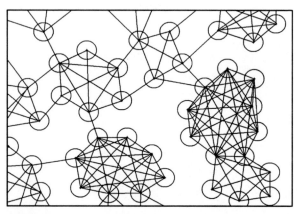

an organized community, comprised of several randomly organized groups

Also, problems will arise within the groups. A part of humanness consists of a variety of personalities and tactics. As in any social setting, cliques will form, power struggles will emerge, and people will clash. It's okay. We all face overwhelming problems in our society. Trying to change culture and the status quo will put anyone under a lot of pressure. As groups progress and grow, feelings of disunity may develop. It is essential to remember that it is good for other groups to develop and organize autonomously. Everything cannot be accomplished through larger groups, nor should it be.

Eventually, after all the struggle, groups will develop a fluid and flexible existence that works for them. Members will know and understand each other better and they will learn from each other. Despite the major differences among people, they will find ways to work together that make sense for them. There were many conflicts in Occupy in Liberty Square and throughout New York. Many groups pulled away to focus more in their own neighborhoods or on specific issues they are passionate about. But we still support each other's work and come together to work on common interests.

Make It Accessible to Everyone: Start a General Assembly

One main factor in creating and maintaining a democratic community is to start holding regular, localized general assemblies. These general assemblies will serve as a platform for people to come together at each level of organizing to share information, build relationships, and make decisions. If we are continuously engaged in the decisions that impact our own lives, we can change anything we need to.

Humanness allows a wide variety of needs and desires to be met simultaneously. Allow the process to happen. If you are a group of progressives, do not be afraid of or closed off to conservative voices. Their views are needed as well. We all have the same enemies: the institutions of the 1%.

General assemblies are great tools for sharing information. Everyone should come together and share things that they know and what they are planning. Methods regarding how we organize the GA in Liberty Square and West Harlem are outlined in the previous section and there are plenty of resources online to get you started (see Appendix). You will have to adapt the methods to work for your own community, but there are some essential things to keep in mind while you develop your GA.

The most important thing to begin with is understanding the principles and processes for socio-political dialogue. Facilitators and participants must create a calm and open environment where people feel empowered to speak, contribute, and participate. It's important to rotate the facilitation team; the assembly can decide how to do this.

At the Liberty Square GA, the Facilitation Working Group also put the agenda together based on the proposals that people brought to them. While anyone can submit a proposal, it may be beneficial to have a group dedicated to organizing the agenda. But no one should have control of the agenda; they should only organize it. Facilitation also must keep the assembly on track. They are responsible for summing up where the assembly is at any point. This can be difficult, so participants have to help and check each other, always encouraging each other to remain on task and reminding each other of appropriate times for other conversations.

Whether just sharing information or making decisions, the focus should always be on practical information and questions (i.e. what is going to take place, what do we need to do, and how are we going to do it). This does not mean that participants' beliefs and political opinions are not valid and important, only that they must be expressed during appropriate times such as break out groups or in settings outside the GA. Logistically, there is not enough time to allow people to express these types of opinions, and participants should not be coerced into listening to irrelevant conversations just because they want to be part of the decision-making process. There should be time limits on speakers, topics, and the assembly, to ensure everyone has time to participate.

Again, decisions are made about topics that are proposed at the

GA through the consensus process. When considering a proposal, it is crucial that everyone have the information they need to understand what the proposal is about. This is the advantage of having regular GA meetings where participants are frequently attending.

In Liberty Square, there were so many new people flowing in and out every day that it was impossible to keep people informed and up-to-date. This is problematic because the purpose of the GA is to participate in decisions that will impact you, not decide on something that impacts a group that you will be leaving the day after. Consensus requires that individuals consider the group's interests. It does not necessarily mean that every person supports what is passed. It means that most people support it, no one is outright against it, and those that do not support it are not obligated to help carry it out. If a proposal does not reach consensus, the drafters rework the proposal and bring it back to the assembly another day.

This process is susceptible to manipulation. Let things develop naturally in ways that make sense in your community, but always be mindful and challenge power structures within the community and within the GA. Democracy relies on public arguments—they must be had and our society will continue to progress because of them. While arguing issues, it is essential that we maintain and act on mutual respect. Through these processes and conflicts you will build a strong community GA.

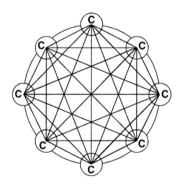

an organized city or town, comprised of several organized communities (C)

These GAs will work together and develop methods to make larger collective decisions. They will be different based on the communities they represent. They will also be autonomous but should create and maintain their connections to other GAs, forming a network around them. As more and more local communities develop GA networks, they will become a nationwide network of local GAs.

This network will be the portal to change the society around you. As trust builds in the community, you can begin experimenting with alternatives to present social structures. You can collectively take control of your local economy, minimize the use of American dollars, create local systems for exchange, and barter whenever possible. This will allow the economy the time to transition to the new economy we are creating, without collapsing it all at once.

You can also decide how to approach local politicians, if at all. Elect local politicians with the purpose of transitioning away from large federal government and representative politics. Even though many participants may want to diverge from the mainstream political system (since you are essentially building your own), everyone should still know who the local officials are and what they are doing. While you organize, politicians are still the ones controlling the public messages. But also, by knowing local officials (school boards, state representatives, mayors, etc.) and understanding what a person or board is responsible for, it will be easy to know whom to pressure when an issue arises.

These methods are not only useful in your community. Bring the same methods of organizing to your workplace and adapt them when necessary. As your assemblies grow and split off into smaller assemblies and groups, you can use online resources to help keep them connected and to tap into larger networks of similar groups. (See Appendix for some resources to help get you connected.) You may also want to create your own.

How Does This Actually Work?

"Our task must be to free ourselves ... by widening our circle of compassion to embrace all living creatures and the whole of nature and it's beauty." —Albert Einstein

Consider how our society functions. Basically, there are two sectors: the public sector and the private sector. The public sector, or the government, has many functions which it levies taxes to pay for. The government provides public goods and services such as housing, healthcare, and education. It provides services that benefit the whole society, but are services that the private sector may not initiate, like building infrastructure. It prints and regulates money. It creates laws and enforces them by maintaining a large military, police force, and prison system. It regulates industry and resources. It conducts large-scale research and development. And it engages in foreign relations and war using embassies, diplomats, and the military.

The private sector produces goods and services for profit. This includes manufacturing (from the extraction and production of resources) to financial and banking institutions. The private sector is also taking on many industries that were previously provided by the government like healthcare, education, and security.

Currently, both of these sectors do not correlate with humanness. Instead, they function to accumulate as much wealth as possible and, to do so, ignore the destruction they cause to people and the planet. Of course, this doesn't mean that every business or government service is destructive; in contrast, it is a small percentage of businesses that do the most damage. The system that people function in is the problem.

In organizing our communities, we seek to change this. Each community will have to figure out their own approach to a new society but it will likely be a multi-prong approach. For example, two major courses of action will likely be pressuring current institutions and creating new alternatives. The assemblies will serve your community as a place to share and coordinate these efforts.

Influencing existing public and private sector institutions will include raising awareness and mobilizing the community for protests, marches, letter writing, lobbying politicians, voting, boycotts, money moving (taking your money out of big banks), and using art to promote social change. The goal of these actions is to make the current institutions work for the community as much as possible—you are fighting for temporary solutions. For example, you may use the GA to coordinate an effort to go to the city council to fight to keep schools open that they are trying to close.

These solutions are temporary because your community will simultaneously be creating alternatives to the current public and private institutions. For example, at the GA you may find that there are many people who need housing and other people who are willing and able to provide it. At Liberty Square a group of people formed a medic working group. They were doctors, nurses, military medics, herbalists, natural medicine experts, and other medical professionals. They offered health services for free to everyone who came to the park. These types of things are possible when people come together and share knowledge and resources.

As your community group grows, you will provide each other with food, housing, healthcare, education, and entertainment. Of course, this will happen a little at a time. Business owners in your community group will run their businesses to serve the community because, in turn, the community will support their business. New businesses and cooperatives will develop from your group. All of these efforts will be coordinated at the assemblies by people sharing information about them.

Most things at the assembly won't need people to come to consensus, and people will simply share what they are doing. Others who are interested will join them. Over time the community will take over more and more functions of their local government and they will need the current government less and less.

The businesses and co-ops in the community will gradually provide all of the goods and services needed in the community and, therefore, the people in the community will no longer need over-inflated corporations and banking institutions. Almost everything will come from the community or nearby communities.

According to the economic measurements of the current economy, things will be very bad. The economy will shrink, people will work less and spend less, and standard of living and quality of life will drop. But in reality, people will be able to live much better lives. Prices will drop significantly because there will be less demand and more free services. People won't need to work as much so they will have more leisure time. The environment will be healthy and everyone will have the food they need. The benefits will be immeasurable.

Actions: Communities Moving for Change

"While we do our good works let us not forget that the real solution lies in a world in which charity will have become unnecessary." ——*Chinua Achebe*

The community is going to want to take action either in support of an issue or against something. If the action is to be carried out in the name of the community, it should be consented on. Groups of people can organize actions autonomously as well, but they should not be promoted as representative of the larger group if they are not.

It is a good idea to start by tackling a local issue you can win in a short time. Of course, this is not always possible, but it is a good way to make allies, build momentum, create collective energy, and dispel any attack that you won't accomplish anything. Remember, this could be as modest as building a community garden—a truly profound accomplishment. As you organize and execute actions, you will continue to expand your group and conduct outreach to others using similar methods as when you started to organize. However, as you carry out actions, you will want to reach a larger audience.

You will likely meet or attract people who are very good at planning protests. You will find that the synergy of people coming together with creative passions for social change will transform the world around you. You are working to transform your community into a democratically functioning society, so your main concern will be helping to create a platform for people to speak and act. But coordinating actions will still be a big part of your group's work.

Chances are, you will not have to organize a protest without help from experienced participants. However, just in case you are the driving force behind a protest, here are a few things to consider.

Non-violent resistance, including sit-ins, marches, and civil disobediences, quickly become confrontational if the police want to escalate the situation. However, an action does not always need to be confrontational. Most people know Occupy Wall Street protests by their disruptive qualities and clashes with police, but most Occupy actions actually are non-confrontational events: free schooling, lectures, community service, disaster relief, theater, art, music, writing, advocacy, and meetings.

Protests are good public awareness events because they are usually a spectacle of sorts. They are an opportunity to engage people who are not participating. They also bring media attention that will spread the message to a wider audience. However, the media will also downplay your numbers, effectiveness, and purpose, so it is crucial to have your own media as well.

Livestream has become the most essential tool for citizen journalists working toward social change. Set your smartphone up with apps, like Bambuser, to stream to the Internet, and start filming. You can learn how to do this just by searching for it online. If no one in your group owns a smartphone, you can use a video camera or take still photos. You will also want to learn how to make, edit, and upload videos onto YouTube, post pictures to Flickr and Facebook, and create your own #hashtags and use existing ones to reach a wider audience on Twitter (see Appendix).

Of course, organizing and actions are only part of the picture. If we are going to create a new world, we have to imagine it.

Imagine Another World

"You have to imagine it possible before you can see something. You can have the evidence right in front of you, but if you can't imagine something that has never existed before, it's impossible." —Rita Dove

Imagine how this pattern, or the humanness version of it (which won't be so mathematically perfect), will expand: community groups will network to make up a town or city group, and the cluster of city groups will network to make up a state group, states a region, and so on, spreading across the country and the rest of the world.

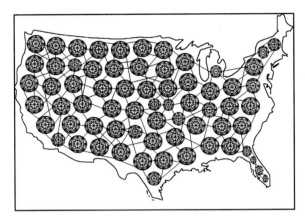

a network of organized communities spreading across the U.S.

All this requires is that people come together in their communities with the purpose of creating space for participatory democracy and self-determination and that they are conscious of others doing the same around the world. With new technology, we have the power to create and maintain global networks based on small, human communities.

The first part of this book illustrates that there is no possibility of total freedom because we live in a world with other people that impact our freedom. Instead of pretending that it is okay for a small amount of people to plunder the earth and exploit the global population in the name of "individual freedom," Part 1 makes it clear that we must consider freedom for all in a society. We must challenge illegitimate power wherever it arises, especially when it's in our own community. By acknowledging each individual's humanness and cooperating as communities of people, we can create a new society that maximizes freedom and self-determination for all.

Part 2 uncovers the major flaws in the foundation of the global economic model. It highlights the falsehoods that political and financial leaderships must project to make the population believe that it is the best system for economic organization. It also shows how by leaving out so many human and environmental conditions when calculating economic activity, the economic structure is detrimental to our humanness. This structure allows corporate and financial institutions to engage in destructive activity without repercussion because it doesn't calculate or consider negative externalities.

What do we want the world to look like?

Imagine that every day you wake up, you might go to work for a few hours, come home to spend time with your family, work on your latest artwork or jump into a pick-up game with some friends, all before you head down to the community park to participate in the weekly GA. Some people will miss the assembly but you're not worried because you know they will catch up online and share their opinions via the online forum.

As our communities begin to value factors of production (i.e. natural resources and human labor) based on humanness, things that we currently produce at almost "no cost," will become much more expensive and less desired. At the same time, things that are currently expensive will be virtually free.

For example, electronics, plastics, and papers will be expensive because we will factor in the environmental and human suffering that goes into producing these types of goods in mass. Perhaps, instead, people will develop more sustainable ways to produce these types of goods at a low cost. However, I imagine that they will look very different than what we are currently used to.

Conversely, things like housing and education will be extremely cheap as the prices of these goods and services are arbitrarily inflated to accumulate wealth for the rich, rather than based on actual costs, supply, or demand. (Part 2 discusses the fallacies of supply, demand, and price.) Additionally, we will provide many of these goods and services to each other for little or no cost.

In a new society we create based on humanness, we could work much less hours at most jobs. People could spend more time working on jobs essential to the health of their communities and on jobs that interest them. Based on the economic model outlined in Section 2:1, we know that society has been inclined to produce more and more until we reached a point where we spend almost all of our time and resources producing things we don't need to inflate the equation of growth (GDP), which only serves to increase the wealth of the 1%. This isn't necessary for survival or happiness and it certainly isn't helping elevate the standard of living of the poorest people of the world. So why are we doing it?

Currently, we do it to pay our bills. We do it to pay for our housing, education, and loans. We do it to pay interest. However, we will never finish paying for these things because the 1% sets prices way above our capacity to afford them to keep us working to build up their wealth. The 1% provides us credit so we can purchase the things we need and many things we don't need, but we will forever be in debt to them. They will continue to profit off of our debt.

Sure a few of us can get those jobs where we can pay down our loans, buy a nice house, and send our kids to college; but there are not enough of those jobs to go around. Most of us will forever remain the slaves of the 1% until we make society what we want it to be. Again, this is not asking the 1% to give us anything; it is demanding that they stop plundering everything and get out of our way so we can live and thrive on this earth as human beings.

Because we don't need to produce the things that we do, and producing most of what we do is not sustainable, notions about jobs and work should drastically shift. We will work much less because there won't be as much work to do. And, we won't have to work as much to fulfill our needs.

Currently, the lack of jobs is a huge problem. People everywhere are fighting for jobs because they have to pay their bills. But machines are taking our jobs and corporate leaders ship our jobs overseas. There are less and less jobs available and, therefore, less and less people who can afford to buy the stuff being produced. This means companies will be forced to stop making stuff because no one will be able to buy it, and then there will be even less jobs.

Our community organizations are going to be able to absorb this problem. We are going to help house, educate, and feed each other based mostly on systems of personal exchange. The things that we do produce will be made in small production systems by workers (not the state, but the people) who collectively own what they make.

People will share more goods within their communities and consumption will be drastically reduced. Most of the goods consumed will be produced in the community or communities nearby so everyone will benefit. With more people involved in the production and distribution of goods on smaller scales, wealth (in whatever form it manifests) will be naturally distributed relatively evenly.

An economic system that favors humanness and sustainability naturally distributes power more evenly among people. In addition, general assemblies will ensure that every individual has an equal voice in their own self-determination. This combination maximizes freedom for all people in the social, political, and economic sphere. While we have to accept certain limits on freedom, we have the capability to nurture and maximize legitimate freedom and equality.

We can not determine exactly what this will look like, but we can imagine community assemblies will meet regularly to manage common affairs, share information, enjoy leisure, and work. Community assemblies will make up the city or state assemblies, which will meet less often. The state assemblies will make up the regional assemblies, which will meet less often than the state assemblies, and so on. All communities will be tapped into a nationwide (eventually worldwide) network of other organized communities.

On one hand, our leveled organization network creates a second bloc to the current social structure—an alternative to the current system. It is a way to live (almost) outside the oppressive economic and political structure of society. The political leadership will still ignore our voices when it suits them, but in matters that our groups control, we will have an equal and empowered voice of self-determination. The economic leadership will still destroy our environment and dehumanize us by exploiting the labor we produce with our own bodies, but we will start to make our own goods using sustainable methods and we will value each other in many other ways.

Over time, our system will meet the needs of society in ways that are completely outside the current system. For example, rather than send our children to state or private universities, we will educate them ourselves, in the community, in free universities, or elsewhere. Rather than buy goods from Nike, we will barter for clothes with members of our community. Rather than pay for costly medical procedures, we will teach each other how to live healthier lifestyles and, whenever possible, we will provide each other with medical treatment.

On the other hand, our leveled organization network is a means to exert significant influence to break the current system down from the inside. As we build our new society and create alternative structures we will vote in such a way that we stifle any political decision that doesn't meet our needs.

We will only vote in candidates that will mimic the wishes of the people, or pressure them so much that they are forced to do so, and eventually, as the people gain more political power, the current government structure becomes irrelevant and governing decisions are made entirely by the people. Simultaneously, we are buying less and less goods and services produced by large corporations and we are taking our money out of the big banks. As we stop buying and using their products and services, and using local ones instead, we are removing power from them and making them irrelevant—when no one is buying Nike products, Nike will no longer exist.

You can take your money out of big banks and invest in local banks and credit unions, and stop using credit cards, especially those from major credit card companies. If everyone pulls their money out of the big banks, local banks will be flooded with money. It will be important to distribute the money holdings to multiple, small banks.

Perhaps you can pressure banks to be transparent about their holdings and how they give out loans, and seek salary caps and profit distribution where additional profits go into a fund to start other banks that can have other owners from the community. With community based banks you can wield significant power and influence because your community will provide the bulk of their customers.

Many banks function based on co-operative principles where members of the bank are owners. In most cases this means that members elect the board of directors, but you can imagine how your community-based direct democracy can apply to a banking model. Perhaps you could start your own bank. Of course it will take a long time to make our current government and economic institutions irrelevant, but as our communities of humanness grow, we will gradually gain the power to make this transition.

Anyone can critique political, social, and economic structures. It's easy to think about what the problems are. What the Occupy Wall Street Movement showed is how to factor in the incalculable human element by bringing people together in open space. It was physically open but also emotionally open (supportive) and spiritually open. People talked, shared, discussed, ate, and cared for each other together in a very human way. It was a reawakening of dissent but it was also an awakening of the human element in society that materialism and consumerism leave out.

We must engage each other with peace, compassion, and love. We must talk to each other and work together to solve problems and enhance our quality of life. We must use horizontal democracy methods to ensure everyone has an equal voice. No single leadership. No hierarchy. Individualism must be respected. Community support must be valued. You can see that these ideas represent the culture shift that is needed.

This book cannot provide the answers. My only hope is that it will inspire you to inspire others. I hope you will help the people around you to see that they are capable of getting together with other people in their own communities; solving problems collectively; and making life better by sharing gifts, talents, and knowledge. You are an autonomous actor. If you believe in freedom, self-determination, democracy, our ability to create a wonderful and sustainable quality of life together, and humanness, then another world is truly possible.

Engage in the many conversations regarding important issues facing humanity. You will see how people can live and work together as a community in a way that is drastically different from current societal and cultural norms. Think about what you can do for your community. We need to carry this momentum and implement these ideas in a very strategic, purposeful, and calculated way. We must focus on liberating more public spaces, building more assemblies, and implementing direct democracy processes. But most importantly, we must focus on the principles of humanness. Together we will make the current economic and political structures irrelevant by creating new political networks and economic structures. We will create a society that cultivates individual self-determination, real democracy, and freedom for all.

But if we are to create this society and take back our humanness, you will have to be a driver of change. Engage with others. Institute consistent discussions. Research. Think. Write. Talk. Teach. Speak. Sing. Film. Photograph. Paint. Dance. Perform. Most importantly, organize!

Be human again. This is what democracy looks like. This is what a sustainable planet looks like. And this is what humanness looks like.

Another world *IS* possible!

Appendix: Organizing Resources

American Independent Business Alliance at amiba.net is an organization helping communities launch successful local Independent Business Alliances.

Bambuser.com is a live video service that allows users to capture live video with a mobile phone and share online.

Business Alliance for Local Living Economies (BALLE) at bealocalist.org provides tools and strategies for local businesses and a national network for local businesses.

Doodle.com provides online tools to help schedule events and meetings. It helps organizers ensure that as many people as possible can attend meetings and participate.

Facebook.com has hundreds of Occupy pages from all over the world. You can also start your own Facebook page for your community or group.

Industrialareasfoundation.org is a nationwide network of local faith and community-based organizations.

Interoccupy.net seeks to foster communication between individuals, working groups, and local general assemblies, in the spirit of the Occupy Movement. It uses direct democratic and horizontal decision-making processes in service of the interests of the 99%. It also uses innovative tools like Internet Hubs to coordinate large-scale events and Maestro online conference calls to connect multiple Occupys.

Localharvest.org provides information on farmers' markets, family farms, and other sources of sustainably grown food in your area. They show where you can buy produce, grass-fed meats, and many other types of food.

National Cooperative Business Association at ncba.coop is a national organization for cooperatives dedicated to developing, advancing, and protecting them.

National People's Action at npa-us.org is a network of grassroots organizations engaging in direct actions.

Nycga.net is the official website of the working groups which comprise the New York City General Assembly. This site helps coordinate work and plug new people into the Occupy Movement in New York.

Occuevolve.com focuses on evolving the Occupy Movement by reaching out to various groups and by organizing and supporting actions throughout New York City.

Occupy.com is a media outlet that helps amplify the voices of Occupy through the publication of articles, music, photos, movies, poems, podcasts, and more.

Occupy.net provides people with software tools—such as online forums, interactive maps, and wiki formats—for Occupy-related documents. These tools align with the values of Occupy—they are free, open sourced, and maintained by communities of people.

Occupyourhomes.org works with affiliate organizations around the country to fight against bank foreclosures to help keep families in their homes.

Occupystreams.org is a hub for up-to-date livestreams from everywhere in the Occupy and global change movements. Here you can watch live coverage of everything happening in the movement in many locations from citizen journalists.

Occupytogether.org provides information and materials to help empower individuals to self-organize and contribute to the movement in whatever ways they find meaningful. This site helps connect all the Occupys across the nation.

Occupywallst.org is an online resource for the Occupy Movement happening on Wall Street and around the world. This is the original site that helped disseminate information about what was happening in Liberty Square to the rest of the world. As the movement grows, it continues as one of the many resources to help coordinate the movement and provide people with news and information about it.

Officialoccupythehood.org unites progressive organizations that existed prior to Occupy, with Occupy groups to help craft a movement that uniquely and directly speaks to the issues of People of Color. Occupy The Hood works to re-establish a goal-based National Black Agenda combining new energy with pre-existing efforts.

Opensecrets.org is an organization committed to following political money and advocating for government transparency.

Organizingforpower.org offers tools and information for organizers working to build and empower communities for sustainable transformation.

Ourgoods.org helps foster a network of shared respect and shared resources rather than in competitive isolation. By honoring agreements and working hard, members build lasting ties in a community of enormous potential.

Peoplesmovementassembly.org provides communities with tools and information to help start their own community assemblies. This site also provides a network of other assemblies that sign up to the site.

Publiccampaign.org is an organization committed to reducing the role of big, special interest money in politics.

Riseup.net provides online communication tools for groups working on social change. They work to make information and communication secure, as opposed to other companies like Google, Yahoo, etc. They provide email accounts, mailing lists, security information, and other tools.

Takethesquare.net was born out of the Madrid uprisings in May 2011. The site connects an international network of activists working to organize a global network of citizen activism based on the ideals of the Madrid protests.

The Institute for Local Self-Reliance at ilsr.org works with citizens, activists, policymakers, and entrepreneurs to design systems, policies, and enterprises that meet local or regional needs; to maximize human, material, natural, and financial resources; and to ensure that the benefits of these systems and resources accrue to all local citizens.

The Institute for Social Ecology at social-ecology.org explores ecological approaches to food production, alternative technologies, and urban design, and has played an essential, catalytic role in movements to challenge nuclear power, global injustices and unsustainable biotechnologies, while building participatory, community-based alternatives.

The National Center for Employee Ownership at nceo.org provides objective and reliable information on employee ownership.

Theteaparty.net is one of the many Tea Party websites. This site promotes campaigns for limited federal government, individual freedom, personal responsibility, free markets, and returning political power to the states.

Theworldcafé.com is a social technology that helps people engage in conversations that matter to them. They provide tools to help organizers facilitate World Café style conversations and share the information that comes out of the conversations on the Internet.

Twitter.com is an information network and social media platform where users can share information and communicate in real time. Twitter is good for sharing events and for instant communication during events.

Unconference.net provides information and resources to people interested in hosting an unconference. Unconferences are participant driven, open space style meetings.

Ustream.tv is a live streaming platform for individuals to engage in citizen's media. Create your own account and your own channel. Groups can broadcast to the Internet from a mobile device. Ustream also provides an online community where people can chat with streamers and each other.

Wearethe99percent.tumblr.com is an outlet for anyone to post their story about why they feel they are the 99%.

Youtube.com allows users to upload and share videos on the Internet. You can use YouTube to post videos of your events and actions on Facebook, Twitter, and other social media sites.

*This list is not exhaustive. There are countless Occupy and social change groups doing amazing work in every aspect of social, political, and economic life with technology all over the world.

Endnotes

1 The American Heritage College Dictionary 3rd Edition. Houghtin Mifflin Company. New York. 542.

2 Jamail, Dahr. "Gulf Seafood Deformities Alarm Scientists." *Al Jazeera English.* Al Jazeera, 20 Apr. 2012. Web. 24 June 2012. <http://www.aljazeera.com/indepth/features/2012/04/201241682318260912.html>.

3 Jamail, Dahr. "Gulf Fisheries in Decline after Oil Disaster." *Al Jazeera English.* Al Jazeera, 19 Apr. 2012. Web. 24 June 2012. <http://www.aljazeera.com/indepth/features/2012/03/20123571723894800.html>.

4 Friedman, Milton. *Capitalism and Freedom Fortieth Anniversary Edition.* Chicago: University of Chicago, 2002. 12.

5 Marx, Karl. *Karl Marx, a Reader*, ed. Jon Elster. Cambridge University Press, 1986. 39.

6 Madison, James. *The Federalist Papers No. 10*. The Same Subject Continued: The Union as a Safeguard Against Domestic Faction and Insurrection. The New York Packet, November 23, 1787. Web. 3 Jan 2013. <http://thomas.loc.gov/home/histdox/fed_10.html>.

7 Adams, John and Charles Francis Adams. *The Works of John Adams, Second President of the United States: With a Life of the Author, Notes and Illustrations, Volume 6* (Google eBook). (Boston, 1851). 484.

8 Transcript: Obama address to U.N. General Assembly. Published September 25, 2012. Web. 5 Jan 2013. <http://www.foxnews.com/politics/2012/09/25/transcript-obama-address-to-un-general-assembly/>.

9 Congress: Trading stock on inside information? A script from 'Insiders' with Steve Kroft which aired on November 13, 2011. Web 5 Jan 2012. <http://www.cbsnews.com/8301-18560_162-57323527/congress-trading-stock-on-inside-information/>.

10 "Interface's Values Are Our Guiding Principles." *Interface Global.* N.p., 2008. Web. 24 Nov. 2012. <http://www.interfaceglobal.com/Company/Mission-Vision.aspx>.

11 "Pro-Life and Pro-Choice Groups Use Dialogue and Shared Concerns to Find Common Ground." *CPN - About CPN.* N.p., n.d. The Common Ground Network for Life and Choice.Web. 8 Jan. 2013. <http://www.cpn.org/topics/families/prolife.html>.

12 Moody, Chris. "How Republicans Are Being Taught to Talk About Occupy Wall Street," Dec. 1, 2011. Web. 10 March. 2012. <http://news.yahoo.com/blogs/ticket/republicans-being-taught-talk-occupy-wall-street 133707949 .html>.

13 Lakoff, George. "How to Frame Yourself: A Framing Memo for Occupy

Wall Street," Oct. 19, 2011. Web. 21 Oct. 2011. <http://www.huffingtonpost.com/george-lakoff/occupy-wall-street_b_1019448.html>.

14 Aristotle. *Metaphysics*, Book 13, 1078b. Web. 4 Dec. 2012. <http://www.perseus.tufts.edu/hopper/text?doc=Perseus%3Atext%3A1999.01.0052%3Abook%3D13%3Asection%3D1078b>.

15 Aristotle and Benjamin Jowett. *Politics* (Stilwell: KS: Digireads, 2005), 20.

16 Smith, Adam and Edwin Cannan. *The Wealth of Nations: Adam Smith, Ed.* Edwin Cannan (New York, NY: Bantam Dell, 2003), Book I, Chapter II. 23-24.

17 Hobbes, Thimas and Richard Tuck. *Leviathan.* Cambridge, England: Cambridge UP, 1991. 105.

18 Ibid, 89.

19 Locke, John and C. B. Macpherson. *Second Treatise of Government.* Indianapolis, IN: Hackett Pub., 1980. 9.

20 Mill, John Stuart. *Critical Assessments*, Ed. John Cunningham Wood. Vol. II. London: Routledge, 1991. 99.

21 Smith, Adam and Edwin Cannan. *The Wealth of Nations: Adam Smith, Ed.* Edwin Cannan. New York, NY: Bantam Dell, 2003. Book V, Chapter IX. 875.

22 The World in 2005, "The Economist Intelligence Unit's Quality-of-Life Index", <http://www.economist.com/media/pdf/ QUALITY_OF_ LIFE.pdf>, 2.

23 Aristotle and Terence Irwin. *Nicomachean Ethics.* Indianapolis, IN: Hackett Pub., 1999. xvii.

24 Plato and Allan David Bloom. *The Republic of Plato.* New York: Basic, 1991. 124.

25 Hobbes, Thomas and Richard Tuck. *Leviathan.* Cambridge, England: Cambridge UP, 1991. 9.

26 Ibid, 10.

27 Ibid, 10.

28 Locke, John and Kenneth Winkler. *An Essay Concerning Human Understanding.* Indianapolis: Hackett, 1996. Book II, Chapter I. 33.

29 Locke, John. *Some Thoughts Concerning Education* (Sioux Falls, SD: NuVision Publications, 2007), 11.

30 Locke, John and C. B. Macpherson. *Second Treatise of Government.* Indianapolis, IN: Hackett Pub., 1980. 46.

31 Bacon, Francis. *Novum Organum*, Ed. Joseph Devey. New York: P.F. Collier and Son. www.forgottenbooks.org, Book I, Aphorism XLI, 20-21.

32 Marx, Karl and Friedrich Engels. The German Ideology: Including Theses on Feuerbach and Introduction to The Critique of Political Economy. Amherst, NY: Prometheus, 1998. 573.

33 Aristotle and Benjamin Jowett. *Politics*. Stilwell, KS: Digireads, 2005. 20.
34 Ibid, 20.
35 Hobbes, Thomas, Michael Silverthorne, and Richard Tuck. *On the Citizen*. Cambridge u.a.: Cambridge Univ., 2005. 4.
36 Locke, John and C. B. Macpherson. *Second Treatise of Government*. Indianapolis, IN: Hackett Pub., 1980. 12.
37 Locke, John and W. Von Leyden. *John Locke: Essays on the Law of Nature: The Latin Text with a Translation, Introduction, and Notes; Together with Transcripts of Locke's Shorthand in His Journal for 1676*. Oxford: Oxford UP, 2002. 207.
38 Locke, John and C. B. Macpherson, *Second Treatise of Government*. Indianapolis, IN: Hackett Pub., 1980. 9.
39 Ibid, 42.
40 Rousseau, Jean-Jacques. *Emile, or On Education*. Sioux Falls, SD: NuVision Publications, 2007. 11.
41 Rousseau, Jean-Jacques and Donald A. Cress. *Discourse on the Origin of Inequality*. Indianapolis: Hackett Pub., 1992. 35.
42 Ibid, 35.
43 Ibid, 35.
44 Rousseau, Jean-Jacques. *Emile, or On Education*. Sioux Falls, SD: NuVision Publications, 2007. 65.
45 Ibid.
46 Ibid, 14.
47 Ibid, 94.
48 Marx, Karl. *The Holy Family*. <http://www.marxists.org/archive/marx/works/1845/holy-family/ch04.htm>, Chapter IV, Critical Comment No.2. Web. 23 March 2012.
49 Hume, David and J. B. Schneewind. *An Enquiry concerning the Principles of Morals*. Indianapolis: Hackett Pub., 1983. 92.
50 Ibid.
51 Smith, Adam and Edwin Cannan. *The Wealth of Nations: Adam Smith*, Ed. Edwin Cannan. New York, NY: Bantam Dell, 2003. Book V, Chapter I, Part III. 941.
52 Hobbes, Thomas and Richard Tuck. *Leviathan*. Cambridge, England: Cambridge UP, 1991. 36.
53 Ibid, 36.
54 Ibid, 119.
55 Ibid, 48.

56 Ibid, 111.

57 Locke, John and C. B. Macpherson. *Second Treatise of Government*. Indianapolis, IN: Hackett Pub., 1980. 11.

58 Ibid, 10.

59 Ibid, 12.

60 Rousseau, Jean-Jacques. *The Basic Political Writings*, Trans. Donald A. Cress. Indianapolis: Hackett, 1987. 150-151.

61 Hume, David. *A Treatise of Human Nature*. Mineola, NY: Dover Publications, 2003. 294.

62 Ibid, 131.

63 Ibid, 295.

64 Ibid, xi.

65 Descartes, René. *Descartes: Selected Philosophical Writings*. Cambridge: Cambridge UP, 1998. 36.

66 Harris, Paul. "Indiana Soybean Farmer Sees Monsanto Lawsuit Reach US Supreme Court." *The Guardian*. Guardian News and Media, 09 Feb. 2013. Web. 12 Feb. 2013. <http://www.guardian.co.uk/law/2013/feb/09/soybean-farmer-monsanto-supreme-court>.

67 Gillam, Carey. "Monsanto Wins Lawsuit against Indiana Soybean Farmer." *MNN - Mother Nature Network*. N.p., 21 Sept. 2011. Web. 24 Jan. 2013. <http://www.mnn.com/your-home/organic-farming-gardening/stories/monsanto-wins-lawsuit-against-indiana-soybean-farmer>.

68 Maynard, Mark. "Bob Sloan on the New Slavery of the American Prison Factory System." *Mark Maynard*. N.p., 19 June 2012. Web. 24 Feb. 2013. <http://markmaynard.com/2012/06/bob-sloan-on-the-new-slavery-of-the-american-prison-factory-system/>.

69 "ALEC Exposed: State Legislative Bills Drafted by Secretive Corporate-Lawmaker Coalition." *Democracy Now!* July 15, 2011. Web. 15 Aug. 2012. <http://www.democracynow.org/2011/7/15/alec_exposed_state_legislative_bills_drafted>.

70 "New Exposé Tracks ALEC-Private Prison Industry Effort to Replace Unionized Workers with Prison Labor." *Democracy Now!* August 5, 2011. Web. 15 Aug. 2012. <http://www.democracynow.org/2011/8/5/new_expos_tracks_alec_private_prison>.

71 Blackhurst, Chris. "The MT Interview: Barclays' Marcus Agius." *Management Today*. N.p., 1 Nov. 2009. Web. 6 Jan. 2013. <http://www.managementtoday.co.uk/news/948496/MT-Interview-Barclays-Marcus-Agius/>.

72 "Barclays Chair Resigns over Rate Fixing." *Democracy Now!* Headlines. July 2, 2012. <http://www.democracynow.org/2012/7/2/headlines#7214>.

73 "Matt Taibbi: Libor Rate-Fixing Scandal 'Biggest Insider Trading You Could Ever Imagine'" *Democracy Now!* 19 July 2012. Web. 21 Jan. 2013. <http://www.democracynow.org/2012/7/19/matt_taibbi_libor_rate_fixing_scandal>.

74 "The Story of SPC Ross A. McGinnis." *Army.Mil.* Web. 3 Feb. 2013. <http://www.army.mil/medalofhonor/mcginnis/profile/index.html>.

75 "Meet Bruce Karatz." *The Keep Your Home Foundation.* Web. 19 Jan. 2013. <http://www.keepyourhomefoundation.com/about/meet_bruce_karatz>.

76 Pfeifer, Stuart. "Friends in High Places Seek Leniency for Karatz." *Los Angeles Times.* Los Angeles Times, 10 Nov. 2010. Web. 12 Feb. 2013. <http://articles.latimes.com/2010/nov/10/business/la-fi-karatz-homeboy-20101110>.

77 Pfeifer, Stuart. "Former KB Home CEO Bruce Karatz Sentenced to Five Years' Probation." *Los Angeles Times.* Los Angeles Times, 11 Nov. 2010. Web. 19 Feb. 2013. <http://articles.latimes.com/2010/nov/11/business/la-fi-karatz-sentence-20101111>.

78 Finkelstein, Sydney. "Rethinking CEO Stock Options." *Bloomberg Businessweek.* N.p., 17 Apr. 2009. Web. 2 Jan. 2013. <http://www.businessweek.com/stories/2009-04-17/rethinking-ceo-stock-optionsbusinessweek-business-news-stock-market-and-financial-advice>.

79 Jaruzelski, Barry, Kevin Dehoff, and Rakesh Bordia. "Smart Spenders: the Global Innovation 1000." Booz Allen Hamilton: 2006. 48-49.

80 Galbraith, John Kenneth. Consumer Behavior and the Dependence Effect. <http://msuweb.montclair.edu/~lebelp/GalbraithDepEffect1958.pdf>, 3.

81 Veblen, Thorstein. *The Place of Science and Modern Civilization.* New York: B.W. Huebsch, 1919. 64.

82 "The History of Tom's of Maine. Tom's of Maine." *The History of Tom's of Maine. Tom's of Maine.* Web. 16 Feb. 2013. <http://www.tomsofmaine.com/business-practices/heritage/early-history>.

83 "Press: News and Media. Tom's of Maine." *Press: News and Media. Tom's of Maine.* Web. 16 Feb. 2013. <http://www.tomsofmaine.com/press/releases/detail/colgate-purchasing-toms-of-maine>.

84 Kloer, Amanda. "Starbucks Ignores Customer Demands for More Fair Trade Coffee," *Fair Trade Coffee News'* 1 Sept. 2011. Web. 23 Mar. 2012. <http://www.fairtradecoffeenews.com/>.

85 Sen, Amartya K. "Rational Fools: A Critique of the Behavioral Foundations

of Economic Theory," *Philosophy and Public Affairs*, Vol. 6, No. 4 (Summer 1977): 342.
86 Polanyi, Karl. *The Great Transformation*. Rinehart & Company, Inc, 1944. Chapter 4.
87 Kahneman, Daniel and Amos Tversky. "Prospect Theory: An Analysis of Decision under Risk" *Econometrica, 47. 2.* <http://www.princeton.edu/~kahneman/docs/Publications/prospect_theory.pdf>, (March 1979) 263-291.
88 Bradford, Harry. "Walmart De Mexico Bribed Local Officials To Open 19 Stores: NYT." *The Huffington Post*. TheHuffingtonPost.com, 18 Dec. 2012. Web. 16 Feb. 2013. <http://www.huffingtonpost.com/2012/12/18/walmart-de-mexico-bribed_n_2324053.html>.
89 "Reps. Cummings and Waxman Release Documents Showing That Wal-Mart's CEO Was Informed of Mexican Bribery Allegations in 2005." *Committee on Energy and Commerce Democrats*. N.p., 10 Jan. 2013. Web. 24 Feb. 2013. <http://democrats.energycommerce.house.gov/index.php?q=news/reps-cummings-and-waxman-release-documents-showing-that-wal-mart-s-ceo-was-informed-of-mexican->.
90 The Bribery Aisle: How Wal-Mart Used Payoffs to Bribe Its Way Through Expansion in Mexico. Democracy Now. December 20, 2012. <http://www.democracynow.org/2012/12/20/the_bribery_aisle_how_wal_mart>.
91 "The Bribery Aisle: How Wal-Mart Used Payoffs to Bribe Its Way Through Expansion in Mexico." *Democracy Now!* 20 Dec. 2012. Web. 14 Jan. 2013. <http://www.democracynow.org/2012/12/20/the_bribery_aisle_how_wal_mart>.
92 Barstow, David. "Vast Mexico Bribery Case Hushed Up by Wal-Mart After Top-Level Struggle." *The New York Times Business Day*. The New York Times, 21 Apr. 2012. Web. 16 Jan. 2013. <http://www.nytimes.com/2012/04/22/business/at-wal-mart-in-mexico-a-bribe-inquiry-silenced.html>.
93 The Bribery Aisle: How Wal-Mart Used Payoffs to Bribe Its Way Through Expansion in Mexico. Democracy Now. December 20, 2012. <http://www.democracynow.org/2012/12/20/the_bribery_aisle_how_wal_mart>.
94 Barstow, David. "Vast Mexico Bribery Case Hushed Up by Wal-Mart After Top-Level Struggle." *The New York Times Business Day*. The New York Times, 21 Apr. 2012. Web. 16 Jan. 2013. <http://www.nytimes.com/2012/04/22/business/at-wal-mart-in-mexico-a-bribe-inquiry-silenced.html>.
95 Procter, Don. "Unprecedented Era for Steel Tech Innovation." *Daily Commerical News*. Reed Business Information, 25 Jan. 2013. Web. 28 Jan. 2013. <http://www.dcnonl.com/article/id53749>.
96 Aquino, Judith. "Nine Jobs That Humans May Lose to Robots." *Msnbc.com*.

NBC News. Web. 24 Feb. 2013. <http://www.nbcnews.com/id/42183592/>.

97 Hill, David J. "1 Million Robots To Replace 1 Million Human Jobs At Foxconn? First Robots Have Arrived. Singularity Hub." *Singularity Hub*. 11 Dec. 2012. Web. 17 Jan. 2013. <http://singularityhub.com/2012/11/12/1 million-rob>.

98 Hargreaves, Steve. "7 Great Government-backed Inventions." *CNNMoney*. Cable News Network, 20 Oct. 2011. Web. 17 Mar. 2012. <http://money.cnn.com/galleries/2011/technology/1110/gallery.government_inventions/2.html>.

99 "What Is ARPANET?" *Computer Hope*. Web. 17 Mar. 2012. <http://www.computerhope.com/jargon/a/arpanet.htm>.

100 Kelly, John. "What High-tech Products Came from NASA Technology?" *How Stuff Works*. Web. 12 Mar. 2012. <http://science.howstuffworks.com / innovation/nasa-inventions/nasa-high-tech-products.htm>.

101 Sen, Armatya. Poverty and Famines an Essay on Entitlement and Deprivation. Oxford: Clarendon, 1982.

102 Davila, Tony, Marc J. Epstein, Robert Shelton, and Robert D. Shelton. *Making Innovation Work: How to Manage It, Measure It, and Profit from It*. Upper Saddle River, NJ: Wharton School Pub., 2006.

103 Goodwin, Neva, Julie A. Nelson, Frank Ackerman, and Thomas Weisskopf. *Microeconomics in Context*. 2nd ed. Armonk, NY: M.E. Sharpe, 2009. 100.

104 Strassmann, Mark. "America's Dwindling Water Supply." *CBSNews*. CBS Interactive, 09 Jan. 2010. Web. 21 Jan. 2013. <http://www.cbsnews.com/8301-18563_162-6073416.html>.

105 "U.S. Unemployment Rate." *Bureau of Labor Statistics*. U.S. Department of Labor, n.d. Web. 14 Apr. 2012. <http://data.bls.gov/pdq/SurveyOutputServlet>.

106 "U.S. Unemployment Rate." (every other year from 1950-2010). *Bureau of Labor Statistics*. U.S. Department of Labor, n.d. Web. 14 Apr. 2012. <http://data.bls.gov/pdq/SurveyOutputServlet>.

107 Sharp, Kathleen. "'Erin Brockovich': The Real Story." Salon.com *Salon.com RSS*. 14 Apr. 2000. Web. 24 Feb. 2013. <http://www.salon.com/2000/04/14/sharp/>.

108 Konty, Melissa Fry, PhD, and John Bailey. "The Impact of Coal on the Kentucky State Budget." *The Economics of Coal in Kentucky: Current Impacts and Future Prospects*. The Impact of Coal on the Kentucky State Budget Mountain Association for Community Economic Development, 25 June 2009. Web. 10 Feb. 2013. <http://www.maced.org/coal/exe-summary.htm>.

109 Jowit, Juliette. "World's Top Firms Cause $2.2tn of Environmental Damage, Report Estimates." *The Guardian*. Guardian News and Media, 18 Feb.

2010. Web. 24 Feb. 2013. <http://www.guardian.co.uk/environment/2010/feb/18/worlds-top-firms-environmental-damage/print>.

110 "Soya Blazes a Trail through the Amazon." *Greenpeace*. Greenpeace International, 12 Dec. 2003. Web. 16 Feb. 2013. <http://www.greenpeace.org/international/en/news/features/soya-blazes-through-the-amazon/?accept=e654f091f9313dcda74f278670b8b201>.

111 Rifkin, Jeremy. The End of Work: The Decline of the Global Labor Force and the Dawn of the Post-market Era. New York: G.P. Putnam's Sons, 1996. 13.

112 Watkins, Kevin. "Growth with Equity is Good for the poor." Oxfam GB. 27 June, 2000. 7.

113 Ibid, 4.

114 Bangura, Yusuf. "Combating Poverty and Inequality: Structural Change, Social Policy and Politics." Geneva: United Nations Research Institute for Social Development, 2010. 32.

115 Beddoe, Rachael, Robert Costanzaa, Joshua Farleya, Eric Garzaa, Jennifer Kent, Ida Kubiszewskia, Luz Martineza, Tracy McCowen, Kathleen Murphy, Norman Myerse, Zach Ogden, Kevin Stapleton, and John Woodward, "Overcoming systemic roadblocks to sustainability: The evolutionary redesign of worldviews, institutions, and technologies" *Proceedings of the National Academy of Sciences*, vol. 106, no. 8. Feb. 24 2009. 2483.

116 "Distrust, Discontent, Anger and Partisan Rancor." *Pew Research Center for the People and the Press RSS*. Pew Research Center, 18 Apr. 2010. Web. 2 Nov. 2012. <http://www.people-press.org/2010/04/18/section-1-trust-in-government-1958-2010/>.

117 Blodget, Henry. "CHARTS: Here's What The Wall Street Protesters Are So Angry About..." *Business Insider*. N.p., 9 Oct. 2011. Web. 11 Oct. 2011. <http://www.businessinsider.com/what-wall-street-protesters-are-so-angry-about-2011-10?op=1>.

118 "Who We Are." *Occupy Wall Street*. Occupy Wall Street, 16 July 2011. Web. 7 Oct. 2011. <http://occupywallst.org/article/who_we_are/>.

119 "#OCCUPYWALLSTREET Update from Adbusters." *Occupy Wall Street*. Occupy Wall Street, 12 Aug. 2011. Web. 7 Oct. 2011. <http://occupywallst.org/archive/Aug-2011/page-2/>.

120 "Who We Are." *Occupy Wall Street*. Occupy Wall Street, 16 July 2011. Web. 21 Sept. 2011. <http://occupywallst.org/article/who_we_are/>.

121 Bates, Daniel. "Women Who Want to Succeed at Work Should Shut up - While Men Who Want the Same Should Keep Talking, Research Says." *Mail*

Online. Daily Mail, 17 May 2012. Web. 6 Dec. 2012. <http://www.dailymail.co.uk/news/article-2146015/Women-want-succeed-work-shut--men-want-talking.html>.

122 Maya. "Study Confirms That Women Don't Speak up as Much When Outnumbered by Men." *Study Confirms That Women Don't Speak up as Much When Outnumbered by Men.* Feministing, 20 Sept. 2012. Web. 6 Dec. 2012. <http://feministing.com/2012/09/20/study-confirms-that-women-dont-speak-up-as-much-when-outnumbered-by-men/>.

123 This section was written using notes from "Intro to Direct Democracy-Facilitation Training," <http://www.nycga.net/groups/facilitation/docs/intro-to-direct-democracy-%E2%80%93-facilitation-training> and documents we made for the General Assembly of the West Harlem 99%.

124 "Intro to Direct Democracy-Facilitation Training," <http://www.nycga.net/groups/facilitation/docs/intro-to-direct-democracy-%E2%80%93-facilitation-training>.

125 Created through use of handouts and facilitation trainings at Occupy Wall Street.

Index

A

accountability 128, 139, 169, 212, 214, 215
accurate information 31, 42, 51, 59, 64, 112-118, 120, 239
activists 186, 188, 191, 199, 201, 203, 208, 214, 216, 220, 236, 237, 238, 254, 255, 281
Adbusters 185
advertisements 193, 202, 211
advertising 26, 99, 102, 112, 114, 115, 118, 123, 128, 137, 157, 191, 196, 258
agriculture 84, 96, 118, 133
ALEC 98, 99, 172
ambiguous language 33, 44
America 3, 13, 14, 20, 22, 24, 25, 26, 27, 29, 32, 44, 45, 47, 51, 55, 98, 99, 100, 101, 104, 129, 147, 148, 159, 166, 168, 172, 184, 185, 193, 217, 238, 242
American 3, 5, 12, 13, 16, 20, 21, 22, 25, 28, 29, 30, 32, 37, 39, 43, 82, 95, 96, 97, 98, 99, 116, 121, 122, 147, 151, 152, 168, 171, 172, 179, 183, 184, 186, 191, 192, 193, 194, 197, 216, 239, 246, 266
Apple 127, 152
appreciative inquiry 236
Aristotle 61, 64, 77, 79-81, 86
assumed truth 90, 157
assuming totality 34
assumptions 58, 59, 103, 107, 112, 120, 121, 135, 145, 146, 162, 164, 170
autonomy 201, 208-209, 229

B

Bacon, Francis 79
banking 14, 50, 101, 138, 152, 183, 267, 268, 276
Bank of America 101
Barclays 99-100
barter 247, 266, 275
big business 85, 123, 142, 169, 182, 183, 238, 246, 247
Bush, George W. 183
business cooperative 248

C

capitalism 18, 53, 56-60, 63, 68, 72, 73, 84, 85, 90-96, 102, 103, 107, 110, 125, 126, 129-132, 134, 145, 156, 162, 166, 170, 171, 173, 183, 185, 191, 192, 194, 207, 211, 222
capitalist 41, 53, 56, 57, 59, 90, 92, 94, 97, 98, 103, 104, 126, 128-132, 167, 170, 171, 173, 181, 188, 198, 211, 217, 219, 246
capitalist economy 97
Cargill 96, 148
CCA 99, 172
centrally planned 92, 95, 125
CEO 109, 183
circle discussions 236

293

class 12, 80, 84, 110, 127, 141, 161, 179, 184, 248
coal 43, 142
Colgate 116
collective 106, 174, 184, 190, 195, 199-202, 206-208, 212, 213, 219, 222, 223, 226-232, 234, 236, 237, 256, 266, 269
collective responsibility 201, 212
collectivism 201, 212, 213, 215
commodification 182
commodities 138, 170, 173, 182, 196
communism 35, 92-95
communist 35, 92-95
community 14, 22, 30, 48, 49, 51, 73, 81, 93, 104, 106, 108, 124, 148, 160, 161, 170, 173-175, 177, 180, 186-188, 195-211, 215-221, 227, 228, 235-276, 279, 280
compete 66, 67, 69, 81, 99, 111, 115, 116, 121, 124, 125, 127, 134, 135, 151, 198, 212
competition 57-59, 63, 66, 67, 82, 84, 87, 96, 102, 105, 111, 118-126, 128, 135, 151, 212, 222, 231
Congress 22, 40, 41, 50, 98, 116, 122, 173, 179
consensus 36, 216, 227-237, 265, 268
conservatives 22, 43, 171, 231
Constitution 18, 24, 39-40
consumerism 135, 142, 179, 276
consumers 38, 57, 58, 63, 66, 67, 68, 70, 99, 102, 111, 112, 114, 115, 117, 118, 122, 134, 138, 139, 149, 173
consumer sovereignty 122, 126
cooperation 62, 170, 173, 196, 212, 231
co-operative 275
corporate 17, 22, 25, 27, 31, 34, 41, 42, 96, 98, 109, 114, 122, 125, 142, 183-184, 186, 190, 191, 193-197, 231, 232, 245, 250, 272, 273
corporations 1, 5, 14, 22, 34, 42, 95, 96, 98, 99, 101, 102, 110, 115, 116, 117, 122, 125, 127, 139, 141, 142, 148, 161, 169-171, 173, 182, 183, 196-198, 216, 238, 239, 241, 247, 252, 261, 268, 275
creating duality 33, 40
cultural 59, 116, 173, 195, 205, 222, 239, 242, 249, 256, 276

D

Da Vinci, Leonardo 132
debt 69, 184, 248, 260, 273
degradation 114, 133, 140, 190, 246
democracy 1, 4, 13, 24-31, 44-46, 50, 51, 93, 94, 101, 170, 173, 174, 185, 192, 197, 198, 200-202, 208, 214, 216, 218, 220-222, 226, 228, 230, 232, 235, 237, 241, 244, 250, 252, 254, 255, 261, 271, 276, 277
Descartes, Rene 80, 88
direct actions 216, 219
direct democracy 30, 198, 222, 226
disingenuous evidence selection 33, 38
diversity 133, 173, 203, 204, 214,

234
divide into sides 41

E

economic growth 5, 35, 43, 56, 57, 60, 67, 69-72, 91, 117, 127, 152-155, 157, 162, 164, 165, 167, 168, 174, 181, 185, 205, 273
economic measures 48, 59, 72, 73, 108, 126, 143, 153-160, 162-166, 174, 181, 200, 268
economic models 65, 120, 262
economics 27, 31, 35, 43, 50, 51, 53, 55-72, 74-76, 82, 84, 89-95, 99, 100, 105-110, 112, 113, 117, 119-121, 123, 127, 128, 132, 135, 138-140, 143, 145-147, 152-155, 157-185, 189-195-200, 203-205, 207, 213, 214, 219, 238, 239, 241-243, 246, 247, 249, 252, 261, 262, 268, 271, 272, 274, 276, 277, 281
economic system 35, 51, 53, 55, 56, 59, 63, 91, 93, 94, 99, 108, 121, 138, 154, 160, 169-171, 173, 174, 180, 198, 238, 274
economic theory 61, 62, 64, 90, 112
economists 58, 61, 64, 65, 72, 75, 85, 103, 113, 120, 127, 153, 155, 156, 157, 158, 164, 166, 175
economy 21, 54-57, 60, 66, 67, 70, 71, 74, 85, 91-93, 95-97, 99, 102, 107, 108, 114, 121, 123, 126, 134, 135, 137, 139, 150, 151, 153-158, 159, 160, 162, 165, 171, 172, 179, 183, 188, 195, 246, 247, 252, 266, 268
ecosystem 56, 95, 114, 140, 144, 147, 148, 149, 161
education 22, 55, 72, 73, 77, 78, 98, 119, 126, 145, 146, 153, 174, 181, 184, 188, 192, 206, 212, 219, 243, 247, 248, 260, 267, 268, 272, 273
effectiveness 17, 50, 121, 127, 128, 200, 212, 240, 245, 251, 257, 270
efficiency 50, 58, 109, 121, 125, 126, 128, 134, 154
Egypt 130, 182, 220
election reform 197
Emergency Economic Stabilization Act of 2008 183
empowerment 62, 188, 195, 197, 202, 203, 205, 207, 210, 228, 232, 239-241, 255, 256, 264, 274
entrepreneurial spirit 129, 175, 246
environment 13, 14, 42, 43, 70, 95, 98, 109, 111, 114-118, 124, 127, 128, 132, 133, 135, 139-145, 148, 149, 152, 154, 157, 159, 160, 164, 171, 174, 179, 181, 182, 185, 189, 190, 196, 198-200, 203, 218, 242, 246, 254, 264, 269, 272, 274
equality 3, 29, 30, 56, 73, 166, 191, 200, 202, 203, 274
ethical business 116, 245
executives 110, 114, 123, 124
exploitation 12, 25, 56, 109, 117, 128, 135, 159, 180, 185, 190,

295

196, 217, 246
externalities 109, 111, 139-141, 143, 148, 154, 157, 159, 164, 170, 174, 249, 272

F

Facebook 220, 258, 260, 270, 279
facilitation 223-224, 227-228, 233-234, 257, 264
factors of production 57, 272
family 5, 14, 18, 21, 34, 43, 46-49, 51, 73, 81, 96, 107, 108, 143, 157, 159, 161, 169, 174, 180, 181, 183-184, 198, 199, 237, 242, 247, 249, 252, 254, 258, 259, 260, 272, 280
Federal Reserve 139, 184, 197
finance 55, 152
firms 57, 58, 63, 65-71, 99, 111, 112, 114, 118, 121, 125, 126, 130, 133, 134, 139, 140, 143, 150, 152, 153, 157, 164, 183
flexibility 77, 214, 230, 257
fluidity 214, 230
framing issues 33, 44
freedom 1, 3-6, 11-20, 24, 25, 28, 29, 30, 31, 35, 37, 38, 44-47, 50, 51, 53, 55, 60, 72, 73, 74, 80, 97, 166, 168, 170, 171, 173-175, 180, 183, 184, 185, 192, 193, 195, 197, 198, 200-202, 204, 221, 222, 230, 238, 241, 242, 271, 274, 276, 277
freedom of speech 16, 202
free market 44, 66, 68, 74, 85, 92, 93, 95-97, 99, 122, 127, 135, 139, 172, 207

G

Galbraith, John Kenneth 112
GDP 60, 69-73, 156-166, 181, 273
GDP per capita 72, 156, 163
general assembly 202, 216, 218, 219, 221, 223, 227-230, 254, 258, 263-266, 268, 272, 274, 279
goods and services 55, 57, 66, 68-72, 74, 102, 106, 139, 156, 163, 247, 267, 268, 272, 275
government 1, 4-6, 13-26, 29, 30, 31, 35, 36, 37, 43, 44, 50, 51, 56, 59, 62, 66, 71, 74, 81, 84, 85, 93-95, 98, 99, 101, 102, 111, 122, 128-131, 148, 152, 159, 168, 179, 183, 184, 188, 190, 191, 193, 194, 195, 196, 197, 220, 238, 241, 242, 243, 250, 252, 261, 266-268, 275, 276
Green Revolution 133-134

H

health 22, 33, 43, 47, 62, 73, 124, 140, 145, 149, 153, 154, 157, 159, 161, 165, 175, 181, 212, 268, 272
healthcare 18, 21, 33, 36, 43, 72, 98, 116, 152, 159, 174, 184, 188, 192, 195, 219, 243, 247, 248, 267, 268
Hobbes, Thomas 6, 13, 62, 77-78, 81, 83, 86-87, 105
horizontalism 201-204, 208-210, 214, 215
human nature 46, 47, 51, 53, 59-64, 69, 74-84, 85, 86-88, 96, 103-106, 112, 125, 132, 150, 173

humanness 1, 45-51, 53, 60, 128, 143, 170-175, 177, 179, 181, 182, 184, 187-189, 193-204, 208-222, 231, 232, 234, 238-242, 245-247, 257, 259, 260, 262, 267, 270-272, 274-277
Hume, David 78-79, 84, 85, 88

I

Idle No More 199, 238, 240
ignoring hypocrisy 33, 37
incentives 18, 57, 59, 63, 66, 67, 106-112, 114, 118, 121, 122, 126, 129-132, 135, 173, 174, 175, 210, 259
inclusion 202
individualism 56, 105, 125, 173
individuality 200, 201, 211, 212, 244
innovation 58-59, 63, 67, 69, 73, 74, 111, 118, 125-135, 150, 151, 153, 155, 168, 175, 181
interest rates 138
Internet 30, 48, 49, 67, 131, 240, 270, 279
irrationality 46, 47, 64, 86, 87, 118, 119, 120, 155

J

jobs 11, 17, 58, 59, 69, 102, 108, 111, 126, 127, 128, 138, 148, 150, 151, 152, 164, 172, 181, 183, 184, 190, 198, 199, 203, 208, 246, 248, 260, 272, 273
John Henry 151

K

Kant, Immanuel 79, 82
Keynes, John Maynard 113

L

labor 12, 55, 57, 58, 65, 68, 69, 71, 84, 98, 110, 111, 114, 127, 134, 136, 138, 143, 146-148, 150, 151, 152, 154, 164, 172, 173, 175, 182, 183, 245, 252, 259, 272, 274
Lake Mead 136
leadership 1, 27, 82, 85, 90, 104, 172, 175, 191, 207, 210, 223, 255, 274, 276
levels 48, 55, 94, 99, 110, 114, 115, 147, 178, 181, 224, 241, 242, 243, 247, 262
liberals 17, 21, 22, 42, 95, 171, 191, 231
liberty 3, 12, 24, 30, 56, 62, 78, 82, 215, 257
Liberty Square 185, 186, 208, 220, 229, 263, 264, 265, 268, 280
LIBOR 100
Livestream 220, 258, 270
local businesses 114, 239, 245, 247, 261
local food 246
local group 252-255, 258, 260, 261
Locke, John 6, 13, 62, 64, 77, 78, 79, 81, 82, 87, 88, 105, 284, 285, 286
love 3, 15, 19, 22, 38, 46, 47, 61, 80, 81, 83, 87, 108, 111, 123, 157, 168, 169, 180, 201, 249, 260, 276

M

marginal cost 68
market 56, 61, 66, 68, 92, 93, 95-98, 108, 111, 112, 120, 122, 125, 135, 136, 138, 152, 159, 245, 287
marketing 102, 117, 137, 153
Marx, Karl 12, 79, 80, 84
McGinnis, Ross A. 104
measurable 107, 126, 127, 141, 142, 143, 146, 157, 199, 247
media 17, 22, 26, 31, 33, 41-44, 48, 124, 135, 157, 175, 177, 186-195, 199, 203, 217, 220, 231, 239, 252, 258, 260, 261, 270, 279
Mill, John Stuart 64
monetary 18, 48, 57, 63, 65, 103, 107, 108, 118, 120, 126, 127, 130, 131, 135, 139, 140, 142, 143, 145, 146, 148, 154, 157, 159, 160, 172, 173, 181, 182, 210, 215, 246
money 6, 18, 21, 23, 27, 42, 45, 55, 57, 58, 63, 65, 69-72, 86, 94, 99, 101, 102, 107, 108, 110, 114, 123, 126, 129, 131, 133, 136, 138, 139, 141, 144, 146, 150, 154, 155, 157, 158, 159, 160, 161, 169, 172, 173, 181-184, 192, 194, 197, 199, 202, 217, 229, 238, 239, 241, 246, 247, 252, 259, 267, 268, 275, 289
Monsanto 96-97
mutual respect 201, 210, 211, 213, 222, 224, 235, 265

N

nature 4, 12, 36, 46-48, 53, 59-62, 64, 75-85, 87, 103-106, 144-145, 148, 154, 160, 173, 182
networks 239, 240, 248, 253, 254, 262, 266, 271, 277
new society 177, 186, 195, 197, 198, 206, 209-211, 215-217, 221, 240, 242, 248, 267, 271-272, 275
news 23, 32, 42, 192, 238, 244, 252, 280
Nike 275
non-violent 270

O

Obama, Barack 28, 29, 33, 182, 183, 186, 187
Occupy Wall Street 21, 44, 105, 175, 177, 185-192, 194, 197-207, 214, 216, 217, 219-221, 224, 226, 228, 235, 236, 238-240, 263, 270, 276, 279, 280, 281
open space 223, 236, 276
oppression 14, 25, 28, 150, 182, 184, 185, 196, 203-205, 219, 236
outdoor spaces 218
owner class 110
Oxfam 153, 154

P

Pacific Gas and Electric 141
participation 17, 24, 30, 93, 113, 183, 194, 203, 208, 209, 218, 222, 232, 236

people's assembly 202
personal responsibility 208, 209, 210
Plato 64, 77, 86
pollution 42, 118, 140, 159, 160, 161
poor 6, 13, 72, 110, 122, 140, 146, 150, 154, 156, 164, 171, 172, 173, 174, 203
poverty 11, 43, 71, 72, 127, 154, 164, 171
price 34, 56-59, 66-70, 72, 97-100, 107, 109-111, 114-115, 121-122, 125, 127, 136-145, 148, 153, 180-182, 260, 272, 273
privilege 33, 204, 205
productivity 69, 70, 71, 109, 164
profits 5, 34, 42, 57, 58, 59, 65, 69, 70, 97, 98, 99, 101, 102, 107, 109, 110, 111, 114, 115, 117, 118, 125, 127, 128, 130, 132, 133, 134, 137, 139, 140, 142, 148, 149, 172, 181, 182, 183, 185, 192, 194, 275
propaganda 22, 60, 75, 94, 107, 125, 168, 181, 196, 197
property 17, 18, 26, 56, 59, 61, 63, 69, 78, 80, 82, 84, 97, 107, 121, 130, 132, 135, 146, 172, 214, 217
protest 185, 187, 219, 220, 232, 270
public spaces 187, 188, 208, 209, 213, 217, 218, 219, 238, 277
pundits 29, 33, 39, 53, 72, 76, 85, 94, 169, 175, 193

Q

quality of life 12, 53, 60, 73, 95, 106, 129, 148, 150-155, 156-159, 162-167, 247, 250, 269, 276

R

race 83, 172, 191, 206
racism 173, 190, 204
rational 46, 47, 53, 59-65, 67, 69, 75, 77, 82, 86, 87, 102, 112, 113, 117-120, 125, 132, 135, 151, 173
rational choices 112
raw materials 136
reason 20, 34, 35, 44, 76, 78, 82, 83, 86-89, 93, 96, 122, 129, 135, 156, 157, 243
regulation 39, 40, 56, 85, 95, 98, 191
renewable resources 56, 137, 149
resources 37, 47, 56, 69, 74, 102, 104, 106, 111, 114, 126, 136, 137, 140, 144-150, 157, 160, 167, 168, 170, 174, 175, 179-181, 197, 210, 212, 217-219, 236-237, 242, 246-247, 257, 258, 261, 264-268, 272, 273, 280
Rousseau, Jean-Jacques 82-84, 87

S

scarcity 56, 102, 120, 156, 160
self-determination 12, 14, 16, 24-26, 27, 30, 31, 45, 46, 51, 55, 171, 180, 182, 183, 185, 187, 191, 193, 197, 198, 200, 208, 212, 221, 222, 232, 237, 238, 241, 242, 251, 254, 255, 256, 271, 274, 276, 277
self-interest 58, 59, 61-64, 66, 67, 69, 81, 82, 84, 85, 87, 103, 106,

109, 112, 114, 118, 119
Sen, Amartya 119, 134
Smith, Adam 61, 69, 85
social change 197, 199, 201, 202, 203, 213, 219, 238, 244, 245, 250, 257, 258, 261, 268, 269, 270, 281
socialism 92-95, 191
socialist 93-95, 130, 168, 192
social movements 175, 177, 185, 192, 199-201, 204, 209, 216, 226, 238, 239
social organization 1, 49, 90, 182, 195, 198, 201, 202, 206, 209, 221, 235, 242, 244, 247, 249, 250, 253, 262
Socrates 61, 62, 76, 77, 86
solidarity 200, 201, 213, 214
standard of living 58, 60, 67, 70-73, 146, 151, 155, 156, 162-164, 166, 167, 269, 273
Starbucks 117
state of nature 6, 81, 83, 84, 86-88, 96, 104, 105, 171
stock options 109, 110
subsidize 142
supply and demand 57, 59, 67, 68, 97, 127, 134-139, 146
sustainability 34, 106, 126, 137, 144, 148, 149, 167, 175, 187, 194, 219, 235, 240, 242, 246, 247, 250, 255, 272-274, 276-277

T

Taibbi, Matt 100, 287
taxes 4, 5, 14, 17, 18, 21, 59, 74, 98, 130, 154, 171, 183, 184, 186, 191, 192, 195, 267
Tea Party 5, 177, 186, 190, 191, 199, 238
technology 30, 48, 66, 67, 114, 127, 129-133, 146, 150-152, 167, 175, 216, 220, 236, 271, 281
the 1% 23, 134, 185, 187, 191, 194, 196, 198, 238, 239, 245, 247, 249, 263, 273
the 99% 21, 177, 187-192, 194, 196-198, 203, 247, 256, 279, 281
Thirteenth Amendment 172
transparency 139, 190, 214, 215, 218, 248
truths 31-38, 45, 54, 60, 76, 79, 89, 90, 91, 105, 114, 121, 128, 145, 170, 196, 213

U

unemployment 21, 73, 138, 152, 166, 183
United States 1, 3, 12, 15, 18, 24, 27, 28, 29, 35, 39, 42, 62, 90, 92, 94, 96, 97, 100, 102, 105, 117, 124, 130, 136, 138, 139, 141, 147, 148, 165, 166, 172, 174, 180, 184, 186, 191, 193, 218, 231, 259, 271, 283, 289
unjustified omission of the other 33, 36
unsustainable 115, 147, 154

V

value 22, 23, 28, 32, 36, 46, 48, 49, 65, 68, 69, 71, 74, 108, 120, 123, 128, 133, 137, 139, 140, 143-149, 154, 157-160, 165,

166, 173, 182, 198, 200, 202, 203, 206, 210-212, 222, 223, 238, 247, 262, 272, 274
Veblen, Thorstein 113, 287
voting 23, 27, 29, 30, 41, 98, 101, 193, 195, 202, 221, 229, 231, 232, 268

W

wages 45, 63, 69, 99, 102, 115, 127, 137, 138, 140, 151, 154, 164, 172, 180, 184, 246, 248
Walmart 123, 124, 246, 288
water 42, 43, 47, 106, 118, 133, 136, 137, 140-142, 144, 148, 149, 161, 182, 200, 243
wealth 12, 14, 18, 27, 57-59, 63, 64, 69, 70, 72, 74, 82, 85, 91, 108-110, 127, 133, 145-156, 159, 163, 168, 170, 172, 175, 179, 181, 183-185, 189, 192, 196, 197, 200, 217, 238, 245-248, 267, 272-274
wealth accumulation 69, 150, 217
worker ownership 248
workers 12, 59, 63, 66, 69, 93, 102, 108, 109, 110, 111, 115, 127, 128, 138, 150, 151, 152, 181, 183, 184, 242, 245, 248, 274
World Café 236, 237

Z

zero-sum 145-147, 150
Zuccotti Park 185

CPSIA information can be obtained at www.ICGtesting.com
Printed in the USA
BVOW030747040613

322337BV00002B/7/P